C

Children with Special Needs

Assessment, Law and Practice –
Caught in the Act

of related interest

Dyslexia: How Would I Cope?
Michael Ryden
ISBN 1 85302 026 5

Talent, Teaching and Achievement
Edited by John Radford
ISBN 1 85302 111 3

A Voice for Children:
Speaking Out as Their Ombudsman
Målfrid Grude Flekkøy
ISBN 1 85302 118 0

Grief in Children
Atle Dyregrov
ISBN 1 85302 113 X

Children with Special Needs

Assessment, Law and Practice – Caught in the Act

Second Edition

Harry Chasty and John Friel

Jessica Kingsley Publishers
London and Philadelphia

First published in the United Kingdom in 1991.
Reprinted in 1991.
Second edition 1993 by
Jessica Kingsley Publishers Ltd
116 Pentonville Road
London N1 9JB

British Library Cataloguing in Publication Data
Chasty, Harry
Children with Special Needs – Assessment
Law and Practice: Caught in the Act. –
2Rev.ed
I.Tit.e II. Frie, John
371.90941

ISBN 1-85302-155-5

Printed and Bound by
The Cromwell Press, Melksham, Wiltshire

CONTENTS

Part I

DEFINING, ASSESSING AND MEETING THE NEED

Chapter 1

The individual's needs and the educational system

INTRODUCTION

In this book, the special needs and special arrangements to be made in schools for the child who shows 'significantly greater difficulty in learning than the majority of children of his age' will be discussed. In considering learning, we usually think of teachers teaching and children as pupils, learning from that formal situation. The fact that in the preschool years children learn very rapidly without a formal curriculum or even a *national* curriculum or organised teaching is frequently overlooked. Learning is normal. Despite Mary Warnock's comment, in her Report, that at some time in their education 20 per cent of children will have special needs, failure to learn is unusual. Parents and teachers must not accept failure to learn as unalterable. Documenting the circumstances surrounding that failure, and making appropriate arrangements which reduce its effects to the minimum, so enabling the student to gain maximum benefit from his education, will be the aim of this book.

KINDS OF DIFFICULTY IN LEARNING

For many years, the ability to learn was regarded as an 'innate skill'. Children either could learn, or could not, and their capability was considered to be unalterable. The learning capacity of the child was thought to be circumscribed by the two major variables, 'ability' and 'environment'. While psychology and education now take a more dynamic view of learning, the practical remnants of outmoded ideas about fixed abilities are still to be seen in special needs provisions made for some children in this country. This attitude must be questioned.

The philosophy of this book is that learning itself is a learned skill. In our schools, there are many children who are unable to use some of the major components of learning to the full, but who could and must be taught to do so.

The approach to meeting the 'special educational needs' of children who show a 'significantly greater difficulty in learning than the majority of children of that age' is to address their problem in very practical terms, asking 'if this child doesn't learn the way we teach, can we teach him the way he learns, and then extend and develop his competences in learning?' The interpretation of the Education Act 1981 and Education Reform Bill 1988 in relation to the national curriculum, by the DES and local education authorities, must take account of this child centred approach, and for each failing child seek to build an individual provision which meets his learning and curriculum needs.

SPLD/DYSLEXIC STUDENTS AND SPECIAL NEEDS PROVISIONS

Definitions of Spld

The legal aspects of this book are relevant for *all* special needs children. The psychological and educational aspects are also broadly relevant for all special needs children but will refer particularly to the abilities and difficulties in learning experienced by dyslexic children, i.e. those with specific learning difficulties. However, it is acknowledged that these special needs are different from those of children whose failure to learn is attributable to some other cause.

Other children with learning difficulties

Different kinds of failure are evident in children's learning. Failure to learn may be very severe and broadly based. For these children, progress is the slow but steady development of the simple skills of everyday living, such as sitting up, walking, looking and paying attention, skills in establishing eye contact, and skills in making and saying simple words.

Failure to learn may be moderate. A child with a moderate learning difficulty will learn to walk and talk. He or she will eventually read, write and spell at a basic level, but all these skills will develop at a slower pace and to a lesser extent than normal. All the child's skills in learning will be retarded.

Failure to learn which is *specific* is limited only to certain skills, particularly those in information processing. These children have deficiencies in a narrow range of abilities which relate to the delivery of learning. Some things they will do well, other things they do rather badly. It is this group of enigmatic learners which engages our special attention in this book.

McDonald Critchley (1970) defines 'dyslexia' as 'A disorder manifested by a difficulty in learning to read, despite conventional instruction, adequate intelligence, and socio-cultural opportunity. It is dependent upon fundamental cognitive difficulties which are frequently of a constitutional character.'

In the period since 1970, research and experience in managing the development of the learning of dyslexic students suggests that 'specific learning difficulties' is a more appropriate title for them. Specific learning difficulties are defined as 'organising or learning difficulties, which restrict the student's competences in information processing in fine motor skills and working memory, so causing limitations in some or all the skills of speech, reading, spelling, writing, essay writing, numeracy, and behaviour' (Chasty 1989 and 1990).

In this later definition, the cognitive factors referred to by Critchley are identified, and the curriculum effects of the difficulties in learning are widened to include a developmental continuum of language based skills, including numeracy and behaviour. Although these may appear to be totally separate skills, they are both rule based and language related, require developed information processing competences and are greatly influenced by prolonged consistent failure in class.

A special needs programme which restricts the aims of provision for Spld children solely to reading or literacy skills neglects vital areas of student development. In managing the education of Spld students, attention cannot be focused solely on reading, literacy or even on the curriculum effects of reading, spelling and writing skills. The important learning skills which are often neglected will be necessary for working in other areas of the curriculum. If the student has not acquired these essential skills from his present experiences, he is unlikely to build them effectively, even from the remedial language experiences provided by his 'special needs' tutors. Teachers must therefore plan for, and have a clear aim to improve, the deficiencies in his *learning skills* which must be regarded as the major causative factors which underlie the literacy failures observed in these students.

HOW DO CHILDREN LEARN?

In early childhood the child develops major skills or competences in learning which he or she uses in organising both the experiences and the teaching provided by his or her school. Reuven Feuerstein 1979 has described these major building blocks or 'prerequisites' of learning which are acquired comparatively easily by ordinary children from their experiences.

He discusses deficient cognitive functions related to failure in learning and groups mental activities into three major stages: (i) input, the process of gathering all relevant information, (ii) elaboration, efficiently using the information gathered to find solutions, and (iii) output, executing tasks and communicating findings and solutions to oneself and others. He points out that much teaching fails to recognise the impossibility of learning in children who have not acquired these basic cognitive skills. Such children have not developed adequate discrimination, or short term memory competences, therefore logical thought is beyond them and they cannot organise or retain their experience. They cannot, therefore, benefit from the broadly based classroom teaching available to them, however wide the curriculum, and they cannot organise or retain that experience. This aspect of Feuerstein's work has significant implications for the learning of Spld students.

Blagg, Ballinger and Gardner (1988) in their 'Somerset Thinking Skills Development Course' based the thinking 'domains' highlighted in their teaching approach, on Feuerstein's work. They represent them as a 'design or performance loop' listing the relevant skill areas, and they interpret them, as: (1) gathering and organising all relevant information, (2) recognising and defining the problem, (3) generating alternative solutions, (4) planning tactics, (5) monitoring performance, (6) checking performance against original aims, (7) revising plans and strategies to meet original aims, and (8) evaluating performance and strategies. They offer a skills training course to develop the child's competences in the management of this learning/thinking system. They consider that their approach is based upon commonly accepted theory but acknowledge that other theoreticians and researchers have adopted different terms for similar concepts.

In the Dyslexia Institute our view of the 'building blocks' of learning shows similarities to these analyses. In practical terms, imagine a young child playing on the floor of the family living room while mother sits in a chair watching television, and father mends the iron on the kitchen table. The child will have available wide ranging sources of information; sights, sounds, feelings tastes and smells from which he or she may learn. If he or she is to learn effectively from this environment, he must (1) *survey* the whole of that environment and attend to all the major sensations from it; (2) *focus* his attention in an analytical way to take in important aspects; (3) *sequence* the results of his analysis of environment into a coherent required order; (4) *move* himself, his limbs or his ideas to explore and give different perspectives to that environment; (5) *integrate* separate aspects of that environment into a more meaningful pattern for him; (6) *represent* that ongoing experience (a) in feeling or motor terms (b) visually in pictures, or (c) verbally in words. The final aspect of this learning package is (7) *recalling* experiences and thoughts for later use through verbal, visual or motor channels, or any combination of these modalities.

While all the learning skills listed in 1–7 may be acquired by the child from experience, children do not *all* acquire these skills at the same rate. Individual differences will be apparent both in overall rate of acquisition and the delivery and use of these skills. The rate of acquisition and the profile of these abilities will be major determinants of the effectiveness of the child's responses in class. In the past teachers have tended to adopt a 'laissez faire' attitude, leaving the child to acquire competences in learning as best he can, from whatever experiences he has available to him. But these skills listed above are *all* teachable. Should our approach not be to teach the child the major learning skills which he or she finds difficult, as a major step on the way to dealing with his 'significantly greater difficulty in learning' which determines his special educational needs? This requirement must be accepted as part of the philosophy of education underlying the basic principle restated in Warnock, that all children are educable.

PRE-WARNOCK DEVELOPMENT OF SPECIAL EDUCATION

Historically, as awareness and sectional interest grew in the particular needs of groups of handicapped children, special educational arrangements were always made for these students in *separate* institutions, which could help even the most severely handicapped. This segregation enabled the establishment of very clear educational aims, which led to the development of appropriate highly specialised teaching programmes. These were often accompanied, rather later, by specialist teacher training courses which were often not located in the colleges of education. The education of clearly recognisable groups such as the blind and the deaf benefited greatly from this specialism and concentrated expertise.

Indeed, the Warnock Report acknowledges that, historically, provision for children with different handicaps was established at very different times:

> 'Special education for the handicapped in Great Britain is of relatively recent origin. The very first schools for the blind and deaf were founded in the lifetime of Mozart; those for the physically handicapped awaited the Great Exhibition; day schools for the mentally handicapped and epileptic arrived with the motor car; whilst special provision for the delicate, maladjusted and speech impaired children is younger than living memory.'

It must be pointed out that special provisions for dyslexics post-date Concord and the Space Shuttle.

Interest in Spld was slow to develop

Dr Pringle Morgan's letter to the *British Medical Journal* in 1896 is the first recorded documentation of the learning difficulties of 'a very intelligent boy of twelve who is unable to learn to read, ...had all the lessons in class been oral lessons, he would probably be the brightest boy, but as it is, he is being kept back by what is, possibly – shall we call it – congenital word blindness.' While research interests in this theme developed quickly, wider public awareness and suitable educational arrangements were very slow to develop. It was only in the 1960s that educational charities and a few research units began to make a provision. This became increasingly informed in the 1970s, but local education authority awareness was still very diffuse and lacked precision until after the Education Act 1981 was implemented.

NEGATIVE EFFECTS OF THE TIZARD REPORT

Attitudes in many local education authorities were unfortunately coloured by the report of the Advisory Committee on Handicapped Children chaired by Professor J. Tizard, 'Children with Specific Reading Difficulties'. The Committee convened at a very important time in English education, but dismally failed to give the necessary direction to practitioners from maintained and independent sectors.

In its conclusions and recommendations the Tizard Report unreservedly condemned the term 'dyslexia'. 'The term "dyslexia" has been very loosely used in educational purposes. In particular, we cannot attach any scientific meaning to the term "acute dyslexia" and we are sceptical of the view that a "specific syndrome of 'developmental dyslexia'" has been identified.' This led many local education authority administrators to deny the existence of the problem, and resources were withheld from the essential research and development necessary to lead to a provision.

Whilst conceding that general remedial teaching offered to Spld students was unlikely to be helpful, 'there is some indication that the remedial teaching given to the general run of delayed readers may prove ineffective for some children with the particular problem of specific reading backwardness.' The Tizard Committee attacked the arrangements for the 'clinic' based provisions usually offered by the voluntary educational charities:

> 'This does not mean that all children with reading difficulties – nor even all children with *severe* reading disability – should be *withdrawn from ordinary schools* for remedial teaching purposes. The great majority of children with reading difficulties, including specific reading difficulties, are best taught in their regular primary and secondary schools, provided that suitable arrangements are made for them. If taken outside the ordinary school they may miss the stimulation of their peers as well as the opportunities of a wider curriculum. Indeed, since reading is a language skill, it cannot be divorced without detriment from the general development of language, which in its turn is impoverished if not related to other aspects of the child's experience. Moreover, progress made with children selected for short sessions of remedial teaching elsewhere is all too commonly lost following return to the ordinary school environment, and better results can often be obtained by remedial teaching within the ordinary school, or even within the ordinary class. In saying this,

> we are aware that at present arrangements made in primary schools for children with reading disabilities are often inadequate, and that in secondary schools the position is still less satisfactory.'

Some local authorities therefore interpreted this destructive criticism of the *arrangements* for 'out of school' teaching as also applying to the *methods*, and consequently refused to permit children to attend such centres – but did not themselves respond to the Tizard challenge to improve the arrangements they made for such children within schools. Their appreciation of the need for detailed assessment and skill based multi-sensory teaching for Spld students was, consequently, seriously limited.

There was, therefore, no opportunity for established assessment and teaching principles to be disseminated and widely accepted into local education authority practice prior to the implementation of Education Act 1981 in 1983. For this reason, provision for Spld students under the Act has been 'patchy' throughout the country. Local authorities have had to face a daunting task of constructing an appropriate provision for the large numbers of these children, in their area, and at the same time, developing their own staff expertise to identify the difficulty and deal with the problems in class.

THE WARNOCK REPORT: THE PRINCIPLES UNDERLYING CURRENT EDUCATIONAL PRACTICE

The very dark and gloomy educational outlook which existed for dyslexics prior to 1978 was relieved by the work of the Warnock Committee, which culminated in the publication of Warnock Report in May 1978. The Committee had very wide representation from education and the voluntary bodies working on behalf of the handicapped. An enormous number of submissions was studied and representatives travelled extensively to view facilities in this country and abroad. The Committee was greatly influenced by developments and legislation in the USA.

The Report itself is a massive document dealing with both philosophy and practice in special education, running to some 400 pages, containing 224 recommendations.

The Report builds upon the fundamental egalitarian principle established in English education in the 1944 Butler Act, that the child is entitled to an education in keeping with his needs. In the Report, the aims of education are considered to be the same for all children. In their quest to develop their potential to the full, all children are equally entitled to what they need from the community. These aims are clearly stated as 'first to enlarge the child's knowledge, experience, and imaginative understanding, and thus, his awareness of moral values and his capacity for enjoyment; and secondly, to enable him to enter the world after formal education as an active participant in society, and a responsible contributor to it, capable of enjoying as much independence as possible.'

THE SIZE OF THE 'SPECIAL EDUCATIONAL PROBLEM'

The Warnock Committee considered that at some time in their education, 20 per cent of children might be expected to have special educational needs. In 1978, when the Warnock Report was published, less than two per cent of children were in special schools. While other children were receiving special education outside these special schools, it is apparent that a considerable increase in the numbers of children receiving a specialist provision was projected by the Report.

This immediately raises major issues of funding. Indeed, Mary Warnock wrote to the *Times Educational Supplement*, towards the end of 1978, to point out that the implementation of her Committee's report needed funding, and, without it, great difficulties would arise. The approach taken by the DES was to fund special education by closing outmoded facilities and transferring the finance saved to the new services required. While this is a laudable financial aim for those who must be careful in their use of public money, it is a debatably questionable practice in both economic and educational terms. The DES failure to fund this important educational advance sent signals to local education authorities which conflicted with the intention of the provisions made in the Act, and must be regretted by all concerned in education.

DEFINITION OF NEED

In every area of handicap, there is a continuum of need ranging from those very seriously affected, through those moderately affected, to those with very mild difficulties. There is no sharp divide between the handicapped and the non-handicapped. Each child is therefore a unique individual on this continuum of need. In Warnock's view this led to the corollary that categorisation and labelling could be misleading and dangerous. Warnock's concerns about categorisation, subsequently gained much support in special needs education in this country. While the egalitarian aspects of this change are laudable, the educational and teaching implications must be thought about very carefully. In defining need there is a requirement to do so with some precision, and one must question whether the avoidance of labelling and categorisation actually facilitates or hinders that vital process of definition. Further, if categorisation of children as, for example, dyslexics, is to be avoided then, equally, categorisation or standardisation of provisions from local education authorities must also be avoided, and education authorities must not think in terms of standard packages available for 'kinds of children'.

SEX DIFFERENCES IN THE SPLD POPULATION

The voluntary educational charities working with Spld students have always acknowledged that this client group is heavily biased in favour of boys, with some 70% of those who are assessed and taught because of their specific difficulties being boys. The arguments which are advanced to support this are neurological, relying on different neurological specialisation in boys and girls, and hormonal, where the foetus seems to be extremely sensitive to testosterone, the male hormone, in uterus. Current research tends to dispute this view, suggesting that just as many girls as boys have specific learning difficulties. Given the wide ranging definition of Spld advanced in this book, it seems credible that boys tend to show the traditionally recognised difficulties in reading, spelling and handwriting, while girls tend to show the more recently recognised problems in numbers/mathematics, routefinding and map work, and higher writing skills.

However, in groups of children currently receiving help boys tend to outnumber girls by 3:1. Throughout this book the Spld student will be regarded as masculine and referred to as 'he', even though later research may prove this assumption to be unwarranted.

TO LABEL OR NOT LABEL?

The practice of not labelling children in special education originated in Dunn (1968) who rightly criticises the negative effects of labels such as 'mentally retarded' as being a 'destructive self-fulfilling prophecy'. Dunn advocates main-streaming as a much more positive response to meeting the special needs of handicapped children. While it is easy to sympathise with the egalitarian aspects of this philosophy, the educational advantages and disadvantages must be considered carefully. Dunn's aim was to enable the child to be taught more effectively, and it must be asked whether ceasing to label encourages the right attitude in teacher or facilitates the development of the child's skills in learning. These two factors should be complementary, but with regard to dyslexic children there is frequently a conflict between shades of meaning in understanding the 'right attitude', which affects the actual teaching, and an attitude which is right for the blind or the deaf is not necessarily right for dyslexic children.

There is no hard research evidence which confirms that by *not* labelling children, their learning skills improve and their literacy deficiencies are reduced. What seems to be at issue is the social circumstances in which children are taught. Whether the best provision is small group skill based and given by a highly trained specialist Spld teacher; or whether it is large class, group related and given by a broadly trained class or 'special needs' teacher.

Such advantages as are evident from not labelling appear to be political and social, rather than educational. The broadly based study carried out by MacMillan et al (1975) concludes that, 'regardless of the dependent measure employed, self-concept, acceptance, lowered achievement, post school achievement, the evidence does *not* support the conclusion that there is a detrimental labelling affect.' There is no clear evidence in the wider literature to confirm that labelling has a detrimental effect upon children.

The implications of labelling in special educational practice has recently been considered by Stobart (1986), who concludes that the British approach to special education in not categorising children does not bypass the problem of labelling, especially for children attending 'special units' in schools. It must therefore be concluded that the extension of Dunn's reservations about labelling the severely handicapped to other kinds of learning difficulty, where labels may have benefits for teacher and taught, appears to be a dubious and questionable educational practice fostered in this country by Warnock Report. This procedure should not go unchallenged.

WHICH LABEL TO CHOOSE

The range of labels used in the dyslexia/specific learning difficulties area of education represents the widely different backgrounds of the workers in this field, and, in the circumstances, is not surprising. Indeed it would be surprising to see unanimity of terminology in a field which arouses such wide ranging professional interests in skilled practitioners whose training, experience, qualifications and professional language vary so much.

Such is the rate of development of thinking in this area of education that experienced practitioners change their label and their stance to the problem regularly. This is a normal part of the learning process related to working in an interesting and much researched area of psychology and education. Piaget had a word for it, and 'accommodation' will affect all learners if their learning about this subject is sufficiently deep.

Parents and teachers should apply, to the consideration of appropriate labels, the views of Hayakawa (1965). He pointed out that the labels do more than classify or provide a useful written or sound link to an idea. The word used to label is not sterile. It can motivate the person labelled. It can also inspire the teacher who uses the label. In the next five years, practitioners working in this area of special education should choose the label which (1) best describes the child in the light of current knowledge of his abilities and difficulties; (2) motivates that child to improve his learning and literacy skills, (3) guides and inspires parent and teacher in the most effective way, and (4) be prepared to change the label. Apply these principles and the choice of label is the reader's, but until the authors learn otherwise, they will use the label 'specific learning difficulties'.

In doing this, the pragmatism of Cornwall, Hedderly and Pumfrey (1984) is accepted. In their conclusion they state 'We (meaning British psychologists) must accept that they (parents) may wish to use the term dyslexia even though we prefer to use specific learning difficulty. We are keener to place the emphasis on the teaching programme than on the label used.' Psychologists, educationalists, parents and teachers need to develop increasing precision in the concept, but flexibility in the use of the label, so that access to appropriate teaching is not obstructed, and learning is facilitated.

The smokescreen, 'We do not use labels to describe children, or we do not use the word dyslexia', is sometimes used in schools or by education authorities to discourage parents who question the literacy failures of their child and enquire about the possibility that the child might be 'dyslexic', in the hope of arranging more suitable teaching. This negatively defensive and impractical position is the reverse side of those egalitarian gains sought by the Warnock Committee. Unsympathetic professionals should not hide defensively behind a 'non-labelling' approach to the education of Spld students.

INTEGRATION

Warnock also followed educational practice in the USA in establishing that, as far as possible, special educational needs should be met in the ordinary classroom of the ordinary school. This right arose from American opposition to segregation in education in any shape or form. However, a range of provisions which met an increasing range of needs was set out in Warnock Report. Most needs could be met in the ordinary classroom, some children with greater difficulties may need support or withdrawal from that classroom, while others, with more severe needs, require greater withdrawal and less linking back to the ordinary school. A few children will need highly specialist help in a 'special' school which is separate from the normal maintained sector, and a very few children may need educating outside the school system perhaps at home or in a hospital. Warnock Report therefore envisages a range of provisions meeting a range of needs, and it must be stressed that no single provision can meet all needs. It is the meeting of the needs which is important, rather than doctrinaire adherence to the principle that this *must* happen in the ordinary classroom of the ordinary school. The key criterion must always be that the child's needs *are* met, and that should take precedence over where they are met. Little evidence is to hand that all children learn *best* in the ordinary classroom of the ordinary school, but is accepted that for social, economical and organisational reasons, this is the most effective way of maintaining their education. However, in making arrangements for the education of Spld students, schools and education authorities must be careful to balance these anticipated, but not yet demonstrated, social gains with the losses in personality and behavioural skills which stem from the student's evident failure to handle the language-based ideas systems offered in those ordinary classrooms.

THE EDUCATION ACT 1981

Major aspects of the thinking in Warnock Report entered into legislation in Education Act 1981, which became law on 30th October 1981, and tentatively creaked into operation on 1st April 1983, supported by its appropriate regulations, Education (Special Educational Needs) Regulations 1983. For some time education authorities were immensely busy establishing the necessary administrative structures, and parents also needed that time to digest the implications of the sections. The arrangements for provisions were developed slowly, but it was soon apparent that this was an exciting and challenging legislation which completely altered the established expectations for children with specific difficulties in learning.

DEFINITIONS

The old 'categories of handicap' were swept away by the Act and are no longer relevant. The issue has changed from whether a dyslexic child is 'handicapped' to how serious the Spld child's special needs are. It is the special educational needs which determine the provision, *not* the particular handicap.

The most important definition in the Act is *a learning difficulty.* A child has a learning difficulty when he has 'significantly greater difficulty in learning than the majority of children of his age.'

The word 'significant' is the key around which this definition hinges. In general use, the word means important or full of meaning. However, psychologists and teachers tend to use the word as part of their professional jargon to mean a difficulty which is unlikely to happen by chance, and is greater than that experienced by at least 95 per cent of the population of this age.

Psychologists may address this problem of deciding whether the child has a learning difficulty very directly through psychometric test procedures such as British Ability Scales. This enables abilities such as reasoning and spatial knowledge to be examined and the child's competence in comparison with others of his age to be established with some precision. Psychologists should therefore have no difficulty in stating whether a particular child has significantly greater difficulty in learning than the majority of children of his age, and psychometric test procedures will give them an answer.

In recent years many local education authority psychologists have abandoned psychometric testing and prefer to use curriculum or classroom based methods. These models, while more practical, and clearly related to needs in one particular classroom, do not sustain the same analysis, and while they may say something about what is happening to the child in relation to others in his class, they are *not* relevant to the 'majority of children of his age' referred to in the Act, and, at present, they can offer no evidence of the comparability of that classroom with the outside world. These methods are therefore of limited value in procedures under the Education Act 1981.

The second definition of a 'learning difficulty' is that the child 'has a disability which prevents or hinders him from making use of educational facilities of a kind generally provided in school, within the area of the education authority concerned, for children of his age'. Books, reading materials and other printed resources certainly come within the meaning of the term educational facilities in this definition. The Spld student with an effective reading age of eight years, who is expected to work on the curriculum of his high school, using a history or biology text book requiring a fourteen year reading competence, would certainly come within the scope of this definition. On both definitions, it is a comparatively straight forward process to establish that a particular student has a learning difficulty.

Under the terms of the Act, a child is considered to have *special educational needs* if he has a learning difficulty which calls for a special educational provision to be made. This should apply to many children with Spld.

This concept of special educational needs removed the education authority's specific duties in relation to dyslexic children, as set out in the Chronically Sick and Disabled Persons Act 1970, Sections 25–27 which were generally poorly observed and enabled these children to be dealt with in a similar way to others with special needs under Education Act 1981.

A *special educational provision*, for children aged two and under, means *any* educational provision; for children aged two and over, it means 'an educational provision which is *additional to, or otherwise different from* the educational provision generally made for children of his age, in schools maintained by the local education authority concerned.

The definition is somewhat ambiguous, and leaves a loop-hole which has occasionally resulted in an unsatisfactory provision for a child. A local education authority may carry out only a limited assessment of a seriously retarded child with specific learning difficulties, ignore the child's problems in learning, identify the all too apparent difficulties in the major curriculum skill of reading, and conclude that reading teaching was necessary for the student. As reading instruction was generally available in the authority's schools, this was a *general*, rather than a *special* provision, consequently the authority considered that child did *not* require a special provision, and so the authority wrongly assumed the child did *not* have special educational needs. Some limited reading teaching was provided but certainly not at a level which met the child's serious problems in learning. By misusing this definition the authority evaded its responsibility to provide the detailed and wide ranging learning programme required by the student. The circularity of the relationship between a 'learning difficulty', 'special educational needs' and 'special educational provision' is immensely frustrating for parents, and can lead to problems in interpretation and implementation of provision.

GENERAL DUTIES

While general duties under the Act cover all children with special educational needs, much more specific and detailed powers cover the assessment and teaching of children whose special educational needs call for the authority to determine the special educational provision that should be made.

In practice children with such serious difficulties that the authority should determine the provision to be made for them are 'statemented'.

Within the context of an educational procedure where labelling has been questioned, the choice of the word 'statementing' seems to be particularly inappropriate. This is an ugly, awkward sounding word, which does not inspire confidence in parents and implies, possibly all too accurately, an awkward and difficult process. Indeed 'statemented' is much too close to 'sectioned' for comfort and many parents have confused the terms with unfortunate results. In Scotland under the Scottish Act, the use of the word 'recording', to describe the establishment of a 'record of needs' conveys a much more positive, smooth and reassuring impression to parents.

Parents of children with specific learning difficulties should be aware of the essential stages in the process which are:

Is the child failing in learning and literacy skills in school and appears to have a learning difficulty?

(i) Establish in an assessment that he has significantly greater difficulty in learning than other children of his age.

(ii) This should result in a special educational provision of some kind. Is this provision required so great, or so complex, that the education authority should determine it? Seek Section 5 assessment of the child's needs under Education Act 1981.

(iii) If the need is assessed as being sufficiently great, then a statement of special educational needs is necessary.

There is a duty laid upon both the parents and the education authority to ensure that this procedure is followed so that the child's needs may be identified and met.

The parent's duty is to see that the child's needs are met by full time attendance at school, *or otherwise*. If the parent, having been advised of his child's needs, considers that these are not being met within the curriculum of the school at which his child is enrolled, then he must make arrangements, 'otherwise' by making an appropriate provision himself. Schools and education authorities will apply pressure to ensure that parental arrangements are made *after* school hours so that the demands of national curriculum can be met. Parents may not be able to meet this restriction, and from both an educational and learning view point it may not be justified by the child's best interests.

The education authority has a duty to ensure that it provides schools sufficiently diverse in 'numbers, character and equipment to afford, for all pupils, opportunities of instruction and training as may be desirable in view of their different ages, abilities and aptitudes.' This requirement places the onus on the education authority to deliver special educational provisions for pupils who have very wide ranging special educational needs.

Generally, the major issue between parents and the authority is not whether the authority can deliver *a* provision, but how appropriate that provision might be, and how detailed.

Formal assessment is only appropriate at stage (ii) of the process above, and is only provided for very much fewer children, whose difficulties are, *a priori*, quite obviously more severe. Great concern often arises because of inconsistencies in this 'ad hoc' assessment procedure which varies greatly in its form and detail from area to area, across the country. The point is rather underplayed by Adams (1986) 'Special Education,' which, because of the nature of its publication and the spread of its contributors, must be taken to represent the views of the Society of Education Officers.

> 'One of the more problematic areas under the new Act is deciding which pupils have, or might have, special educational needs at a level which requires the education authority to determine provision. The procedure of formal assessment is clearly laid down in Act, but there are a great many pupils with additional needs who are being helped and assessed from time to time, for whom the procedure of formal assessment is considered inappropriate. Usually many more children are involved in the ongoing process of assessment and guidance than are involved in the procedure of formal assessment. The point at which formal assessment under Section 5 of the Act is indicated will be determined by many factors, including local arrangements and provision and the views of parents and involved professionals; it is not an area in which precise guidelines or criteria will be meaningful for all cases'.

This paragraph has, if anything underplayed the grey area between informal observation and assessment which is subject to the pressures and limitations of local skills and resources, and the formal assessment procedures under the Act. Clearly it is for children considered to be in this sector that parents must be most vigilant, and make the strongest representations to the education authority to ensure that the child's abilities and difficulties are known in full, and his special needs are met in full.

UNDERACHIEVEMENT

For parents of children with specific learning difficulties, decisions about provisions for children in the 'grey area' are always about underachievement. For good decisions and positive action, home and school must appreciate each other's perspective and communicate. As the professionals dealing with a complex issue, education authority and school must accept that their perspective is different from the parent's and so must listen with great care to what the parents say.

The school's perspective is usually group based, and determined by what is being achieved in a particular class. If the child conforms to expectations for that group, he is learning effectively and performing up to school's expectations. School will not see a particular child who achieves the group standard as having a problem which merits consideration and additional teaching.

Parents are not fully aware of group standards, nor are they particularly concerned by them. They have lived with their child from birth. While they may not experience how other children learn and organise the experience they gain from their world, and may not be acutely aware of detailed patterns of abilities and difficulties, they are very perceptive about their own child's rate of skills acquisition. From the child's responses at home they will have formulated judgements about his general level of ability. If, in school, the child does not acquire literacy skills at the expected rate, or shows skills in some areas and difficulties in others, these anomalies will result in questions to school about individual differences in learning which rightly threaten that cosy group standard adhered to in school.

Chapter 2

The assessment process

TYPES OF ASSESSMENT

In this section reference will be made to the *Advice on Assessment* document in Appendix 1. Regardless of which procedure is followed, an assessment presents a model of how a child learns, and the areas of success and failure in that learning. The perspective taken can be classroom based, on a model constructed by the child's teacher or the local educational psychologist using materials and skills directly relevant for children in that particular class. It can be based upon wider national implications, given by a chartered psychologist with much training and experience in psychometrics using norm referenced tests which have an accepted national or international validity. The assessment may be language based and given by a speech therapist. It may be given by an occupational therapist or physiotherapist and look searchingly at the hierarchical development of the child's gross and fine motor skills. It may by given by the child's family doctor, or the schools medical officer of health and look at the health of the child over a period of time, discussing illness patterns, vision or hearing. It may be given by a psychiatrist (who is a medically qualified expert in child mental health and behaviour), or a clinical psychologist who is usually a hospitals based expert in abnormal behaviour who looks at the child's behaviour and social adjustment in the learning situation.

Each of these models has its limitations. The real skill of assessment is in the construction of a coherent picture which represents the essential elements of all of these perspectives and leads to relevant practical initiations which help the student. The aim should be to present as wide a picture as possible, containing all the elements which affect the child's learning. Classroom based assessment is practical and relevant for the class teacher, but limited in scope, and says nothing about the child's learning outside the classroom. Teachers should not forget that their classroom may not present the best circumstances for learning for the individual student under consideration. Clinic based assessment, which looks in detail at the individual child's abilities and difficulties, neglects the classroom at its peril.

PURPOSE

The purpose of the assessment process must be to survey all the influences on the child's learning, so enabling a teaching programme to be implemented which meets the child's needs. The wider and more 'in depth' this process is, the more likely it is to convey an accurate picture of the range of abilities and difficulties apparent in the child's learning, and the more appropriate the provision will be.

MONITORING AND ASSESSMENT UNDER THE 1981 ACT

In Section 18 of DES Circular 22/89 clear guidance is given to the local education authorities on the breadth and scope of the assessment process.

> 'The assessment of SENs (special educational needs)is not an end in itself; it is the first step towards a better understanding of a child's learning difficulties for the practical purpose of providing guidance to the education needed and establishing a basis upon which to monitor the child's progress. When carrying out assessments, the LEA should ensure that clear distinctions are made between:
>
> (i) the child's relevant past and present levels of functioning, emotional states and interests and how these represent resources and deficiencies in relation to the educational demands which will be made on the child.
>
> (ii) the analysis of the child's learning difficulties;
>
> (iii) the specification of goals for change in the child and environment (including school, home and the wider community);
>
> (iv) the specification of the child's requirement for different kinds of approaches, facilities or resources, in order to facili-

tate access to the National Curriculum, with any modifications which are considered essential;

(v) the perceptions and wishes of the parent and child;

(vi) the special educational provision and services required to meet the identified needs.'

All of these are of such vital importance to the understanding of the background to the child's abilities and difficulties in learning, that it is regrettable that the DES did not word that section more strongly, requiring not just 'clear distinctions to be made between', but a detailed appraisal to be made of each of these factors, with due account having to be made in the provision to be constructed for the child.

ABILITIES

Understanding the actual performance of the child, in a given learning situation and a given classroom environment, is as much about his abilities and the efficiency with which they are applied, as it is about his difficulties in learning which appear to be the real cause for concern to parents and teachers. In addressing the special needs of children who fail to learn, their abilities and how they are used must be considered.

As was pointed out in the introduction to this section of the book, children do not only learn in school, in class, in a national curriculum. These are artificial structures which seek to facilitate, control and direct the natural learning inclinations of the child, enabling these to be channeled into ways which meet the long term goals of 'those who know best' in the education system. The trouble about that class based judgement of failure is that it is accompanied by a 'class based' concept of how the material is to be taught which may not meet the learning needs of the Spld student. We must come back to the vital question. 'How does this child learn at this moment? How efficiently are these abilities applied, and over what time scale? What are the individual personality and social factors which he brings to learning which influence his application of his intellectual skills? What levels of anxiety and stress does he experience in the learning process, and, perhaps most significantly, how does teacher present information to the child? These are the issues which must be examined in the assessment process to enable the child's needs to be determined, documented, and an appropriate provision to be specified.

These major questions are addressed in some detail in Annex 1 of the DES Circular 22/89 and it is an immense pity that this excellent checklist (previously available in Circular 1/83) is not used on *every* assessment. All too often major aspects of it are seriously neglected.

ADVICE ON SPECIAL EDUCATIONAL NEEDS: SUGGESTED FROM DES CIRCULAR 22/89

(a) DESCRIPTION OF THE CHILD'S FUNCTIONING

1. Description of the child's strengths and weaknesses

   Physical state and functioning (physical health, developmental function, mobility, hearing, vision and continence)

   Emotional state (link between stress, emotions, and physical state)

   Cognitive functioning

   Communication skills (verbal comprehension, expressive language, speech); perceptual and motor skills

   Adaptive skills

   Personal and social skills

   Approaches and attitudes to learning

   Educational attainments

   Self-image and interests

   Behaviours.

2. Factors in the child's environment which lessen or contribute to his or her needs

   In the home and family, and including the language of the home

   At school

   Elsewhere.

3. Relevant aspects of the child's history

   Personal

   Medical

   Educational.

(b) AIMS OF PROVISIONS

1. General areas of development

(Reference should be made to the relevant attainment targets of the national curriculum wherever possible.)

Physical development (eg to develop self-care skills)

Motor development (eg to improve co-ordination of hand and fingers, to achieve hand-eye co-ordination)

Cognitive development (eg to develop the ability to classify)

Language development (eg to improve expressive language skills)

Social development (eg to stimulate social contact with peers)

2. Any specific areas of weaknesses or gaps in skills acquisition which impede the child's progress

Eg short-term memory deficits

3. Suggested methods and approaches

Implications of the child's medical condition (eg advice on the side-effects of medication for epilepsy)

Teaching and learning approaches (eg teaching methods for the blind or deaf, or teaching through other specialised methods)

Emotional climate and social regime (eg type of regime, size of class or school, need for individual attention)

(c) FACILITIES AND RESOURCES

1. Special equipment

(eg physical aids, auditory aids, visual aids)

2. Specialist facilities

(eg for incontinence, for medical examination, treatment and drug administration)

3. Special educational resources

(eg specialist equipment for teaching children with physical or sensory disabilities, non-teaching aids)

4. Other specialist resources

(eg nursing, social work and welfare support, speech therapy, occupational therapy, physiotherapy, psychotherapy, audiology, othoptics)

5. Physical environment

(eg access and facilities for non-ambulant pupils, attention to lighting environment, attention to acoustic environment, attention to thermal environment, health care accommodation, privacy of continence care)

6. School organisation and attendance

(eg day attendance, weekly boarding, termly boarding, relief hostel accommodation)

7. Transport

INTELLIGENCE? OR THE EFFICIENCY WITH WHICH ABILITIES ARE USED IN LEARNING?

Research in psychology and education is moving the thinking of teachers much beyond the dated concept of fixed intelligence or ability. A typical example of this kind of development of ideas is seen in Michael J. A. Howe (1989). 'Separate skills or general intelligence: the autonomy of human abilities.' In this paper Howe directs attention towards the relevance of a range of separate abilities in the learner in determining successful performance, and questions the validity of the concept of general intelligence.

> 'First, once it is apparent that what a child is capable of doing largely depends upon particular abilities which that individual has acquired, rather than upon the presence or absence of some mythical quality or power of intelligence (or "intelligences", in Gardner's 1984 conceptualisation, for that matter), it becomes clear that the way to help the child to gain a valued intellectual ability is to maximise the chances of the individual acquiring the particular skills and the particular kinds of knowledge which that ability depends upon. In deciding what is required, the concept of intelligence is redundant and unnecessary. Introducing it only confuses the issue'.

Parents of Spld students will wish to ask how the interplay of the child's abilities and difficulties in learning affect the development of the essential literacy and numeracy skills required on the curriculum. They must therefore be looking at the profiles of abilities and difficulties in the major prerequisites to literacy; motor skills, working memory skills, perceptual skills, and knowledge of the language upon which later speech, reading, spelling, and writing competences are built.

It is therefore apparent that 'intelligence' *per se* is of little relevance in determining whether or not a child has specific learning difficulties. Its only value is to give some indication of language expectations from a particular student, and when used for that purpose some care must be exercised. The efficiency with which the skills available to the student are applied in a range of problem solving situations and in language training is a much more relevant matter.

Work by Tyler and Elliott, (1989) and Elliott (1989) has identified profiles on British Ability Scales indicating different patterns of abilities and difficulties in students with specific learning difficulties and relating to these profiles to their failure in development of literacy skills. Similar patterns of abilities and difficulties underlying failure in the acquisition of literacy skills have been identified in the Dyslexia Institute from detailed analysis of some 10,000 case histories. In Table 1, given below, the profiles of three students failing literacy skills are presented. It should be noted that in fact these represent very large groups of children, not single students.

Table 1. Profiles on Wechsler Intelligence Scale for children (Form R) of students failing in the acquisition of literacy skills

Verbal Scale (Problem solving in words)				**Performance Scale (Problem solving using visual and hand skills)**			
Child	*1*	*2*	*3*	*Child*	*1*	*2*	*3*
Information	7	12	7	Picture Completion	13	9	13
Similarities	9	16	14	Picture Arrangement	12	7	6
Arithmetic	6	10	8	Block Design	13	6	10
Vocabulary	9	15	15	Object Assembly	16	10	15
Comprehension	9	17	16	Coding	12	6	7
Digit Span	(5)	10	(5)	Mazes			
Sum of scores	40	70	60		66	38	51
Verbal IQ	87	125	112	**Performance IQ**	123	84	101

Child 1 shows low average verbal problem solving competence. He has average skill in verbal reasoning in similarities, similar ability to define words in common English use in vocabulary, and oral comprehension. Marked difficulty is evident in the auditory short term memory competences required in digit span, and related weakness is evident in the working memory processing required in information and arithmetic.

On the performance scale, Child 1 shows well-developed visual analysis in picture completion, competent visual sequencing in picture arrangement, and good visual perceptual skills in block design. His constructive visual thinking in object assembly is excellent, and in coding he shows adequate fine motor skill and competent visual short term memory for the abstract shapes he is required to copy. This student is visually able, and has well developed skills in art, design and creative practical work. He is consequently well adjusted to school, and is not too concerned by his language failures, but needs help to develop competences in verbal learning and literacy skills. He is easy to work with, enjoys his special language and learning lessons, but is relaxed rather than highly motivated to succeed in this area of his education. He expresses himself through his art and creative practical work, and knows he will enjoy his work in this field when he leaves school. He is tolerant of the use school makes of his time, but his priorities are often different from the teacher's.

Child 2 shows a very marked contrast. He has competent verbal skills, but has marked difficulties in visual sequencing in the picture arrangement subtest, very poor visual perceptual skills in block design, and shows limited visual short term memory capability, and very uncertain fine motor skills in coding. Child 2 shows good oral verbal skills, but is unable to express himself adequately through written language, drawing or art, and is consequently frustrated and aggressive in class. His need is for help with visual learning and literacy, and he can be very demanding in his special language and learning lessons, and his cooperation is limited.

Child 3 shows fluctuating abilities and difficulties in both verbal and visual problem solving areas, and displays the classic ACID profile researched at the Dyslexia Unit at Aston University and discussed subsequently by Newton and Thomson. His learning and literacy needs are different from Children 1 and 2.

These children show contrasting patterns of abilities and difficulties in learning. They all experience significant retardations in the basic literacy skills of reading, spelling and writing, but show differences in their literacy failures related to the contrasts evident in their learning difficulties. They may all be categorised as dyslexic, but for teachers this is not a particularly useful term in highlighting the abilities and difficulties in learning which underlie their literacy failures, and lead to the individual and distinct learning programmes which should be constructed for these disparate students. Teachers must look at the underlying patterns of abilities and difficulties in learning to identify the student's special needs and build an appropriate special provision for him.

A further point must be made which underlines the irrelevance of the student's level of ability. For all these children, IQ scores in the average ability range might be quoted, but it is noted that psychologists would hesitate to quote a Full Scale IQ score for children 1 and 2. Clearly none of these students would work in class in any 'average' way. The abilities and difficulties which underlie their literacy failures will also greatly affect their day to day work on the curriculum. Some things they will do well, but others they will do very badly. Their major problems relate to the delivery of their knowledge through literacy. These very similar IQ scores say nothing about the sharply contrasting skills in learning these students bring to the curriculum, and the differences in their attitude to school, which must be the starting point for the teaching provision.

LEARNING SKILLS

1. Fine Motor Control

The assessment process should look in some detail at the child's learning skills in fine motor development. He will need this competence in manipulating the book, turning the page and in controlling the pencil in writing. The developed ocular motor skills required in controlling and moving his eyes from left to right across the page so that he takes in the printed words should not be underestimated. Much evidence is available from Dyslexia Institute assessments indicating that children with manual/fine motor skills inadequacies also show increased incidence of ocular motor difficulties. Serious deficiencies in these early skill areas should be noted for inclusion in the teaching programme.

Special needs teachers must be interested in the development of hand and eye skills, their eventual automatic control, and integration into a complex processes of reading, thinking and written expression of ideas. The special needs of children with difficulties in fine motor manipulation, for whom this writing process is different and less efficient, must be considered.

Groden (1969) quotes fascinating incidence figures which have been substantiated by later research. He indicates that 81 per cent of the child population in schools is right handed and 6 per cent left handed. Teachers should be aware of these figures, and must consider the special needs of the remaining 13 per cent of the child population in schools who are uncertain about which is their preferred hand.

If the child has no sense of left or right, how does he know where 'begin' or 'end' is?. How can he sequence or organise his activities? These children show problems in hand skills at the preschool stage, and later sequencing difficulties which alter the structure of their learning and experience. The ability to use fine motor skills is one of the major channels for registering information leading to long term storage and recall. This important aspect of the learning process must be available to all children and special arrangements made to ensure its development in children with specific learning difficulties from their enrolment in school.

2. *Working Memory Competences*

In enabling the understanding and definition of the working memory inefficiencies in the Spld student's learning skills the assessment process makes a vital contribution to the formulation of the provision which will meet the student's difficulties in learning. The nature and extent of the student's working memory difficulties must be investigated in detail, so highlighting the adequacy or inadequacy of the links between auditory, visual, motor, and semantic aspects of learning, which the student brings to the development of literacy skills.

Baddeley (1976), and others, have argued that short term or primary memory is more appropriately labelled working memory to emphasise the fact that it is used as a work space while operating a skill, or thinking about something. Baddeley argues that we should regard working memory as a system involving constituent skills which are employed on some occasions, but not on others, depending upon the subject's strategies and the particular learning task being undertaken.

The constituent systems within working memory have been discussed in detail in the literature. A central executive has been postulated, (Baddeley 1982) linked to a range of 'slave systems' which function as information holds. The major sub-systems are (a) *auditory*: primary acoustic memory (Colle and Welsh 1976, Colle 1980, Salame and Baddeley 1982); and articulatory rehearsal loop, (Baddeley and Hitch 1974, Baddeley 1978; and Salame and Baddeley 1982; and (b) *visual*: the visuospatial scratch pad, (Baddeley, Grant, Wight and Thomson 1974; Kolers and Smythe, 1979 and Baddeley and Lieberman 1980).

These systems are discussed by Reisberg, Rappaport and O'Shaughnessy 1984, who argue that the properties of working memory are extremely flexible and strategy dependent. They consider the constituents of working memory to be activity-based strategic processes or skills available in learning, and suggest there are no limits in principle to the constellation of constituent skills comprising working memory, and thus on the *extent to which it can be expanded*.

Working memory has also been regarded as a process, rather than a structure; (Craik and Lockhart 1972; Craik and Levy 1976; Cremark and Craik 1979; Crowder 1982; and Reisberg, Rapport and O'Shaugnessy 1984). This process has four major functions:

(i) to provide short term storage in strategy dependent systems related to the five major sense areas which may be used in learning, but particularly auditory, motor, and visual information processing.

(ii) to facilitate the encoding of incoming information for effective storage and retrieval in long term memory.

(iii) to enable recall of already learned material from long term memory to the 'executive', to facilitate perception and problem solving using the past experience already available to the child.

(iv) to enable the automatic control of a previously learned skill, while other incoming or recalled information is processed simultaneously in the sub-systems.

WORKING MEMORY INEFFICIENCIES IN STUDENTS WITH SPLD

The child with specific learning difficulties has not acquired the skills and strategies referred to by Reisberg, Rappaport and O'Shaughnessy (1984), and has difficulty in developing working memory competences. Often the child's parents and teachers will have gained some knowledge of his difficulties from his fluctuating skills in recalling, and his varying competences in long and short term memory.

Although Spld children show difficulties in the peripheral aspects of working memory, such as auditory and visual short term recall, the most significant difficulty they experience is in the fourth area of working memory described above, that is, the automatic control of the subskills in a major schema such as reading, when the peripheral subsystems are heavily committed in contributory recall tasks. (Perfetti and Lesgold 1972, Daneman and Carpenter 1980; and Chasty and Zdzienski 1986). The argument advanced is that children with limited working memory capacity will experience a conflict in the use of working memory for temporary storage, as well as for processing the skill. This will reduce the effectiveness of one or other of these functions. For example, in reading aloud the child may say the words correctly, but be unable to store and recall the sense effectively in comprehension. However, when required, he can switch priorities, using available memory capacity for retaining the sense, but in doing so, makes many more word recognition errors.

Learning inefficiencies such as this are referred to specifically in Annex 1 of DES Circular 1/83 and again in Annex 1 of Circular 22/89, where in Section 1 cognitive development is listed; and again Section 2 of the Aims of Provision, in considering specific areas of weakness or gaps in skills acquisition which impede the child's progress, direct reference is made to short term memory deficits.

PERCEPTION

Testing of the integrity of perceptual skills must be included in the assessment procedure. The important process of perception has been investigated in some detail by the teaching profession and teachers are generally aware of the need to develop the child's competences in perception. Perception should now be regarded as a sub-skill of working memory, related to, and dependent upon, the establishment of appropriate competences in storage and retrieval of previously encountered information. How can the child make sense of shapes, when exercising visual perceptual skills, if he is unable to hold in visual short term memory the basic shape he is trying to recognise? How can the child perceive and label the shape appropriately, if, while holding the shape in visual short term memory, he is unable to recall from long term memory the previous recollection of that shape which enables the match to be made? The efficiency of operation of perceptual skills must be a part of the assessment process.

SPEECH SKILLS

The Spld child's speech difficulties are more readily evident to his parents and teachers who observe him in a range of meaningful contexts than to the psychologist working in a limited clinic based assessment process. In a psychometric assessment procedure the tester must make a deliberate effort to monitor and think about the range of speech skills the student has available, and report on his competences. In cases where the child shows some limitation in speech skills, further testing by a speech therapist will be necessary and should be recommended.

EXPRESSIVE LANGUAGE PROBLEMS

Initially, in expressive speech, the Spld child may have problems making certain sounds. Usually, the high frequency sounds such as f/th. v/th. s/sh, are badly made in speaking, and often poorly recognised and spelt.

Difficulty is also evident in using sounds sequentially as parts of words. Many Spld children experience sequencing problems in speech, long after other children have overcome this difficulty. They will still be mispronouncing words, saying 'aminals' for animals' or 'suspectable' for 'susceptible'. They may report, 'My dad was pushing a "mow lawner" across the grass' or 'He left his car at the par cark'. They get sounds in the wrong places in words. This is often regarded by others as amusing, and when children are laughed at for producing such utterances they become sensitive and learn not to expose themselves to ridicule by risking spontaneous communication in class.

An equally serious problem is often evident in expressive language skills where a child must formulate an idea as a spoken or written sentence.

All too often the Spld student has no sense of the range of purposes of speech and uses the communicative 'vernacular' form when the purpose is representational in the thinking process. His friends in the playground may understand him, and his mother will know intuitively what he means. As communication the speech may be effective in a limited way, but language such as this is not so useful in the classroom as a basis for thinking, reading, spelling and higher writing skills required in examinations, nor indeed for handling the range of activities required in the national curriculum.

RECEPTIVE LANGUAGE PROBLEMS

The Spld child's difficulties in receptive language are much less obvious, but no less serious. Teachers tend to build lengthy sentences, and give spoken instructions in long sequential lists which are often incomprehensible to the dyslexic child. An instruction such as 'Before you go home, do your spelling corrections', is wrongly comprehended by many Spld children who take in the key words 'go', 'home', 'do corrections,' and dash immediately for the door.

A basic speech principle which is too often neglected by teachers is 'order of mention'. Teacher must give instructions to the child in the order they should be done. If teacher varies the order in the way illustrated above, she gives the child the additional problems of (i) recognising the obliqueness of the form of communication, and (ii) holding the instructions in working memory, while resequencing to the required operational order. This is a totally unnecessary complication to teacher-child communication which reinforces the question posed earlier: 'If this child doesn't learn the way we teach, can we teach him the way he learns?'. Teacher's duty must be to give the child the information he requires in a way which is acceptable and usable by him.

READING SKILLS

Reading is not a single skill: it is a linked series of sub-skills which leads to information-processing competences with a very wide range of purposes and applications. The testing carried out in reading should look at the range of reading skills, monitoring the student's competences in a variety of situations.

Single word recognition tests

These tests are much loved by teachers because of their ease of administration. Parents also favour them because they offer a crude definition of level of skill which they can readily relate to. Recent 'guides' to tests have attacked word recognition tests as being unhelpful. Vincent, Green, Francis and Powney 1983 amongst others, have commented very negatively on the Schonell Graded Word Recognition Test, 'Judged against contemporary theories of reading and reading curriculum, the continued use of either test is to be deplored. Repeated use of the test on the same children, either yearly or termly, is not unheard of, and this merely increases the pointlessness of using the tests'. While reading theorists, looking at the development of reading in children with competent learning skills, may attack this kind of test, it should be accepted that for Spld students who bring rather different competences to the learning of reading, word recognition tests enable a searching analysis of one sub-skill of reading which is difficult for them, i.e., the link between the shape of the word and its sound. Psychologists and teachers interested in the reading sub-skill weaknesses of Spld students will find that with a little ingenuity, these single word recognition tests can provide information about their reading strategies which is not readily discernible in other circumstances.

Much useful information can be gleaned from a word recognition test which contains a balanced word repertoire relating to the vocabulary of the children concerned. The British Ability Scales Word Reading Test (A) seems particularly appropriate from this point of view.

It is suggested that by timing this test from the start to the point of discontinuation as given in test instructions, two additional calculations may be made:

(i) *Mean response time*: the total time the child takes from the start of the test to the point where he must discontinue is divided by the number of words attempted, to give the average or mean time taken to respond to each word. Some children achieve a very low average response time of 1 second or less, others record a very high time of 5 seconds or more. This enables qualitative differences in speed of processing to be determined in aspects of the student's word recognition strategies.

(ii) *Accuracy of response expressed as a percentage of words attempted*: it is important to know whether the student attempted a great many words and got most of them wrong. The child with the 45 per cent accuracy level has a qualitatively different word recognition system from the child with an 85 per cent accuracy level.

A practical illustration will clarify the advantages of adding these extra dimensions to the test procedure. On British Ability Scales Word Reading Test (A), Bill and Charles both recognise 50 words correctly and can be credited with reading ages of 7 years 7 months. However, Bill read 50 words correctly out of a full 90 attempted, and records an accuracy level of 55 per cent with a mean response time of 1.2 seconds per word. He is clearly using a very fast but inaccurate visual recognition strategy.

Charles, on the other hand attempts only 60 words, has an accuracy level of 83 per cent and a mean response time of 6.4 seconds per word. He is using a very slow but accurate 'analyse, sound out, then blend', phonic strategy. Although both boys have exactly the same overall word recognition competence at the 7 year 7 month standard, a little extra time spent in analysis after testing allows the test procedure to be used much more efficiently, so enabling teacher to relate the learner to the important teaching implications relevant for dysphonetic or dysedictic learners. The element of consistency or accuracy of response in a given time is very important in assessing students with specific learning difficulties.

Continuous reading

In the assessment process it is essential to listen to the student reading aloud from graded materials of increasing difficulty.

(i) Sentence reading tests. The Salford Reading Test by Bookbinder gives a useful example of this procedure and the rather more dated Holborn test provides a wider age range on older and less certain norms, and using less acceptable words and sentences.

(ii) Continuous prose. Tests such as Macmillan Reading Analysis or Neale Analysis of Reading Ability (Revised British Edition) give important information about skills levels in reading aloud. In this complex sequential skill the reader must recognise letter,

word or phrase shapes. The size and complexity of the visual unit processed will depend upon the skill and sophistication of the reader. He must link the sounds accurately and quickly to the shape, control and coordinate muscles of tongue, lips and teeth to say the words, whilst simultaneously extracting and storing the meaning in small sections and building it into an understanding of the whole. In both these tests, word recognition skills largely determine comprehension competence. Given a fixed working memory capability, if the complex continuous reading process is too large to be managed within the available capacity, will the child focus his/her attention on word recognition – or to processing meaning? He may read all the words correctly, but how effectively does he process, store and recall the meaning in the time scales available to him! Alternatively, he may use much of his available working memory capacity to process the meaning and, by doing this, make a very much higher frequency of errors in the word recognition process. The variation of comprehension competence in relation to speed and text difficulty is a vital dynamic relationship in continuous reading which must be documented in the failing Spld reader.

This may also be done by observing the reader in class, working on a structured text, but this is not necessarily the most efficient way of gaining this information about the student's skills.

Spelling

Norm referenced spelling tests give a useful but crude indication of student spelling competence. Tests such as Schonell A and B, Burt, Vernon, Daniels and Dyack are now rather dated, and only indicate spelling competence in the situation where the child's total available working memory capability is focused directly on spelling the single target word given. An example illustrates the point. Teachers may spell the word 'onomatopoeia' totally accurately in a spelling test, where they have much time, can focus attention on that single word, and use auditory analytical, visual, and motor strategies to support each other to make an accurate response. A much more important measure is the ability to spell the word automatically in a written examination – when addressing a complex question such as 'Discuss the use of onomatopoeia as a technical device in English 19th Century poetry' when there is just five minutes of examination time left, and the candidate must write the word eight times in these five minutes – while drawing together the threads of a complex verbal thinking sequence.

Spelling tests should therefore be augmented by analysis of spelling accuracy levels in *timed free writing* about a complex subject related to the student's curriculum interests. The writing of Pearse (see Appendix 2) makes the point. At age eight Pearse is very bright – with a WISC (R) Verbal IQ of 136 and a Performance IQ of 120. On a Vernon Graded Word Spelling Test he achieves a 7 year 10 month level and on this test cannot be considered to have serious spelling difficulties. Yet on his free writing in his history he makes a very high percentage error rate which indicates that when working memory is heavily loaded with ideas and strategies in history, Pearse has little available space to devote to the mechanics of spelling, and consequently produces a much higher spelling error rate. What is important is not his level of skill in uncomplicated conditions, but the efficiency of application of that skill to the delivery of knowledge in a complex situation.

The timed free writing test gives teachers and psychologists an opportunity to observe the dynamics of the free writing skill. All too often this opportunity is missed in a busy class teaching situation. How effectively does the student hold and manipulate the pen? What is his writing style – block capital, print, cursive? How effectively does he carry out the motor movements necessary to make the letters and words? What is his percentage spelling error rate? How well does he apply punctuation rules? How efficiently does he build and sequence sentences to convey his ideas? It is in this process, which enables the coherent expression of ideas in writing and the effective delivery of knowledge in class assignments and examinations, that the most significant effects of specific learning difficulties are most frequently observed.

NUMERACY

The difficulties in learning evident in fine motor skill and working memory competence can also lead to difficulties in calculation competence. Weaknesses may be observed in oral calculation. This procedure places a heavy load on skills in memory, where information has to be taken up from words, spoken or read, held, and manipulated using an appropriate sequential order process requiring the application of recalled tables. Most Spld students are unable to manage without a calculator.

Written calculation is an essential curriculum skill. This complex process of reproducing figures accurately, placing them in a very specific location on a page determined by the demands of 'place value', and following the process sequence through to its final conclusion while recalling the essential tables, is often carried out very inefficiently. Instruments such as British Ability Scales Basic Number Skills Tests give useful information about the efficiency and integrity of these basic processes. The British Ability Scales Procedure is particularly useful because it enables student performance on the test to be expressed both in terms of age competence and centile rank, or T score, thus facilitating comparison of the child with others of his age as required by Education Act 1981, and enabling judgements to be made about the relative severity of his reading or numeracy difficulties.

A good alternative system with rather higher diagnostic potential is provided by The Basic Number Screening Test by Gillham and Hesse.

BEHAVIOURAL/SOCIAL SKILLS

The difficulties in learning experienced by dyslexic students may also lead to social and behavioural difficulties in class, or at home. The frustrations of prolonged failure on a range of curriculum subjects, resulting in feelings of insecurity and lack of confidence can have profound effects upon social status, friendship patterns in class, and acceptance and adjustment in the rough and tumble of the playground. Stress and insecurity can lead to an accentuation of information processing difficulties. Aggressive and anti social behaviour may result from these tensions.

It is important to note these factors which clearly relate to the student's efficiency of learning. If from the indications given by home and school, behaviour is thought to be an important factor then some measurement of social and personality skills is desirable. Tests such as Children's Personality Questionnaire by Porter and Cattell; and the 16 Personality Factor Test by Catell, particularly in its C, D, or E forms, give a very useful personality profile which enables the identification and documentation of factors such as sociability, emotional stability, impulsivity, conformity, sensitivity, insecurity, self sufficiency, self discipline, tension, and a anxiety. These factors will assist teacher in understanding the efficiency with which a particular student relates to teacher and others in the learning group and learns from his teaching provision. Useful information about the personality of the student in relation to his learning may also be obtained from the junior and adult forms of the Eysenck Personality Questionnaire.

Learning does not happen with equal effectiveness for *every* student in the large, often unstructured group of thirty plus students encountered in the ordinary classroom of the ordinary school. If the child has failed to learn in these circumstances, the social background to that failed learning process must be one of the variables manipulated to improve the child's learning competences.

These matters seem to be given little consideration by psychologists or education officers who write the psychological advice for education authorities. They make the assumption that the ordinary class of the ordinary school is always the best place to learn. But this assumption must be open to question. On the way to improving the child's learning, there is a clear need to establish the present base of his social, emotional, behavioural and personality skills so that appropriate action and management of the learner's group size and structure may be built into his learning programme.

PROFILES IN LEARNING

The research of Tyler and Elliott 1988, and Elliott 1989, points to the need for the student's cognitive profile to be understood and related to the individual teaching provision made for the child.

From a study of the student's profile in the skills of learning, literacy, numeracy and social and behavioural skills, teacher gains real understanding of the full nature and extent of the student's abilities and difficulties, as they influence the direction and pace of his development. It is this understanding which enables appropriate priorities to be established for the student's learning, and a provision to be devised which accurately meets his needs.

TEACHING PROVISIONS

The range of teaching provisions to be made for students with specific learning difficulties will be wide and varied. The provision made must be individual and relate to the abilities and difficulties in learning experienced by the student. The provision should cover (a) learning skills, (b) (i) language skills, (ii) numeracy skills, (c) study/ thinking skills, and (d) behavioural skills, and (e) link effectively to the school curriculum. For the majority of students this can be arranged and managed in the ordinary school. Others with greater difficulty will need to be withdrawn to a unit for small group teaching. A few will have such serious difficulties that they cannot sustain the broad curriculum of the ordinary school and must be sent to a school which makes special provision where skill development is directly related to curriculum load.

The skills list to be covered is set out below:

A. Learning skills

1. Fine motor skill development (train the hand).
2. Laterality-sequencing training (where do I start).
3. Working memory training: develop deliberate control of available capacity, extend capacity, teach discarding of irrelevant information, choose time for learning, switch modalities frequently, multi-sensory is best.
4. Visual perceptual training: skill in recognising shapes consistently.
5. Auditory perceptual training: skill in recognising sounds consistently.

B. (i) Language skill

6. Language development through talk:
   (i) getting sounds and words right
   (ii) getting sentences right
   (iii) concept/idea/labelling.
   (iv) creating an organisation for talk.
7. Structured multi-sensory training to develop simultaneous skills in reading, spelling and writing and making most effective use of deficient memory skills.

B. (ii) Numeracy skill

8. Number language training: using structured multi-sensory methods.

C. Study/thinking skills

9. Extraction, representation, storage and recall of ideas.
10. Expression of ideas in writing.
11. Development of active control of the learning/thinking process in metacognition.

D. Behavioural skills

Developing the competences to enable the learner to operate effectively in a range of social and learning groups with varying purposes, structures, climates.

RELATE TO THE CURRICULUM OF THE SCHOOL

Much thought must go into balancing the demands for fast gains in the student's literacy skills against broad curriculum experience, which may be meaningless unless these skills are at an acceptable level.

It is in this area of provision-making that the real skill is necessary to ensure the student's future success. The student's profiles, detailing abilities and difficulties in learning, will have stimulated a full consideration of his/her special educational needs, leading to an appraisal of the skill areas where development is necessary, and the establishment of priorities in the student's education.

In the evaluation of that student's special needs in relation to the curriculum of his/her school and the national curriculum, a high level of understanding of the student's difficulties, current educational practice and much skill and tact are necessary. Although it is expensive of time, it is usually best if the teaching programme is negotiated at a case conference which reflects student, parent, school, and education authority interests.

TIME ALLOCATED TO SPECIAL NEEDS PROGRAMME

Throughout the country, education officers are very aware that in meeting the special needs of any student, they are obliged by Education Act 1981 to 'take due account of the efficient use of resources'. This is a very interesting and challenging requirement which is too often misinterpreted as 'making the cheapest possible provision in terms of cost in a given financial year'. In an educational service which prides itself on the care and consideration given to children who have special educational needs, it is self evident that 'resources' should not be regarded solely as the cost of the teaching provision. Use of resources should involve the child, and his learning time, and teacher and her teaching time, as these must be part of the resources marshalled and manipulated to meet the child's needs.

If a programme is constructed which aims to keep costs down to a minimum, will this make the most positive and practical use of the child's learning time, and the teacher's teaching time?

In making a provision the education officer should be interested in achieving maximum skills gain for minimum cost, so making most efficient use of child learning and teacher teaching time in school. Is this aim facilitated by making a minimum provision in terms of hours per week, or is it possible to arrive at an educationally and economically efficient provision?

INDICATIONS FROM UNFINISHED RESEARCH

Research still in process of completion, relating progress in word recognition skills as measured by gains on British Ability Scales Word Recognition Test (A) in children of generally average ability, who were at least two years below their chronological age level in this skill, suggests that progress is not directly proportional to teaching time.

With a very limited provision of one hour per week or less, only limited overall gains are recorded. Because the limited time available is usually allocated in one or two spaced session per week, this intermittent provision results in a considerable loss of learned information through forgetting, and the effects of the forgetting curve greatly reduce the overall efficiency of the teaching.

Most effective gains are recorded in multiple short sessions amounting to between three and six hours per week. Above this level, the effects of saturation or boredom seem to reduce the efficiency of the teaching/learning process.

This research is still unfinished but the figures currently to hand translate relatively easily and quite strikingly into costs of provisions. A skill gain of one year in word recognition skills can be achieved on a provision of one hour per week, but will require some 114 hours of teaching. Given normal teaching terms and the usual school distractions, this might occupy three academic years, and at a guestimated cost of £10 per hour would entail the expenditure of some £1140 by home, school or education authority. If the provision is increased to two hours per week the teaching time necessary falls to some 76 hours with the cost being £760. At three hours per week the required progress can be achieved in 57 hours at a cost of £570. At 8+ hours per week the required gain takes 72 hours and costs £720. It is therefore apparent, even from this crude analysis of a very limited aspect of reading skill, that in any financial year, a low cost provision is not an efficient use of resources. However, it is possible to calculate an educationally and economically efficient teaching programme for a particular student.

CONSTRUCTION OF PROVISIONS

The major problem currently arising is the impact of the demands for time and teaching resources made by national curriculum. Headteachers and class teachers are currently overwhelmed by work in this area, and look searchingly at time allocated to meeting special needs by developing individual skills. Not only do we face a demand for special needs to be met wholly in the mainstream school, this is linked to a whole school approach often linked to topics set within a national curriculum where individual skills development in children is regarded as an alien idea. Parents rightly question where the individual child is, in this very 'system' based approach.

Chapter 3

The national curriculum

The national curriculum is the Government's major initiative towards educational policy reform leading to the year 2000 and is legislated for in the Education Reform Act 1988. This sets out, in its first section the important aims and general principles which must be reflected in the curriculum of all pupils.

PRIORITIES

The Department of Education and Science requires all children enrolled in state schools in England and Wales to study a specified group of essential subjects to ensure that (1) they receive a broad education. To this end the system seeks to keep the subject range wide by (2) preventing students from dropping subjects which might be of value later in employment.

AIMS

The aims of the national curriculum are wide ranging, and will have a considerable influence upon the development of thinking of all children. The change in learning processes and the range and depth of thinking implicit in the curriculum is so great as to be revolutionary in effect.

The basic aims enshrined in the act are very laudable:

(a) To promote the spiritual, moral, cultural, mental and physical development of pupils at the school and of society; and

(b) Prepare such pupils for the opportunities, responsibilities and experiences of adult life.

These basic aims have important implications for the school curriculum: and establish the following principles used to determine classroom practices.

(1) That each pupil has a legal right to a broad and balanced curriculum which is also relevant to his or her particular needs.

(2) It is not enough for such a curriculum to be offered by the school: it must be fully taken up by each *individual* pupil.

(3) The curriculum must promote development in all the main areas of learning and experience which are widely accepted as important.

(4) The curriculum should also offer a range of personal and social opportunities and responsibilities to each pupil so that he/she may develop as an individual, as a member of society and as a future adult member of the community.

While specific aspects of the national curriculum may not be appropriate for some pupils with special educational needs and particularly those with Spld, special arrangements may be made for such pupils. However, the general principles established in Section 1 of the Act apply to *all* pupils and must be reflected in all special arrangements made for them. It must be noted that a curriculum which meets the major criteria outlined above is regarded in the Act as an entitlement for *all* pupils.

The problem for parents and teachers of Spld children is that their special skills and difficulties in learning have not been full understood or considered in relation to the proposals now being implemented, and there is a real danger that the important aims and principles outlined above, and now being thrust at parents as an 'entitlement', will take precedence over the major priority to meet the special educational needs of the Spld child *appropriately*. Within a curriculum with such wide ranging opportunities there is a real danger that the teacher will concentrate upon giving the child experiences from which he might learn, rather than developing his thinking skills and strategies to enable him learn more fully and meaningfully from *later* experiences.

AREA OF APPLICATION

All state schools in England and Wales must comply. While the Act does not apply to independent schools, city technology colleges must follow the required curriculum. It is understood that the CTC Trust now wants to develop a separate curriculum specifically for the city technology colleges.

COMPOSITION OF THE NATIONAL CURRICULUM

The core subjects of the national curriculum are English, Mathematics and Science. Seven other subjects are required: technology, history, a modern language, geography, music, art, and physical education.

The elevation of science to the higher status of 'core subject' has been particularly challenging and clearly appropriate for children who must face the demands of the as yet unknown information processing problems relevant to life and work in the year 2010. Teachers generally have welcomed and praised the 'Programmes of study' for science. Particularly reassuring has been the weight given to enabling children to *be* scientific, and *think* scientifically, as opposed to accumulating scientific knowledge and mastering facts which will become irrelevant all too quickly in an age of rapidly accelerating technological change.

It is hoped that in the curricula still to be developed, there will be a similar concentration upon the establishment of *systems* to enable the student to represent knowledge in a range of ways, rather than imposing upon him a heavy burden of verbally stored inert *facts*.

ESTABLISHING THE CURRICULUM

The procedure followed to establish the content of each section of the curriculum has been the same in all subjects. Initially the Secretary of State appoints a working group which writes a draft curriculum. This is published, comments are invited, and the draft is revised in the light of feed back from interested parties. The revised curriculum then goes to the Secretary of State who, even at that final stage, can introduce changes, and is seen to have the last word.

TIME SCALES FOR THE CURRICULUM TO BE FOLLOWED

Children will study the listed subjects up to the age of 16 years, but not all pupils will take GCSEs in these subjects.

PROCEDURE FOR INTRODUCTION

The full range of subjects in the national curriculum will be introduced on a 'rolling basis' and is not expected to be complete until 1997. Even so, teachers are bewildered and perplexed by the rate of change which requires them to absorb an immense burden of information related to the new and developing systems and procedures.

The national curriculum for English has been introduced only to pupils aged between 5–7 years. Mathematics and science curricula were imposed on all but the eldest band. Other subjects such as art and physical education are still in the early stages of the drafting process, so much still remains to be done.

Key stages in English

The first of the key stages in English which covers pupils aged 5–7 was published in late 1989 and the other stages are to follow soon. Five attainment targets are set out for pupils in this stage: (1) speaking and listening (2) reading (3) writing (4) spelling (5) handwriting.

Each of these attainment targets has 10 levels, which cover all children from age 5 to 16. It is expected that only the brightest students will reach level 10. At age seven years, an average child will have mastered level 2, but a bright seven year old might have reached as high as level 6.

TEACHING OF ENGLISH IN THE NATIONAL CURRICULUM

Parents of Spld children will need to be very fully aware of the aims, structure and format for teaching English within the national curriculum. 'The overriding aim of the English curriculum is to enable all pupils to develop to the full, their ability to use and understand English. Since language can be both spoken and written, this means the fullest possible development of abilities in speaking, listening, reading and writing'.

While this explicit aim is totally reassuring, teachers, psychologists and educational administrators still have to understand that the language use of Spld students is subtly different from other students. These children may have both receptive and expressive language difficulties, which are deeper than the processing and production of sounds and words, more far reaching than varieties of English, and have much to do with the management of what Chomsky referred to as the 'deep structure of language', which relates to the number of transformations used in deriving and expressing its meaning, and the amount of memory required to process and store it.

In the English curriculum, it is expected that speaking and listening, reading and writing should be developed through purposeful activities arising out of a range of curriculum contexts. In the advisory document published by the national curriculum Council specific activities considered to be relevant are:

(a) Language use for other readers/listeners

This will involve children in giving and receiving simple explanations, information and instructions, and asking and answering questions. They will need to present their ideas, experiences and understandings in a range of contexts which require an increasing awareness of 'audience' in the determination of purpose in using language.

Reading is seen as being closely related to the curriculum, with reading activities being curriculum based. In Stage 1, reading can arise from role-play and dramatic play. Children will be encouraged to frame questions about texts arising from the curriculum. While this approach to reading is not quite 'top down' is very different from the 'bottom up' step by step construction followed in structured multi-sensory teaching, which aims to build the skill. While the two approaches are *not* mutually exclusive, it is doubtful whether a busy class teacher managing a lively class of young children will have the time to facilitate the use of both approaches *simultaneously*. The implicit principles, and explicit curriculum demands will make the in-class provision of individual structured multi-sensory programmes for Spld students that much more difficult.

Writing is expected to arise naturally from the activities of the curriculum, and opportunities should be given for 'publishing' stories and newspapers for other children and writing for different audiences.

(b) Collaborative learning in language work

It is anticipated that individual children will participate in problem solving collaboratively with the class. They will take part in shared reading experiences with teacher, and the other children. Opportunities will be given for discussing information books, and developing an understanding of the ways in which information can be organised and presented. Such collaborative work is seen as giving opportunities for children who lack detailed writing skills to participate in composing at greater length, by working *with* other children who have developed the necessary competences . On reflection some parents and teachers consider that this will further reinforce the failing Spld child's low self concept, and rejection within the system.

(c) Reflection of language use

A feature of the activity of the English curriculum will be opportunities to discuss work with teacher and colleagues. This will involve reflection upon the progress of a piece of work; discussing ways in which language is written down; reflecting on what has been read, and commenting on the content of reading in a thoughtful way; reflecting on the child's own writing, sharing it with others, and discussing what has been written.

It is apparent that all of this, laudable though its aim is, could be traumatic for a Spld child, unless it is handled very sensitively and skillfully.

THE SPLD CHILD AND ATTAINMENT TARGETS

In the preliminary training given on implementing the national curriculum, some education authorities have suggested that the Spld child at age 7, on attainment target (1) speaking and listening, could be on level 3, or higher; but on attainment targets (2) reading (4) spelling and (5) handwriting could be at a very much lower level, and may even fail to satisfy level 1 requirements. Teachers have been advised to consider the variability in the child's levels of attainment on the national curriculum, studying carefully his/her overall attainment profile. It has been anticipated that a spiky profile will give a clear indication of the existence of specific difficulties in learning in the vital core subjects of the national curriculum. This makes overly simplistic generalisations about the spoken language competence of the Spld child, and one must be concerned that many Spld children with some spoken language deficiencies will show a uniformly low attainment profile, and their thinking competences will be concealed by the speech, reading and writing difficulties which are a part of their specific learning difficulties.

FACTORS RELATING PARTICULARLY TO CHILDREN WITH SPECIAL EDUCATIONAL NEEDS IN THE NATIONAL CURRICULUM

General position

All pupils share the same statutory entitlement to a broad and balanced curriculum, including access to the national curriculum. The national curriculum framework, and specific provisions within it, will offer very wide scope for teachers to deal with the full range of individual needs. But in some cases it may be necessary to make exceptional arrangements.

Meeting different needs within the statutory framework

The basic requirements of the national curriculum may be modified so that children with special educational needs can benefit from it *as far as they are able.* (Though it must be questioned whether with more teaching targeted towards individual skills development they might benefit from it much more fully at a slightly later stage in their school career). The advantages of meeting special educational needs in the national curriculum are:

1. The establishment of objectives for attainment on ten levels covering the period of compulsory schooling means that both normal progression for a pupil over time, and differences in ability, performance and maturity can be accommodated. Virtually all pupils will be able to record some progress through these levels.
2. The overlap of levels of attainment and of programmes of study between the four key stages in each foundation subject implies

that pupils will be able to work according to their own abilities and needs at each stage.

3. The avoidance of over-prescription in programmes of study in each foundation subject, and the fact that teachers are free to determine their own teaching approaches and ways of delivering the programmes, enables the adoption of different ways of doing things. This should be helpful for those with a physical or sensory handicap.

4. Each key stage is defined by reference to the age of the majority of pupils in that class or teaching group. Individual pupils may work with a class of older or younger pupils, for some or all subjects. It is not intended that pupils should have to be kept down, or moved up, on the grounds of how they do, solely on the basis of the formal assessments. Such pupils will not need a different programme nor will they have to be assessed at a different time. The headteacher may decide that pupils should be assessed when they are 7, 11, 14 or 16, regardless of the age of the majority of the teaching group, if their educational level is different from that of their class-mates – for example, in a mixed-age class. However this will need to be handled very sensitively if pupils with special needs are not to be made to feel very different from their peers.

Adaptations to national curriculum to enable individual needs to be met

The national curriculum may be adapted to meet individual special needs. As indicated in DES Circular 22/89 Annexe II Section III, and in accordance with Section 18 of Education Reform Act 1988, modifications to the national curriculum necessary to meet the child's special educational needs in terms of (i) programmes of study (ii) attainment targets (iii) assessment and testing (iv) exemptions from foundation subjects must be *specified* in Section III of the child's statement of special educational needs. It is also required that details of proposals to replace the exempted programme in order to maintain a broad balanced curriculum should also be given.

There are three main ways of adapting to the national curriculum:

1. For groups of pupils defined in terms of particular cases and circumstances: by including exemptions or modifications in the

Orders which lay down the attainment targets, programmes of study, assessment arrangements and in the information requirements. Alternatively special regulations may be made to exempt such a group of pupils or modify their curriculum.

2. For individual pupils with continuing special education needs which are covered by a statement under the 1981 Act: The statement may be used to modify or disapply national curriculum requirements (as described above).
3. For individual pupils for whom the national curriculum is temporarily inappropriate, including those awaiting the preparation of a statement or a reassessment under the 1981 Act, the headteacher is enabled to disapply or modify the national curriculum in circumstances set out in the regulations.

ASSESSMENT

Purposes of assessment?

The main purpose of assessment in the primary school is regarded by the teaching profession as being formative i.e. helping teachers to identify the next steps in children's learning. The extent to which assessment has a summative purpose, i.e. recording the achievement of the pupil is questioned by many teachers. Yet the Secretary of State has indicated that assessment should have both *formative* and *summative* purposes at ages 7 and 11.

What is an assessment?

The problem is accentuated by wide divisions between practising teachers and the strong government lobby not just on the aims of assessment, but on what constitutes an accurate assessment. Teachers understandably take the view that an assessment should be informal, and is, a teacher watching children undertake an assignment. The government's view of assessment is much more formal and presumes written testing of the student's competences from the assignment. Naturally both sides of that debate are aware of the often quoted comment, that an assessment tells one more about the assessor than it does about the student being assessed. At this stage in the development of the dialectic process, all that can be said is that everyone agrees that assessment is fraught.

Assessment by teachers

The individual subject curricula include definitions of 'attainment targets' which require teachers to assess and upgrade the skills of pupils on a scale of 1–10.

The individual child's performance in relation to attainment targets will be assessed and reported on at ages 7, 11, 24 and 16. It is noted that for this purpose attainment targets will be grouped into profile components to make the teacher's task in assessment and reporting more manageable.

The different levels of attainment and overall progress attained by a student on tests and assessment will be registered on a 10 point scale covering all the years of compulsory schooling. In order to safeguard and facilitate comparability, these teacher assessments will be compared with the results of the national tests, standard assessment tasks, (or SATs) and with the judgements of other teachers.

It is planned that assessment will be a combination of national external tests and assessment by teachers. At age 16 the GCSE will remain the main form of assessment, especially in the core subjects of English, mathematics and science.

The DES in its guidance document 'national curriculum, from Policy to Practice (1989)' advises that the results of tests and other assessments should be used both formatively to help facilitate better teaching and to inform decisions about the next steps planned for a pupil, and summatively at ages 7,11, 14 and 16 to inform parents about their child's attainment progress.

Use of results to formulate judgements about schools

The detailed results available from assessments of individual pupils should be given in full to parents, and the DES attaches great importance to the principle that these reports should be clear, simple, and readily understood by all parents. While parents receive their own child's results these will not be published generally, but made available as aggregated results for the whole school, at ages 11, 14 and 16. This should enable the wider public to make informed judgements about attainment in a school or LEA. The DES considers that there should be no legal requirement for schools to publish the group results of seven-year-olds, though it is strongly recommended that schools should do so.

Assessment of English

Parents of Spld students will be particularly interested in the assessment of their child's language development. The Guide to national curriculum published for teachers makes clear the complexity of judgements made upon this area of child development.

> 'Language development is a complex process and cannot be defined as a linear sequence. Children do not learn particular features of language once and for all at any particular stage; they continually return to the same features and refine their competence; language development must be conceived, fostered and assessed in terms which are broad enough to accommodate variations between individuals in the sequences followed (English for ages 5 to 11).
>
> For the teacher, this means that monitoring is needed of both the individual child's progress and the opportunities provided. Records are needed, for example of the child's attempts at a particular form of writing such as non-chronological descriptions (Attainment Target 3, levels 2 and 4) that will demonstrate both the progress made with that form and the experiences that will have affected that development. Teachers will need to include in their records information about a child's home language(s) or dialect and his/her awareness of the appropriate use of different language varieties.'

Concerns about assessment in national curriculum

This area threatens to become a major problem which could bring the whole national curriculum structure crashing down in chaos. Teachers will have to make as yet vaguely defined assessments to monitor the progress made by children towards complex attainment targets, across all ten subjects of the curriculum. The glibly stated aim is that the 'assessment of children's learning in classrooms will have to be derived from normal classroom practice as far as possible, with assessment activities fitting unobtrusively into such practice.' While this sounds reassuring it leaves the whole of the assessment process still largely undetermined.

Commenting on the huge problems raised by assessment, Kate Hinton, Chairperson of the National Science Advisors' and Inspectors' group, the Association of Science Education said, 'It (assessment) is a daunting prospect for primary teachers. They face total overload once they have to assess attainment targets right across the curriculum. We are likely to have a system that is not workable.' Her Majesty's Inspectorate share this view. In a report issued in November 1989 on the implementation of the national curriculum in primary schools, they comment, 'there is considerable uncertainty and anxiety in most schools about the statutory requirements for assessing and recording children's progress'.

SUCCESS OR FAILURE IN THE NATIONAL CURRICULUM

From the perspective of Spld children who must work in schools obliged to apply the national curriculum, it is evident that some pupils with low levels of literacy skills may be good at science, and so may able to carry out the practical assignments, but be unable to write about their knowledge in a formal test. Consequently, their achievements, and ultimately their success or failure in the education system, may be determined by the form of assessment chosen, and the way in which it is applied, rather than by their ability to think positively about the subject, and carry out the practical assignments at the required level. This raises major concerns about whether learning relates to the child's practical abilities to understand and do, or to his ability to deliver a theoretical knowledge through the speaking or writing processes. This fundamental issue threatens the educational integrity of the national curriculum procedure, and ought to have been resolved long before this stage in the process.

The form of assessment chosen has other serious implications which will certainly affect Spld students, but may also have implications for *all* children. What effect will the assessment system have on the teaching approach? As always, there is a genuine risk that the test system finally chosen will circumscribe teachers' options in the classroom and determine the teaching approach, so negating much of what is good in the new proposals.

TEACHER USE OF CLASSROOM TIME

One of the greatest freedoms available to the class teacher has been substantially curtailed by the introduction of the national curriculum. For many years, heads and class teachers jealously guarded their freedom to allocate teaching time to aspects of children's skills development which they, in their professional judgement, considered to be important in their local community. Within that freedom, time was usually available to meet the skills development needs of the Spld child.

However, pressures on teaching time have been increased greatly due to the introduction of the national curriculum, with teachers being required to specify, in writing, how they will use the 902.5 hours per year teaching time required on the obligatory curriculum subjects in the junior school. It is interesting to note that though the total teaching hours devoted to national curriculum are very precisely defined, the hours to be devoted to the important core curriculum subjects are not distinguished from the total time required.

In most junior schools usable face to face teaching time is substantially less than 1,000 hours in an academic year. The disposable time left is very severely restricted and, if schools are to maintain their broad creative, artistic and games procedures, careful time management is necessary. Consequently some heads and class teachers are unwilling to allocate required special needs provision time to Spld students.

Recently a student was acknowledged by his local education authority adviser in special needs and educational psychologist to require a total specialist teaching programme of six hours per week. Because of national curriculum demands, this time could not be found. Yet the head was adamant in refusing to disapply this student from national curriculum. A conflict will frequently be evident between the student's priorities in learning which tend to be individual, and determine his special needs, and the demands of a rigid national curriculum, which at this early stage in its inception seems to be administered with a surprising degree of inflexibility, so inhibiting the school's ability to meet wide ranging special educational needs. The head has the power to apply for disapplication for a student with serious special needs and particularly for statemented students, but many seem unaware of their responsibilities or unwilling to take the necessary action.

This lack of consideration for individual special needs does not augur well for the later success of the currently popular policy, of meeting wide ranging special needs in the ordinary classroom.

Chapter 4

Difficulties related to the formal procedures under the Act: some practical advice to parents

Mary Warnock perceived the need to have access to the national special needs provision through many open doors. Parents, teachers, heads, psychologists, speech therapists, physiotherapists, doctors; whoever first noticed that a child had a problem could alert others so that the child's difficulties might be examined in detail, and a decision made about whether these could be dealt with in the local school, or whether they were of sufficient severity to warrant statementing. It was thought that in an informal, flexible but many-sided access procedure the child's needs would be identified and met, at as early an age as possible.

Sections 23 and 24 of Circular 22/89 indicate that these arrangements are largely a matter for schools and local authorities – and the governors particularly have a responsibility to ensure that pupils with special educational needs are identified and met.

For a range of reasons, the most pressing of which is scarce resources, the system has not worked as smoothly as expected. The increasing frequencies of the differences of opinion between parents, schools,and education authorities about (i) the severity of the child's needs, or (ii) how particular needs might be met, is confirmed by the backlog of cases waiting for statements or appeals and the increasing delay evident in the local authorities' ability to respond to such parents.

The area about which most controversy rages is the refusal of an education authority to make a statement, in cases where a child with Spld is considered by his parents to be failing very badly. In such cases education authorities should be obliged to produce a detailed summary of the evidence they have considered before rejecting the parent's request.

While the parents have a right of appeal to the Secretary of State, most parents who have operated the system do not feel that this is as 'impartial' as it might be, as Secretary of State, county council, or metropolitan borough, and local education authority are pressured by resources and provisions problems. At the end of the process too many parents are left as dissatisfied customers of the education system.

In cases where the education authority has decided that it is not called upon to make and maintain the provision, this *does not* mean that the child should receive *no* specialist teaching, but simply devolves the responsibility to the school for the arrangements, and the provision made must still meet the child's needs. Clearly if the child's later development with this school based provision is monitored for some time, and progress in learning and literacy skills is still demonstrably limited, then the parents may rightly reopen the issue of the suitability of the provision, and the need for statementing.

In cases where the education authority decides to make a statement, parents should submit in writing their perspective on the child's difficulties, and if they have one, a copy of an independent psychologist's report on the child as their evidence to statementing procedure. This is important and failure on the parents' part to record their views will be listed in the documentation in the appendices to the statement and will be interpreted as disinterest by some professionals or members of the appeal tribunal.

When the draft statement is received, parents should read it carefully noting the details in Section 2 of the statement and asking whether these actually give an accurate description of the difficulties in learning which give rise to the child's special needs. It is important that all their child's deficient learning skills are listed.

In Section 3 of the statement, the provision described should actually take account of the needs listed in Section 2, and provide a programme which meets those needs. The requirement of Education Special Educational Needs Regulation 10, that the statement shall 'specify the special educational provision' (in terms of facilities, and equipment, staffing arrangements, curriculum or otherwise) which the education authority considers appropriate to meet those needs, should be noted. The education authority should also specify any modifications required to the national curriculum to enable the child's needs to be met. These may affect programmes of study, attainment targets, or the assessment and testing of the child's standards. Exemptions from the foundation or core elements of the national curriculum should be specified, and details given of the proposals to enable the child's curriculum to be broad and balanced'. Again, parents should note the possible conflict between the priority of maintaining the child's access to that broad curriculum, and the need to develop his learning and literacy skills so that he might learn more effectively from that curriculum.

The student's need for additional items of equipment, such as a word processor or 'lap top' computer should be documented.

In Section 4 of the statement, the authority should specify the type of school which can meet the needs appropriately, and name the school if this is possible.

In Section 5, additional non-educational provision should be recorded. If the child needs speech therapy, physiotherapy or occupational therapy, this should be recorded in this section.

The appendices to the statement are usually lengthy and detailed, and contain the evidence given by the parents, the child's school, the medical officer from the district health authority, the school psychologist, any other advice obtained, and non-medical information furnished by the district health authority, or information provided by the social services department.

Only when the parents are satisfied that the draft statement (1) complies fully with the requirements of the appropriate regulations, (2) describes the child's difficulties accurately; and (3) meets his/her needs, should they sign the statement.

If the parents disagree with aspects of the statement, the most effective way to take the issue forward is to seek an immediate case conference with the representatives of the school, the education authority, and their own advisers. This enables the child's difficulties and the provision to be made to be discussed informally. This is usually much quicker and often more effective than seeking a formal appeal hearing, which may take some months to arrange, and in the more rigid circumstances of the appeal, it may not be possible to explore the issues as positively.

APPEALS

In the event of irretrievable breakdown of discussions between parents and the Authority it will be necessary to ask for an appeal hearing.

In preparing a case for appeal, parents should note that reports, letters and other written documentation to which they intend to refer, should be submitted about a fortnight in advance, to the Clerk of the Appeal so that it may be circulated to the independent panel, and the representatives of the education authority.

The panel

There are very firm regulations controlling the composition of the independent panel at appeals against statements of needs. It should consist of three, five or seven persons, with the 'authority members' of the committee never outnumbering other members by more than one. The appropriate regulations are to be found in Education Act 1980 Schedule 2, Part 1. While there is an opportunity to include parents on the panel, members are usually selected for other qualities and experiences, often relating to education or local government. Unfortunately this gives parents the impression of bias towards the 'establishment', i.e. the education authority, which clerks to appeal committees and committee chairpersons must work hard to overcome. As the appeals system has developed, some individuals appear with noticeable regularity on the appeals committees of certain education authorities. In these circumstances there is a risk of attitudes of panel members to local authority officers and parent representatives, which have been determined in one case, being carried over to another. The effects of members of panels appearing regularly on the conduct of the appeal should be monitored by the Secretary of State through the independent clerks.

The reasons

The reasons for appeal are always because the provision as drafted in the statement does not meet the child's needs. Often this may arise because the description of needs in Section II is insufficiently detailed, but technically the appeal must be against the provision.

APPROPRIATE SCHOOL

The general principle applied by many education authorities is that all needs should be met in the local school, in the ordinary classroom, without withdrawal, using methods related to topics determined by the national curriculum. This certainly takes a very limited and restricted view of the learning process which seems very much at odds with the philosophy 'If this child doesn't learn the way you teach, can you teach him the way he learns, and can you then extend and develop his competences in learning.'

Some schools may operate this system relatively effectively, but others may be less sympathetic and bring a sense of priority to the challenging process of meeting wide ranging individual needs in the ordinary classroom, which puts the needs of the *class* as paramount and the special needs of the individual *'others'* a long way second. The frequent adjustment of focus from group to individual, required to make such a group centred approach work, is often impossible in the busy classroom working towards the national curriculum attainment targets.

John Fish has expressed his views on such option difficulties quite outspokenly in his book, *What is special education?* He says, 'Although many local education authorities have reorganised their special education services, relatively little attention has been devoted to the nature of special education systems within which to meet individually assessed needs. The issue of what range of options should be or, in times of resource restraint, can be made available has not received serious attention. The relatively *ad hoc* accretion of facilities and services has rarely been subject to rational analysis. All too often sensitive assessment is followed by crude choices within a traditional pattern of provision'.

SCHOOLS' SUITABILITY

Parents and their educational advisors should be prepared to visit the school/schools nominated in the statement to assess the suitability of the provision available to meet their child's needs. The checklist in Appendix 1 may be found to be helpful in this visit.

Preliminary research is essential to ascertain the local education authority's policy in meeting special educational needs. If your authority has no documented policy available, ask why not. Some are more 'integrationist' than others. Some make much more individual provision than others. Try to assess the authority's attitude to the important balance between developing your child's individual skills in language, learning and literacy, and providing him with what are euphemistically referred to as 'opportunities' on the national curriculum which may be relatively meaningless in the light of his learning and literacy skills limitations.

Ask to receive, in advance, copies of the school's prospectus and handouts and circulars sent to parents of special needs children in the last year. This will give some indication of school's attitude and development work being forwarded for special needs children.

Parent governors of the school have a responsibility, laid upon them by Education Act 1981, to ensure that children with identified special educational needs *do* receive the provision they require. Talk to the parent governors. Try to determine what the extent of their knowledge on dyslexia is, as this will largely shape the response they make to their duties on behalf of these children. How effectively do they carry out their duty to see that statemented children actually receive the provision they are entitled to? Some comment from them upon the schools established practices and systems would be helpful.

Do some research in your local public library, referring to the *Education Year Book*, to establish the size, resources, and specialities listed by the education authority for the nominated school, and the number of teachers on the staff. This will enable you to calculate average class size, and give some ideas about the complexity of the school's organisation. These facts and figures should, naturally, be checked and reviewed on your visit to the school, but will give you the essential background information to ask pertinent questions on your school visit about what school is and does, and how it does it.

Look carefully at the number of similar schools maintained by that authority, trying to estimate how 'special' the maintained school is, and what its extra resources in terms of additional funding or allocation of specially trained teachers might be.

Try to get some estimate of the burden faced by the special needs department working in the school. In the Warnock Report it is suggested that, *at some time*, 20 per cent of the population may have special needs. While these needs may not *all* happen at the same time in this school, use this figure to guestimate the kind of loading faced by the special needs department as this will give a perspective on the time available to manage *your* child's difficulties in that school.

It should also be appreciated that inner city schools are much more likely to face a greater demand for 'special needs' help than suburban schools. This research will provide essential background to substantiate the information obtained on your visit to the school.

VISIT THE SCHOOL

It is essential to talk to the headteacher to gain some knowledge of the school's major educational aims and achievements, his attitude to (i) special needs children, and (ii) the special educational needs policy in operation within the school. Remember, school policy may reflect what is required by principles and practice in that education authority, and the head may have individual personal views which are worth evaluating and noting.

What is the headteacher's attitude to specific learning difficulties / dyslexia? Try to determine what the head sees as being the *major* special need in the school community. This will often indicate the school's priorities and the consequent allocation of its resources. Does the headteacher regard the abilities of the school's special needs students as fixed, or variable? How many statemented children attend the school, and how many of these have specific learning difficulties? What record of success has the school in dealing with students with similar difficulties?

Ask the head about average class size in the school, and check this quoted figure against your earlier calculations. Ask about obvious discrepancies. Remember that class sizes of greater than 20 will provide very difficult learning conditions for children with serious specific learning difficulties.

HOW EFFECTIVE IS THE SCHOOL'S IN-SERVICE TRAINING PROGRAMME?

The in-service training policy maintained in the nominated school is a clear indicator of its attitudes and competences. Inquire of the head about the school's in-service training policy to acquaint *class* teachers with the 'in-class' learning problems of dyslexics and how their presentation and representation of ideas for their students might be varied to enable the special needs of dyslexics to be met more effectively. Ask about the school and the local education authority's policy in training the specialist teachers who must provide the targeted skills teaching required by dyslexic children.

If the local education authority is advocating a particular 'diploma' course for these important staff, ask how practical, as opposed to academic, the course is, and what arrangements are made on that particular course, to ensure that the teacher is given sufficient supervised practical teaching experience to develop the 'in class' competences necessary for effective teaching of Spld students. Parents should note that some courses in higher education institutions offer *no* practical teaching element whatsoever, and are simply theoretical. Others require students to keep a teaching diary of their own unsupervised or very occasionally supervised work. This approach is, at best, subjective. Still other courses require some thirty hours carefully supervised and developed practical teaching experience. In teaching Spld children a very practical training course which develops teaching competences is necessary. The tendency for local authorities and the Department of Education and Science to overlook practical courses and give credibility to academic courses which are cheap to run but much less effective in developing appropriate levels of professional skill in the participating teachers should be resisted, and seen as 'window dressing' of a particularly unfortunate kind.

Remember that a school which is making a claim to meet a particular special need, or indeed *all* special needs, must have taken its in-service training programme for the difficulty experienced by *your* child seriously. If it has not, then parents must be very vigorous in the other checks they make on that school's special needs programmes.

ENQUIRE ABOUT THE CURRICULUM

Comment has been made in an earlier section on the national curriculum. At present some educationalists are raising the national curriculum to the status of unquestionable holy writ which is sacrosanct and must not be tampered with. The great benefits accruing to all children from its full implementation are increasingly cited as reasons for not offering targeted individual skills based teaching to dyslexics.

The reality is that benefits from that national curriculum need to be acquired through representation of the ideas in memory, and delivered by means of literacy skills which are an integral part of the learning difficulties experienced by the dyslexic child. The assumption that all special needs have equal effects on that national curriculum is certainly not justifiable in cognitive psychological terms. Matching that curriculum to individual learning needs, and maintaining a sufficient degree of flexibility in it to meet these individual needs, is a much more significant aspect than its breadth, or the inherent advantages its *full* implementation might or might not bring to the Spld child.

Ask the head about the way in which national curriculum will be implemented in the school. Will Spld students be disapplied if their difficulties in basic curriculum skills are serious? Ask about the individual arrangements made to help those who are weak in the fundamental skills. Enquire about the vital balance between targeted individual skills teaching, and broadly based 'in class' teaching related to topics on the national curriculum subjects. This will indicate the extent of the individual teaching your child is likely to receive in that school.

Look closely at the relative importance of the delivery skills of learning, reading, spelling, writing and written calculation in the ordinary classroom. How much use does the head see for efficient calculating, note taking and essay writing competences in the students?

Many dyslexics show high levels of skill in practical subjects such as the sciences, art, home economics, design and technology or computing. Look carefully at the facilities available in these important areas of the curriculum, and try to assess the status of the more practical subjects in the school, and the share of the school's resources allocated to this section of the curriculum.

Enquire about school's attitude to 'missed' teaching, checking on arrangements which can be made to make up teaching which has been missed, either because of late entry, or the effects of the student's specific learning difficulties. Try to find out what will happen if your child falls significantly behind his age peers on national curriculum attainment targets.

Ask about arrangements for Spld students to have instruction in keyboard skills, and regular access to typewriters, word processors or computers. Look carefully at some of the textbooks and printed resources available for your child's age group. Take a sample of the text, or note the name of the text book and later, if you have the competence, calculate text difficulty using Fog Index or one of the other measures of text difficulty. Relate the level of difficulty of the text to your child's competence in reading, and ask what arrangements are made to enable children who, because of reading difficulty, are unable to make use of that text or resource, to have access to that aspect of the curriculum.

TALK TO THE HEAD OF SPECIAL NEEDS

In middle or high schools, there may be a member of staff who carries special responsibility for special needs throughout the school. Ask this teacher about their attitude to (i) special educational needs children, (ii) Spld or dyslexic children, (iii) to indicate for you the major problem(s) faced by the school's special needs department. It is useful to check whether the department regards its purposes as (1) containing broadly based literacy difficulties in children from a range of language and experiential backgrounds; (2) teaching basic skills competences to slower learning students (3) dealing with social, emotional and motivational problems; (4) meeting wide ranging individual special needs.

Ask to see the rooms used by the 'special needs' department. Does it have its own accommodation, or does it have to use the rooms vacated by other departments, or fall back on other equally questionable transitory or *ad hoc* arrangements. What additional resources and equipment are available to the department? What teaching procedures or multi-sensory programmes are available? The department may claim to be eclectic, i.e. to follow a wide range of methods or approaches. Remember that eclecticism is a laudable academic attribute, but in practice, it is better to be a *master* of one particular specialist approach to dealing with the learning problems of dyslexics and be able to apply it, than to have a much less full acquaintance with ten, and *unable to apply any* of them effectively. It is also important to stress that successful eclecticism requires a very high level of skill in *many* methods and is a very much more difficult goal to achieve.

If the school's teaching approach is 'objectives'-based or linked to 'targets' in the national curriculum, how realistic are the objectives, and how well do they link to make a coherent structured programme for a dyslexic to learn the language skills he has been unable to build for himself from the previous experiences provided by his school.

How different will these *new* experiences be from those previous *unsuccessful* experiences, and what steps will be taken when providing them, and what principles followed to ensure that the student's individual needs in learning are met within the group structures proposed by the local education authority and school?

VISIT A CLASS

Try to ensure that the class visited contains a statemented pupil, preferably with specific learning difficulties. Initially, check the class size, its organisation and structure against the details already gleaned from previous researches. Note the sense of purpose (or otherwise) in the class activity, and the degree of student practical participation required.

Look at the teaching methods employed, and try to assess the way in which the information is presented. Is it formal verbal with a heavy loading on reading and writing skills, visual/practical, or multi-sensory using verbal, visual and motor skills? How much reading, note taking, writing, spelling and formal essay writing would be required for survival in that class?

Note any special arrangements in operation for individual children. At the end of the lesson try to talk briefly to the class teacher. Was the teacher aware of the presence of, and the detailed special needs of the statemented child? The need for confidentiality can be maintained because it is not necessary to identify or name the particular statemented child to respond to this question. How sympathetic to, and knowledgeable of, the problems of Spld students is that particular class teacher?

DECISION MAKING AND SUMMING UP

At the conclusion of your visit, parents should now be able to answer these key questions:

- How appropriate are the buildings, layout, classrooms, and resources to meet the special educational needs of Spld students?
- How sympathetic are the staff of this school to special educational needs students, and particularly those with specific learning difficulties? How knowledgeable and well

trained are they in meeting the 'in-class' and individual learning needs of Spld students?

- How suitable is the school's general curriculum?
- How detailed and individually appropriate is the school's special provision? Is this school conversant with the particular special needs of my child?
- Can it make and maintain the required provision now (rather than in six months or a year)?
- Does this proposed provision take due account of the efficient use of relevant resources, i.e. my child, the teacher, and the local education authority's finances?
- Will the provision result in fast gains, and good morale, or slow gains, low curriculum success, and falling morale in my child?
- Can it competently meet my child's special educational needs?

Accept or reject the provision, giving your reasons, which should be quite clear to you.

Part II

A GUIDE TO THE LEGAL RIGHTS OF PARENTS

A guide to the legal rights of parents

The object of this part of the book is primarily to inform parents, teachers, and other professionals and administrators in the area of education of the legal rights that a child with special needs and his or her parents have under the Education Acts. This is not a legal textbook but the matters of law considered will, it is hoped, be of use to legal advisors also.

Both the authors of the book have been approached on many occasions by parents wanting to know what they can do for their child, whom they either know or believe has a problem, who is doing badly at school and is often a problem at home, and where nothing has been done; for example when a child, whom the parents know is both bright and intelligent, is suffering emotionally at home, and possibly at school, and achieving nothing at school. We have written the book from the approach of the parent in this situation who wants to know what to do. Many such children are picked up by the local education authority and given a great deal of help. The authors acknowledge the excellent work done in this field by LEAs, and the Department of Education and Science itself in administering the system. However, where proper provision is not being made parents will need help and proper advice. For such parents, and for those working in the area of special needs, the purpose of this part of the book is to explain the legal implications and, for the sake of completeness, we approach this as from the situation of a child with special needs for whom no provision has been made.

Any parent, teacher or administrator will find the law in this area very complex. Those who have needed to come into contact with it have found this to be so and most have been surprised to find that

that is so. No non-lawyer should in fact be surprised, since the courts themselves, including the Court of Appeal, have found the law in this area to be complex and difficult to understand. So it is hardly surprising that the average parent finds it both difficult and confusing. In this book we attempt to simplify the law as much as possible.

Since the first edition of this book was published there have been changes in the law. First, the Children Act 1989 has come into force. Although provisions in the Children Act interrelate with the 1981 Act, the main issue arises in cases where the child will be before the Courts for other reasons. Unfortunately, in practice the situation is that there should be more assessments made under the 1981 Act and it is likely that the implications of the 1981 Act will not be fully recognised for these children. The significant change, however, is the fact that a child in need can be assessed under the provisions of Section 43 of the Act. Although the procedure is not simple, where the LEA maintains that the child does not have purely educational problems and that the other problems are not their responsibility, there is now a statutory duty in appropriate cases to consider *all* needs in the case of children with special needs. The problem with this particular section is that it is only the local authority, or an authorised person as defined under the Act, who has the responsibility to apply to make such an order. However, this is a welcome addition to the powers of the Courts to help children with problems.

The second development relates to a number of decided cases in the Courts. The most important case is *R v The Secretary of State for Education and Science ex parte E* Court of Appeal 1992 Family Law Reports p.377 which has very important implications for all children with special needs. The case clarifies the rights of parents and children and supports fully the view of the authors expressed in the first edition of this book, rejecting the contrary view (namely that statements do not need to detail each and every problem possessed by a child and make provision for every item). However, the Court of Appeal also raised a number of other interesting issues, the implications of which are considered in Chapter 12.

Practice has also shown that, in the first edition of the book, Chapter 12, when dealing with reviews of Statements, did not adequately go into detail on this procedure. These reviews are very important indeed as they check whether the provision is working or whether the child's needs change or even if there are needs which were undiscovered. Again, there has now been case law which involved the issue of the obligation to review, which is considered in Chapter 12.

Perhaps the most interesting point to be made is that, in these cases, the applicant won in Court. These were all cases of judicial review and what is noticeable is the high proportion of cases which succeed in the Courts. The reason for this is that there have been some grave errors made by local authorities or the Minister for Education. This has resulted in new amendments proposed to Circular 22/89 which are to be welcomed as making clearer the obligations of the local education authorities. This circular is reproduced in Appendix 6. What is, of course, surprising is the high level of judge-made law in this area which is correcting mistakes made by the Minister and local education authorities. There has not been an enormous number of cases heard by the Courts; a large number of cases has gone to the level of applying for judicial review, and once the Court has granted leave to proceed, the local education authorities have settled the cases; usually they settle them in a manner favourable to the applicant. These trends indicate that there is still too little attention paid to proper practice and procedure and the requirements of the law in cases of children with special needs.

THE 1988 EDUCATION REFORM ACT

The amendments made in this field by the 1988 Act and the national curriculum have created considerable changes and have, furthermore, changed the law in an involved and circular manner. This is because many changes were, in fact, the work of reformers and not initiated by the government, so that no systematic attempt was made to alter the law as a whole.

A CIRCULAR SYSTEM

The reforms have resulted in a system which is now more complex and confusing than before. For this reason, parts of this book are unavoidably repetitive. One such confusion arises in the system of the 1988 Act appeals procedures relating to exemption by statement, which are not stated in the Act to be an appeal against a refusal to make a statement. In fact, such appeals are, in effect, exactly this. They must be therefore logically considered as they arise, as they constitute the following:

1. Appeals against refusals to exempt and
2. Appeals against refusals to make a statement or to make better provision.

For this reason, the question of appeals must be dealt with twice in the text. Where a child has special educational needs the assessment of those needs and the provision to meet those needs is always a matter of professional expertise. The 1988 Education Reform Act has in this and other areas made substantial changes to the law.

In this book we have focused upon the dyslexic or learning disabled child. The reason for this is that more problems appear in this area than elsewhere, probably due to the fact that dyslexia is not an obvious or visible disability. The guidance on the law is the same for all children with special needs, and is of general application. Whether it be a dyslexic, a child with personality problems, or a disabled child, professional advice will be needed from, at the least, an educational psychologist in addition to the teaching staff concerned. In many cases, reports from other experts such as doctors, psychiatrists, and speech therapists are also absolutely essential.

It is important that the reports prepared by experts actually deal with the issues that affect the child's problems, in the light of the law. The preparation of good expert reports for the parents in situations where there is a disagreement with the LEA is often crucial to the case. In many cases the reports are not adequate because they do not deal with the legal issues. In the majority of cases a lawyer will not be involved but rather the parents, the child and the professional advisors.

So far as parents, local authorities, teachers and administrators are concerned, an expert report that does not deal with the child's needs, and the provision to meet those needs is of no value. It is right to note that parents who are seeking expert advice must ensure that they do get a report that lists the needs plus the provision; if this is not done it is of no help to anybody. As the Courts have required the statement to diagnose all needs and all provision, it cannot be done without proper expert advice; the independent advice must deal with these issues.

The parents in many such cases employ independent professional advisors, but lawyers are involved in only a small number of cases. Some of the reasons for this are, in general, because of the lack of legal aid and the fact that few lawyers are familiar with this field of practice.

There are many reasons for this, and it is not the task of this book to consider them. However, appeals and issues under the 1981 Education Act involve, in terms of future expenditure, complexity and detail of evidence, issues which are normally within the jurisdiction of a High Court Judge and in those circumstances there is an increasing role in difficult cases for both lawyer and professional advisor. But in fact no case can be prepared without a professional advisor and it is essential to realise that this is so at the outset.

When we decided to write this book we hoped that the combination of a lawyer and an educational psychologist with experience in this field would provide parents, teachers, education officers and others interested in the field with a different outlook and a useful and positive approach to this difficult area.

CHILDREN WHO ARE DISABLED OR WHO HAVE OTHER NEEDS

The intention of both authors is to give guidance to those advising in the cases of all children with special needs. We stress that this section is of general application. The advice contained therein is based on experience of children with many different needs – not just dyslexia – and includes the most severely handicapped.

THE FUTURE

The new bill before Parliament is due to come into force in April 1994 and will change the law very substantially; in general, we welcome these reforms. If passed, a complete revision of this part of the book will be required.

Chapter 5

How to approach the problem

We approach the legal issues of helping a child whom a parent, teacher or other professional believes has a special educational need which requires special educational provision from the point of view of parents, teachers and such professionals. We start, therefore, with the following questions:

1. How do you find out if there is a problem?
2. If there is a problem, how is it assessed and recognised by the local education authority?
3. Once a problem has been recognised and an assessment has been made, what provision must be made to meet a child's needs, particularly by the local educational authority?[1]
4. If the parents disagree with the LEA's assessment what rights have they to dispute the assessment?
5. If the parents are unable to succeed in this country can they challenge the decision anywhere else? This question is answered first.

Where a parent has lost an appeal in its final form to the Minister there is a right to appeal either to the European Commission of Human Rights or to the High Court for Judicial Review. Applications in England and Wales to the High Court can only be on a point of law. Applications to the Commission of Human Rights are somewhat less restricted. These problems are solely the province of lawyers and any person in this position should consult a lawyer. There are strict time limits from the date of the adverse decision – six months for the Commission of Human Rights and three months for the High Court. It is in certain cases possible to extend the limit for the High Court, but not for the Commission of Human Rights. This is an extremely complex issue, further consideration of which falls outside the scope of this book.

Experience shows that these are the crucial questions to be asked in the case of any child for whom no provision is being made. We therefore start with the issue *how do you assess the child's needs and ascertain what the provision is for that child?* This book is written against the background of difficulty in some parts of the country where a few local education authorities appear reluctant to make any special provision for a child who has a unique or individual problem. In those circumstances there is a widening gap between parents who realise that they are being offered less than second best, and the local education authority. In other areas, provision and help are steadily improving.

It ought to be said that it is a very shortsighted policy where second best is offered to a child, particularly if the child has a problem which is not manifested in a medical or behavioural condition. A child who has a problem such as dyslexia, who, with proper education and proper help in particular areas, could achieve an enormous amount and contribute a great deal, but who, without this, will do little, is not properly helped. Some authorities attempt to provide second best or less in this area, knowing that the child needs more and better. In fact, this long term cheap provision is more expensive in the end than short term but expensive help. The approach is not only wrong but more costly.

A further problem arises as a result of professional incompetence or ignorance. For example, one still comes across professionals who state there is not such a thing as dyslexia. Obviously, dyslexia is not a specific definition of a problem. However, it plainly exists and, so far as the law is concerned, exists beyond legal dispute.[2] The important case of *R v The Secretary of State for Education and Science ex parte E* The Court of Appeal 1992 FLR p.377 dealt with a case where a child suffered from a dyslexic problem.

As will be seen later in this part of the book, the local authority is under a general duty to identify children with special educational needs under Section 4 of the 1981 Act. As this book is written for a parent who has not had an assessment carried out under Section 5, the question here will involve a child who has not been assessed. The child will be either a child who has no statement, or a child who has been assessed but no statement made, or who has a statement which is not working so that the child's condition is reassessed. In the circumstances it is advisable for the parent to obtain a professional report (the contents of which are considered in detail in the next chapter) which will advise them both of the child's needs and of the required provision, and this report will form the basis of a proper case to put to the LEA. It is at this point that a request for assessment under Section 5 is best made.

However, many parents do not have the means of obtaining an independent report of the nature described. In such a case the parents' only recourse is either to request an assessment by the LEA (or more generally to go through the school itself), or to request a reassessment. In such cases the parents will be reliant upon the procedures of the local authority, and their relationship with the school and those working most closely with the child concerned. In these cases, some parents do experience difficulties in persuading either the school or the local authority to look at the case under the statutory provisions and to carry out an assessment and provide help. The Act itself and its workings are considered in detail from the next chapter onwards. However, there is a practical difficulty that must be referred to here: the authors have often had parents and teachers tell them, 'You have told us what the law is but it simply does not work in this manner.' Obviously it is impossible to judge the true position from questions put at a conference or lecture. It must, however, be stressed that the law in this area is concerned with helping children with specific learning difficulties and special educational needs. It sets out a series of rights and duties which have in fact been expanded rather than contracted in recent years. If it has not been properly applied, then the only recourse is either to use the Appeal System provided for by the 1981 Act or to have recourse to Judicial Review in the High Court of Justice to compel the proper observance of the law.

In this context the Children's Act 1989 has changed the situation for children with special educational needs who require help further. The Children's Act 1989 remedied a very substantial injustice created by the financial provisions of the legal aid system. Though it is not the province of this book to consider legal aid matters in detail, it must be pointed out that where the law is disobeyed or a wrong approach of the sort outlined above takes place, legal aid is now available to a disadvantaged child irrespective of parental means. This effectively redresses the unjust situation that existed before the

Children Act 1989 came into force, whereby only the rich or the relatively poor had recourse to the courts.

The law, therefore, provides a remedy. Although there are obvious defects in the 1981 Education Act as amended by later statutory reform and it requires improvement, it is in general a system which has done a considerable amount for children with these problems. It is therefore up to the parents whose children are disadvantaged by a wrongful approach to the law to enforce their rights, and that, of course, is an individual decision. It is important that parents and teachers realise this. A major problem here is that often there are very substantial problems or stresses at home that arise out of the child's problems; also, in, for example, dyslexic cases, parents themselves may be dyslexic and have great difficulty in dealing with authorities or matters in writing. Many did not enforce their rights because, for varying reasons, it was impossible for them to stand the pressure of such a process, or to take such a risk.

While such a decision is entirely understandable it is hoped that the change under the Children's Act will assist parents in difficult situations.

However, neither the 1981 Act assessment procedure nor the appellate procedure provided for under that Act are at present eligible for legal aid. We must assume that the parents have sufficient means to undertake the preparation set out, but are not wealthy. In some cases it may be possible for those who have no means at all to obtain some help by way of the Green Form legal aid system, though experience shows that such help is not quickly forthcoming and very limited. Those parents who cannot afford the independent professional help considered later must rely on the local authority's own advisors and the independent advisors that the local authority must consult during the statutory process. If in any case there is dissatisfaction with the approach of the local authority, then it is those independent advisors (i.e. doctors or social workers) who are most likely to be able to provide a different viewpoint and independent approach to the problem. Parents must therefore make their point to the independent advisors and seek their assistance in putting in writing where they disagree with the approach of the local authority. Parents must also put in writing those matters that they themselves consider to be important.

Before closing this chapter, it should be said that the most important independent advisors in cases involving children with special needs are generally at present educational psychologists, and that their advice is not in modern terms expensive, save in exceptional cases. Speech therapy and medical advice will often be available under the National Health Service, although it may take both time and effort to obtain such advice. The authors do not therefore regard the idea of using an independent as described in this book to be unrealistic. It is an approach designed for those with some means; it is not an approach advised for the very rich, because such people will in any event be able to pay for a child's special educational needs at a specialist school and are unlikely to wish to enforce their statutory rights through the processes described below.

PROFESSIONALS AND THE LAW

Those who advise parents of children thought to have or suspected of having special educational needs must know and use this basic structure of the law. This provides as a minimum the potential right to a statement, and an assessment by the local authority, and the right to have the appropriate provision which is reasonably needed for the child. It should be pointed out that whether the professional advisor works for the LEA or is an independent, non-LEA advisor, if the parents or the LEA are not properly advised, the right to sue for negligent advice is open to the parents. Little has happened in this field so far, but there is no doubt that more will happen as time goes on.

The right approach to a child's needs has been set out in the judgement of Lord Justice Nolan in the Divisional Court *R v The Secretary of State for Education and Science ex parte E, Times* 17/1/91, *Independent* 24/11/91 and reported in detail in the Court of Appeal Report 1992 FLR p.377,[3] namely that a statement must in Part II contain all the needs and is comparable to a medical diagnosis and in Part III must be a prescription or deal with all the needs diagnosed. The Minister's approach to the compilation of statements has, as a result of this case, changed and his changes to Circular 22.89 plainly adopt this format. (The circular now appears in Appendix 6.) If there is any doubt, obviously the interpretation applied by the courts takes precedent. The Court of Appeal in considering this case on appeal might actually be said to have taken an even stricter view than Lord Justice Nolan. His approach was adopted by all three members of the Court of Appeal. However, Lord Justice Balcombe stressed the

1981 Act looked at 'the whole child'.[4] The LEA must maintain a statement in respect of the child, not in respect of any particular learning difficulty he or she may have. Further, the LEA is obliged to determine the special educational provision that should be made for the child in respect of each and every educational need identified in the statement. Such a determination involves deciding that in respect of each and every need the LEA should intervene so as to make the provision from their resources or to establish whether the school was already or is capable of providing for that need.

Therefore, the LEA must identify and make provision for each and every need. It is therefore an obligation on any expert, whether working for a local education authority, or as an independent expert to identify each and every need.

Where, for example, an independent expert detects needs which require provision and which are yet unidentified it is therefore very important that these issues are made clear. In all expert reports it is quite obvious that if the law requires such a detailed exercise the expert must comply with the requirements of the law. Reports which do not do this will be of no assistance to parents, education officers, or anybody else.

NOTES

1. Section 8 (1) 1981 Education Act.
2. *R v. Secretary of State for Education and Science ex parte L* 1988 86 LGR p.13. See Lord Justice Dillon's judgement.
3. *Ex parte E* 1992 FLR p.377.
4. 1992 FLR p.388 E to F.

Chapter 6

Statementing: identifying children

IS THERE A PROBLEM?

The parents of a child who believe that there is a problem will not normally think 'does my child have a special educational need?' But it will be obvious to the parents, possibly to the child and often to the teacher that something is wrong. The educational aspects of assessment and recognition are dealt with elsewhere in this book; this chapter is therefore solely concerned with the practical and legal means of recognition.

Before a parent or an education authority can know whether or not there is a legal obligation to make provision under the Education Act 1981 for a child's needs, and the provision to be made for a child that child must first be assessed. The Act of 1981 first identifies the child, then assesses the needs and then makes provision.

HOW IS A CHILD ASSESSED?

There are two principal ways to obtain an assessment of a child under the 1981 Act. The first is for the LEA to make an assessment under the 1981 Act and the second is for the parents to request an assessment. We consider here the parents' request.

(a) The approach

The parents of a child who believe the child has special educational needs can, under the provisions of Section 9 of the Education Act 1981, request an assessment of the child. The assumption, in such a case, is that no statement (as described in the last chapter) has been made under the 1981 Act for the child; obviously, if there is one which has proved unsatisfactory, the question is one of re-assessment.

The Education Act 1981 – a rough guide

Assessment procedure

1. (a) Decision to assess: either by LEA, or parents request that LEA assess.
   (b) LEA must normally act if required by parent.
   (c) If LEA refuses to assess, the parents will be best advised to apply for judicial review. Alternative remedies are a complaint to the Minister under Section 68 or the Commissioner for Local Administration. Experience has shown that judicial review is quite often far quicker than either remedy.

2. LEA proposes to assess – writes to parents and:
   (a) proposes to assess
   (b) gives details of procedure
   (c) gives name of officer for information
   (d) states parent's right to make representations/submit evidence – 29 days minimum allowed.

3. If the LEA decides to assess or not to assess, it must notify parent in writing.

4. If LEA decides *not* to determine special educational need, parent may appeal to Secretary of State. Secretary of State may direct LEA to reconsider.

5. LEA decides to *determine special educational needs*: it must send parent a copy of the draft statement.
   (a) Parent may make representations or further representations – fifteen days minimum allowed.
   (b) Parent may require Authority to arrange discussion with officer of Authority – 15 days allowed.
   (c) Parent may require Authority to arrange meeting to discuss 'relevant advice' in statement (with which parent disagrees) with the professional giving that advice – 15 days allowed.

6. Meeting - can be very important to resolve disputes.

7. LEA decides to make a statement as originally proposed, or to make a statement in a modified form, or not to make a statement. LEA must notify parent in writing. Such notice must include:
   (a) a copy of the statement
   (b) notice of right to appeal against educational provision specified
   (c) name of officer for further information.

8. Parent may *appeal* against the needs and the special educational provision specified in the statement. An appeal goes to an appeal committee.

9. The appeal committee may confirm special educational provision in statement or remit this statement to LEA for reconsideration.

10. In case of remit, LEA reconsiders and notified parent of decision.

11. Parent may appeal in writing to the Secretary of State, who determines the appeal in writing and may:
    (a) confirm special educational provision specified in statement
    (b) amend the statement and the special education provision to be made
    (c) direct the LEA to cease to maintain the statement.

If a parent believes that a child has a special educational need which requires provision and the LEA has done nothing, the LEA must assess if requested to do so, unless the request is not reasonable (a definition of what is considered 'unreasonable' is given later in this chapter). Section 9 of the 1981 Act and Paragraph 33 of Circular 22/89 on Assessments and Statements makes it clear that the LEA will normally be bound to assess. In our view the parents should, before making a request for such an assessment, obtain at least one expert report stating that the child has special educational needs and requires provision. In some cases, more than one expert report will be necessary; for example, a child may have a medical condition which will make an expert report from a doctor, preferably a consultant, necessary. If there is a speech problem, a report from a speech therapist will be necessary. There may be other difficulties for which a proper expert report should be obtained. Obviously, expert reports cost money, although generally charges are reasonable. However, for those of limited means there is some help available.[1] Even if means are limited, if something can be afforded, at least one report from an educational psychologist should be obtained. In cases of severe disabilities, consultants and doctors are normally extremely co-operative in writing brief reports or requests, and in such cases the doctor's report is the essential one. One would expect the LEA, as a matter of course, to introduce assessments in cases of severe disabilities at an early age.

If the expert, who will normally be an educational psychologist, recommends, for example in the case of a dyslexic, a placement outside the LEA's maintained system in an independent specialist school, or some form of therapy or other provision which requires expenditure, then in our opinion it is absolutely essential that there be, if possible, two expert reports to deal with this main area of provision, and that the reports in general agree with each other. A backup report can be obtained following a written request to the LEA, under Section 9 of the Education Act 1981. In urgent cases, however, a written request under Section 9 will have to be made giving reasons, and the parents should follow it as soon as possible with a report, or reports.

(b) The contents of the report

Essentially, four major questions should be addressed by the main expert, normally an educational psychologist)

Too often expert reports are compiled without reference to the structure of the law and the legal obligations of the LEA concerned. All expert reports should approach the child's problems by asking the following questions. The first two are:

1. What is the problem (the need)?
2. What provision is required to deal with the problem?

Expert reports in this area are often extremely deficient. The regulations require that the statement specifies the special educational provision in terms of facilities and equipment, staffing arrangements, curriculum or otherwise which are appropriate to meet the needs. The report should therefore go into detail describing the need and necessary provision, regarding staffing, equipment, curriculum and so forth and not simply be in general terms.[2] The expert should say how many hours are required for specific needs – for example, literacy 5 hours; numeracy 2/3 hours; access to the curriculum 5 hours; learning skills, 1 hour. The terms of Paragraph 62 of Circular 22/89 should be borne in mind always. If teaching by a special system is needed then it should be stated.[3]

So long, therefore, as expert reports approach the child as a whole and look at all the needs there can be no complaint. It is a practice in some local education authorities for others than the educational psychologist then to compile the statement. Where, however, the parents are seeking independent advice, it is impossible to see how the independent expert can give proper advice unless the expert advises what is the provision to meet the child's needs. If a statement or a suggested statement is accurate there will be little difficulty. If, however, there is either a valid disagreement, or needs and provision to meet those needs have not been determined or detected, then it is very important that these issues should be raised and dealt with.

At some stage, an appropriate officer in a local authority will decide exactly how much extra provision will be made for the child. It will be determined exactly in so far as humanly possible. It is obviously necessary for the independent expert to advise on the extent of provision required where there is a disagreement.

In some cases, the only initial issue for a report to cover will be the question of whether the LEA should assess, as the question is whether a statement is required, and that will be when an expert is being asked to deal with a child who has not been assessed by the LEA. Unless the expert report at least justifies the reasons for the making of the statement and gives some idea of the provision, the report will not do the job.

The authors would point out that the law of contract does require an expert report to be reasonably fit for its purpose, and the law of negligence means that if an expert does not provide a competent report, the expert may well be liable. The propositions that are put above, are therefore based on the basic principles of contract and negligence, and are unsurprising. Some experts have commented upon the views set out above; however, it is only right to point out that these views simply express the law as it stands on the drafting of statements as expressed by the Court of Appeal and the basic law of contract and negligence.

The two other major questions are:

3. What is the appropriate school or type of school for the child? If a specialist independent school is needed, this should be plainly stated and reasons should be given (these cases will not be common).

4. If other provision is required, reference should be made to it or a specific recommendation made. If the expert is unable to cover that area, then he or she should recommend a further expert report from somebody properly qualified in the area concerned.

The existence of behavioural or other particular problems or their existence in the past should be clearly stated. The implications of such problems, actual or latent, should be covered in the report, and advice given in the context of the four questions posed particularly when discussing need or provision.

Regulation 10 of the 1983 regulations governing assessment has now been amended. The amended regulation is as follows:

10. **Contents and form of statements** (1) A statement of a child's special educational needs, made in pursuance of Section 7(1) of the Act of 1981, shall also –

(a) specify (i) the special educational provision (in terms of facilities and equipment, staffing arrangements, curriculum or otherwise) which the education authority consider appropriate to meet those needs;

[(ii) any modification to the provisions of the National Curriculum (in terms of attainment targets, programmes of study and assessment arrangements) in their application to the child which the education authority consider necessary to meet those needs;

(iii) any exclusions from the application of the provisions of the National Curriculum (in terms of attainment targets, programmes of study, assessment arrangements and foundation subjects) which the education authority consider necessary in view of those needs; and

(iv) the provision which the education authority propose to substitute for any such exclusion in order to maintain a balanced and broadly based curriculum, being a curriculum which meets the terms of paragraphs (a) and (b) of Section 1(2) of the Act of 1988 for the child;]

(b) without prejudice to the generality of sub-paragraph (a), specify either –

(i) the type of school which the education authority consider would be appropriate for the child and, if they consider that a particular school would be so appropriate, the name of that school, or

(ii) if they consider it appropriate that the child should be provided with education otherwise than at a school, particulars of the provision which they consider would be appropriate;

[(c) specify any non-educational provision –

(i) which the education authority propose to make available or which they are satisfied will be made available by a district health authority, a social services authority or some other body, and]

(ii) of which, in their opinion, advantage should be taken if the child is properly to benefit from the special educational provision specified in pursuance of sub-paragraph (a) and (b) above, and

(d) set out the representations, evidence, advice and information taken into consideration in pursuance of Regulation 8.

(2) A statement shall be in the form set out in the Schedule hereto or a form to the like effect and shall be authenticated by the signature of a duly authorised officer of the education authority concerned.

The regulation itself is not clearly drafted. However, it is plain that any expert report must deal not only with exemptions from the national curriculum, which is easier to state, but also with the issue of attainment targets. The only difficulties that will arise in practice will be where the child is older, but can hardly read or write. Children with very specific problems such as dyslexia who ought to be capable of achieving normally or near normally, or even above, may not be able to cope with certain parts of the national curriculum for varying reasons. A severe dyslexic, for example, who is not identified under the age of 12 to 13 (or more), may need to be taken out of the national curriculum for a period and given intensive specialist remedial education in order to be brought back into the national curriculum and have a good chance of at least obtaining GCSE passes.

Clearly, disabled children may benefit greatly from the national curriculum but their attainment levels will obviously be limited. Such children do undoubtedly benefit from involvement with the national curriculum. Obviously, in their case some items of the national curriculum will not be appropriate. Some disabilities will preclude children from various parts of the national curriculum and where such an obvious need for an exemption arises, the expert should deal with that issue. However, the issues are different, where involvement is beneficial, from those issues where the whole curriculum has failed the child.

Section 19 of the 1988 Act only allows temporary limited exemptions for non-statemented children on a six-monthly basis. This means that, if the child should be exempted from the whole or any part of the national curriculum, this consideration will be a crucial factor in the decision as to whether to make a statement, and must now be covered in all reports.

Professionally, the expert should bear in mind the factors as they are set out in the Minister's Circular when making the assessment. Circular 22/89 (the new post-1988 Act Circular) has a checklist and is set out in Appendix 6 to this book. Some LEAs have adopted and expanded these guidelines. It should be borne in mind that, although integration into ordinary schools is an aim of the 1981 Act (Section 2 (3)), this is only the case if the child and its needs are compatible. This factor can be lost sight of in some cases. Some children will have individual problems that cannot be provided for in ordinary schools, or have severe and complex problems that will need a specialist placement.

The report by the advisers employed by the parent should finish with a clear conclusion summarising the issues, and with details of recommended provision. If a statement is needed the report should say so. The parent is paying for this advice.

Legal aid is not available in cases under the 1981 Education Act. Therefore, the parent will normally have to pay for the case privately. If means are limited, parents can obtain proper advice from a number of local bodies; in the case of a dyslexic, the Dyslexia Institute or British Dyslexia Association or local BDA (there are local branches all over the country); in the case of the disabled, from bodies such as RADAR, Network for the Handicapped Ltd, ACE (Advisory Centre for Education) and many other well known bodies. However, the green form legal aid scheme is certainly available to be used by a parent with limited means who wishes to obtain an expert report from an educational psychologist or a doctor, or both, in order to determine whether the local education authority is in breach of statutory duty in not making available proper education to the child.[4] The major problem here is not that a solicitor cannot obtain green form legal aid, but that many solicitors are not aware of this field of law and therefore do not know which expert to consult or how to go about it. It is important, therefore, that parents should consult an expert solicitor or one of the bodies who are expert in promoting the interests of children with problems and who are experienced in advising parents. In general they will at least be able to recommend either a solicitor who can assist in the area or an appropriate expert. In this area of the law, the formation of the

Education Law Association, a body comprising solicitors, barristers, and experts, which is given to the object of increasing legal knowledge and good practice in the area of education law is a welcome development. Appendix 10 deals with legal aid in more detail. Appendix 11 lists useful names and addresses. The green form can also be used to obtain a barrister's opinion, if it is believed that there are good grounds for getting legal advice.

(c) The request for an assessment

This request is made under Section 9 of the 1981 Act. It should simply enclose an expert report, and give reasons why an assessment is requested. It is essential that such a request states specifically that it is made under Section 9 of the 1981 Act.

A parent should send the expert reports obtained, together with a written request for an assessment under Section 9 of the Education Act 1981 in relation to the child to the local education authority. The LEA must then comply with the request and assess the child's needs unless it considers the request to be unreasonable. The word 'unreasonable' means 'conduct which no sensible authority acting with due appreciation of its (his or hers) responsibility would have decided to adopt.'[5] In effect, this means that a local authority must comply with the request unless it is obvious that there are no grounds for it.

The duty of LEAs in this regard was considered in the case of *R v Surrey Education Authority ex parte B*, Mr Justice Kennedy, Crown Office Digest 1991 p.293. The judge decided the case on other grounds and his decision on Section 9 was not essential to his judgement and is therefore not a determinative of the issue. In that case a parent, whose child was about to leave school, after saying that the child would be leaving school and going to the college of secondary education, changed her mind and requested an assessment under Section 9, and that her daughter remained in education at school until the age of 19. There had been a number of previous requests, and these requests had been accompanied by expert reports; the reports were quite detailed and effectively supported a statement. The judge decided that the local education authority should probably have assessed the child under Section 9 in relation to the earlier requests, but that, in relation to the last request, as the local education authority was only requested to assess under Section

9 after it had refused a request to assess because the child was going to leave school in June, the parent lost. The judge also decided that the technical interpretation of the word 'reasonable' contained in *The Secretary of State for Education and Science v The Metropolitan Borough of Thameside* 1977 AC p.1014 was not appropriate but he failed, in fact, to define what 'reasonable' meant. In deciding that the LEA was wrong in failing to assess the child's needs earlier, when supported by a proper request, he actually added little to the law. The judge appears to have been saying that the word 'unreasonable' should be looked at as used in everyday life. However, there would actually appear to be little difference between the word 'unreasonable' as used on an everyday basis and the legal interpretation. The authors stand by the House of Lords judgement in the Thameside case as the appropriate usage of the word 'unreasonable' in the 1981 Education Act Section 9.

The case, however, draws to the attention of the unwary parents the fact that many local authorities do not now retain children at school after the age of 16. A number of colleges of further education are not schools as defined by the Education Act 1981 and parents should be aware of this problem. Although a child is approaching the age of 16, a parent must make it clear with their request for an assessment that they require the child to be educated until the age of 19 and that the child is not going to leave school. The case highlights the important requirement that a parent clearly requests assessment under Section 5 and accompanies their request, if possible, with some cogent evidence.

Where a request for an assessment is refused, there is at present no appeal to anybody. This position is considered later in this chapter.

(d) Children with statements

Section 9[6] can also be used by the parent of a child for whom a statement has been made, who is dissatisfied either with the provision originally made for the child or, alternatively, with the provision as it now stands. It may well be that the child, after initially doing well, has slipped back or that further problems have arisen. As long as the child has not been assessed for six months before the date of the request, the authority must comply with the request, unless they are satisfied that the assessment would be *inappropriate*. *Inappropriate* is not as strict a test as the word *unreasonable*, which in ordinary (and indeed legal) language means that there is no reason, before a local authority can refuse to assess. The use of the word 'inappropriate' would on the other hand clearly mean that, in the case of a child who has a statement and is receiving education under it, there would have to be no new grounds for saying that a reassessment is needed before an LEA can refuse. If the parent can show that there has been a change of circumstance or that something was missed or not fully appreciated upon an assessment then a reassessment must be made.

(e) The LEA's duty to assess

The duty of an LEA is twofold. First, there is a general duty of the LEA towards all children for whom they are responsible with special educational needs and second there is a specific duty to assess special educational needs and provide for them itself in certain cases. This is the means whereby the LEA itself identifies children with special needs.

(f) The duty to identify pupils

The LEA is under a duty to identify those children within its area with special educational needs whose needs are (or probably are) such as to require the LEA to determine their special educational provision. The LEA must then decide, after assessment, whether to make a statement in the child's case. A statement is made where the LEA determines the child's special educational needs and provision.[7]

(g) For which children are the LEA responsible?

1. The LEA is responsible for a child with special needs if the child is registered as a pupil in a school maintained by the authority or if it makes arrangements either at an independent school for his or her education, or at a school maintained by another LEA.

2. The LEA is also responsible if the child is brought to its attention as having or probably having special educational needs and is registered as a pupil at a school in the area of the LEA. This also holds if the child is not at one of its schools or at a school at which he or she has been placed by the local LEA but lives in their area. This would therefore include a child resident in the area by

virtue of his or her education at an independent school, and equally, one who is resident in the area but attends an independent school elsewhere. (Obviously, in both these cases it is assumed that no other LEA has taken responsibility.)

3. The LEA's responsibility also extends to a child who is not registered as a pupil at school and is not under the age of 2 or over compulsory school age, and probably has special needs. This will be a child who is being educated at home by his parents either with the assistance of a private tutor or tutors or by the parents themselves.

The Act therefore covers all children who may be within the local area of the LEA and it requires the LEA to identify them. It does not matter whether a child is at a maintained school or an independent school or, indeed, whether the child is being educated at home.

(h) The LEA's duty to assess under Section 5

This duty arises where it is believed that a child has a learning difficulty which might require the LEA to make provision. In these cases the LEA will assess if it has reason to believe the child has or probably has such a learning difficulty. This test has a very low threshold in that there must simply be a reason to believe. The basis of such a reason and such belief need not therefore be a very strict requirement. In practice, however, any LEA which is acting of its own volition will normally require evidence of a learning difficulty before an assessment under Section 5 takes place. Generally, the parent and the school will have brought problems to the attention of the LEA, and those concerned with the case, who may at this stage include an educational psychologist, will be satisfied that there are substantial problems in the case.

The duty of the LEA under Section 5 is different from that under Section 4 which is one of mere identification. If there is no parental request under Section 9, which for practical purposes means that the LEA must make an assessment under Section 5, then there are three criteria which compel an LEA to make an assessment of a child's special educational needs. If any of the criteria are met, the Act is mandatory and they must make an assessment of a child's needs. The criteria are as follows:

1. If the LEA is of the opinion that the child actually has special educational needs which call for the authority to determine the special educational provision that should be made for him or her; or
2. That he or she probably has such special educational needs; or
3. If the LEA considers that the child does or might need exemption from the national curriculum as a result of the 1988 Act. (The effect of the 1988 Act is a third factor to be read into the law. If the 1981 Act is adhered to properly these should be rare cases.)

The duty on the LEA is therefore less onerous where there is no parental request, because the LEA must either be of the opinion that the child has such needs or that the child probably has such needs or may require exemption, and such an opinion is at the discretion of the LEA.

All assessments under the Act must be made in accordance with the provisions of Section 5 sub-sections 3 to 10 of the 1981 Act. The criteria for identifying children requiring help varies. In paragraph 29 of Circular 22/89 (see Appendix 6) the Minister draws attention to lack of progress by a child who has special needs. Where a child may need provision additional to or otherwise different from provision made generally in LEA maintained schools in the area then an assessment should be initiated.

(i) Other duties which require assessment of children under school age

Sections 5 and 9 do not deal with the cases of children under the age of 2. Section 6 deals with the case of a child under the age of 2 who, in the opinion of the LEA, either had or probably has special educational needs and this permits the LEA to make an assessment.

Sub-section 2 of Section 6 allows an LEA to maintain a statement of a child's special educational needs following an assessment, prior to the child entering school. It gives very wide powers in that the LEA has powers to maintain a statement in such manner as it considers appropriate. Section 6 is used rarely, normally in cases of children who are mentally or physically severely disabled.

(j) Duties of the health authority

A health authority which forms the opinion that the child has or probably has special educational needs is also under an obligation under the 1981 Education Act. Section 10 of the Act requires that the health authority shall, if it is of the opinion that the child has special needs, inform the child's parents of that opinion and of its duty under that section. Having given the parents the opportunity to discuss that opinion with an officer of the health authority, it is obliged to bring the opinion to the attention of the appropriate local education authority. Further, if the health authority is of the opinion that a particular voluntary organisation is likely to be able to give the parent advice or assistance in connection with any special educational needs that the child may have, they are under an obligation to inform the parents accordingly.

(k) What if the LEA refuses to make an assessment?

If there is a request for an assessment under Section 9 there is, strangely enough, no appeal provided for under the Act if there is an initial refusal to make an assessment. The reason is presumably that it should be impossible for the LEA to refuse a reasonable request. In these circumstances the main remedy of any parent faced with refusal should always be an application for a judicial review to the High Court of Justice. Any citizen is entitled to challenge the decision of an LEA or any other administrative body which, it is believed, has gone wrong in law. The normal means of such challenge is to ask for a judicial review by the Queen's Bench Division of the High Court of Justice Divisional Court. Legal aid can be obtained to make such an application. If the local authority, as a result, is compelled to make an assessment, the local authority will have to pay the costs of the proceedings. Plainly, in challenging an LEA in this way, the parent should not proceed without the benefit of some legal advice – one does not seek a judicial review lightly. Legal aid is available to the child on this issue.

Alternatively, under the provisions of Sections 68 or 99 of the Education Act 1944 a parent can complain that the LEA has acted or is proposing to act unreasonably, or in breach of statutory duty, in not making a statement. If the Secretary of State is satisfied that the LEA has failed to discharge any duty imposed upon it, then the Secretary of State has powers to order the local authority to reverse its decision. For practical purposes this particular route is open to parents who cannot obtain legal assistance. Such a complaint does, however, in reality require professional knowledge and advice.

Although LEA offices or civil servants dealing with such complaints may disagree, an examination of complaints made by those who do not have recourse to legal advice or the advice of an educational psychologist or other professional adviser (such as an adviser with the Citizens Advice Bureau, Network for the Handicapped or some other expert body) shows that the Minister will often miss important points in such complaints because they are not brought clearly to his attention and the LEA is not concerned with doing anything more than justifying its view. The law in this area is complex, and experience has shown that the Minister has missed important points on complaints of this nature. It is also true that where parents act for themselves, civil servants do their best and do often pick up difficult points which relate to mistakes made by the LEA. Nonetheless, it is advisable that there be professional legal advice relating to such complaints, or at least knowledgeable advice by a person who knows both the child's difficulties and the legal structure.

It must also be said that the system of such complaints takes far too long. It is not possible to give an estimate here as accurately as we give in relation to appeals under the 1981 Education Act Section 8; however, it is not unknown for the Minister to take at least nine months and more often over a year to deal with such complaints. A simple urgent point can be dealt with on judicial review in under three months. An application to the High Court is quicker, more effective, and easier.

The last body to which a complaint could be made is the Commissioner for Local Administration. However, the experience of the authors has shown on this issue that the Commissioner is not quick enough. While his staff do a good job, they are not familiar with this area of law and need a great deal of guidance. This will be the slowest remedy.

Where a local authority refuses a request for an assessment which is reasonably made or where there is a statement which is not appropriate, the remedy should always be judicial review. It is quicker than either of the other two remedies. In the case of the *Surrey Education Authority exparte B*, Mr Justice Kennedy expressly criticised the Minister who, by the time the case had come to court had actually done virtually nothing with the case, and appeared to be going to do nothing with it. Mr Justice Rose has also voiced similar criticisms in a different case.

Appeals to the Minister under Section 5, where the LEA agrees to assess but refuses a statement take about one year. This is far too long for a child who has special educational needs. The Divisional Court has generally been able to deal with these cases within a timescale of roughly three to four months. The courts have therefore shown themselves to be the only efficient means of dealing with these problems.

The system of complaint to the Minister still takes far too long. Although it is not possible to give an accurate estimate, as these complaints are rare and no obvious pattern has emerged, they are certainly slow – much slower than they ought to be when dealing with the problems of children with special needs. The delays under the appeal system set up by Section 8 of the 1981 Act and Section 5 on Appeal were extreme and inappropriate for children with severe problems. The issue of these delays is considered in more detail later, when dealing with appeals. However, it was not unknown for the Minister to take over two years to deal with appeals under Section 8, and over one year to deal with appeals simply against a refusal to decide to statement under Section 5. An application to the High Court is now probably still quicker, more effective and actually easier, in practice, than an appeal to the Minister. This, of course, should not be the case.

As a result of the flood of interest in this area, the next chapter is a very brief examination of the issues the courts have been prepared to grant judicial review or allow cases to proceed in the High Court. It is not intended to be an extensive analysis of the law on judicial review, but merely a guideline to parents and advisers in this area. We would warn against always seeking judicial review, but for practical purposes, where an appeal to the Minister takes so long, it appears to be the only effective remedy in urgent situations – and many cases of children with special needs, if not all, involve urgency.

In this chapter we have considered the methods whereby the LEA is requested to assess a child under the 1981 Act. The LEA does not have to make a statement, but obviously should do so in appropriate cases, where it is clear that the child has a severe or complex difficulty.

It should be pointed out that the Education Act 1944 identified, in Sections 33 and 34 and Section 8 of the Act (prior to its amendment by the Education Act 1981), a category of pupils who needed special educational treatment. Under the 1981 Act that category was increased rather than decreased, for it was not the intention of the 1981 Act to restrict the previous legislation but to widen its scope (this aspect of the Act was considered by Mr. Justice Taylor in *R v. Hampshire Education Committee ex parte J* Vol. 84 LGR p.547).

The last means of initiating an assessment is under the Provisions of the Education Reform Act 1988, and this will be dealt with in Chapter 9.

NOTES

1. Legal Aid Green Form.
2. See Regulation 10 of the Education (Special Educational Needs) Regulations 1983.
3. A sample report, and guidelines are in Appendix 3 of this book.
4. Legal Aid Green Form by extension.
5. *Secretary of State for Education and Science v Metropolitan Borough of Thameside* 1977 AC p.1014.
6. Section 9 (2).
7. This does not mean that a school can determine the provision for a child, and the LEA supply all or most of it and not make a statement. If an LEA rather than the school makes the provision, even if it is given at the school, the LEA has determined the provision.

Chapter 7

Judicial Review on the 1981 Education Act System

INTRODUCTION

The 1981 Act provides a careful system of assessment of children with special needs for the purposes of a statement, and leaves those who are not assessed as potential children for statement within the general system. In general, therefore, the main issues which concern parents and judicial review are as follows:

1. Refusal of an assessment.
2. During an assessment improper delay or an improper or defective assessment.
3. An assessment commences but the statement is wrongly refused. (N.B. There is an appeal to the Minister also.)
4. There is a statement, it goes to appeal and the appeal goes wrong. (An appeal is available here also.)
5. The appeal wins, yet statutory reconsideration goes wrong. (An appeal is available here also.)
6. The Minister rejects an appeal either under Section 5 or Section 8 of the Act.

JUDICIAL REVIEW

Judicial review is available where the procedure under the Act has gone wrong and been operated either unlawfully, or unfairly and in the legal sense unreasonably. It is not available where there is a disagreement between the LEA and the parents as to issues covered by the appeal rights under the Act.

Although there is an appeal system for some of the issues under the Act, on two points there is, in fact, no appeal provided for by the Act itself. In those circumstances the only effective remedy is judicial review.

For those areas where there is an appeal, the situation is different. Although normally the courts allow the appeal system to sort out the problem, the appeal under the 1981 Act is not a true appeal. For this reason judicial review is available.

The powers of the appeal committee under the Act in Section 8(4) are only to make observations and include no binding orders. The Secretary of State on appeal and an appeal committee cannot re-assess or assess. If, therefore, the early progress of the case is defective in assessment, all that can be done is to compel the local education authority to go back and do the job properly. An appeal to the Secretary of State from an appeal committee has taken, in some cases, well in excess of two years. This is gravely wrong for children with special needs. Judges in two cases have criticised the Ministerial delays.

The appeal system is not a full appeal yet; the appeal to the Secretary of State is in some ways a lesser appeal, (and different from) that to the appeal committee. The Court of Appeal, and the High Court, have allowed judicial review applications to go ahead and have interfered. However, floods of improper applications would undoubtedly cause the Courts to take adverse views on education cases and it is noticeable that the cases that go before the courts are cases where very significant errors have been made. The courts apply the test of procedural error, fairness and unlawfulness very carefully. On this basis we now turn to areas in which judicial review can be of use.

REFUSAL OF ASSESSMENT UNDER THE ACT

Section 9 allows a parent to request an assessment of a child's special educational needs if there is no statement, or if a statement has been made for a set period of time, say six months. A request, where there is no statement, cannot be refused unless the parents' request is unreasonable or, in the case of a child with a statement, the request is inappropriate. There is no appeal against the refusal of such a request. As the majority of cases in this area relate to children without statements, a parent must be silly indeed to request an assessment and be unreasonable. Judicial review is plainly an appropriate remedy here. So long as the parent has some reasonable reason, such a request cannot be refused. In *R v Surrey Education Authority ex parte B* COD 1991 p.293 Mr. Justice Kennedy did not grant judicial review on the facts of the case, but he did hold that the LEA was wrong to refuse an earlier request. He seemed to place the word 'reasonable' in the common dictionary sense of the word rather than the legal sense. So long as the parent, therefore, makes the request backed by at least some good reason, it must be granted.

If there is already a statement, the word 'inappropriate' is a much higher threshold, but as long as the parent provides evidence that the LEA ought to act on, such as a reason why the statement is not working, or that needs have increased or were missed on assessment, they ought to proceed.

There have been a number of cases on these issues go to court but they have all been settled, the majority in the parents' favour.

THE ASSESSMENT

We have no doubt that there are many ways in which an LEA can get things wrong. However, the main areas where an assessment can go wrong are, first, that the LEA delays. The Minister's Circular 22/89 recommends six months to the draft statement. Many LEAs ignore this time limit and, if the case is urgent, an application for judicial review is appropriate. In *R v The Islington LEA ex parte S. Poppewell* unreported, CO/1120/91 a statement was ordered to be made in a case of excessive delay. Second, where the assessment is plainly defective, when a local education authority ought to obtain reports from other experts and refuses to do so, an order can be obtained to compel them to do so in accordance with the regulations which are 1983 Statutory Instrument No. 29.

Third, the issue of temporary provision. A local education authority may agree to assess and accept that a statement is necessary, but not make any provision. The Minister's Circular 22/89 plainly indicated that there is power to make temporary provision. Although no case has come to a final decision before the courts, where it is obvious that a child needs help and none is being given, the parents who have gone to court have managed to agree temporary provision in appropriate cases. These cases are obviously very extreme, where there is no room for disagreement that at least some help of a specialised nature is necessary.

THE STATEMENT AND APPEAL AGAINST THE STATEMENT

Section 7 provides a very careful system for considering statements. No case has yet emerged where Section 7 has not been properly operated by a local education authority in this regard. Obviously, if it happened the judicial review would be available. However, if a statement is not accepted by the parents, the parents have the right to appeal.

The appeal committee must act fairly, and give detailed reasons for its decision. In the case of *R v Surrey Education Committee ex parte H* 83 LGR p.219, the Court of Appeal applied the duty to give reason to this Committee, although it is under a duty to give grounds as a result of Paragraph 9 of Schedule 2 to the 1980 Education Act and detailed reasons as a result of the Tribunal and Enquiries Act 1971. This was reaffirmed in *R v Salford ex parte L* CO/1120/91 *Times* 17/4/92.

If such detailed reasons are not given, it is impossible properly to conduct an appeal to the Secretary of State, particularly as, where the appeal committee recommends a change in the statement, the appeal is against the failure to consider their observation, and if the appeal loses, it is against their decision itself. Such reasons that they come to are, therefore, crucial in the statutory process.

However, cases have emerged where appeal committees have tried to limit the evidence by saying the case will take an hour and then it is stopped, or they refuse to hear important witnesses. This plainly is unfair and improper and the courts have held that it would be proper to interfere. There is no full decision on these issues as, whenever the cases have gone to the Divisional Court, they have been settled. However, in two unreported Court of Appeal decisions – *R v Kirkless Metropolitan Council ex parte Jackson* unreported, 10/7/89 CO/4901/89 and *R v Somerset LEA ex parte Hamon* unreported, 10/7/89 CO/470/89, both decided by the same court on the 10th July 1989 – the Court of Appeal held that such allegations justify the grant of leave, and that it was wrong for the High Court Judge to refuse leave in those circumstances on the basis of an appeal made to the Secretary of State.

The other area in which the appeal committee can get things wrong is where they act unlawfully. Despite being given details of the law, appeal committees have often, for example, refused to accept a transcript of the Court of Appeal that speech therapy is an educational provision, or although all the evidence indicates there are special educational needs which are not in the statement and there is no disagreement between the parties on that evidence, they still refuse to change the statement. As the insertion of such a need still requires the assessment of provision which will take time, at least two years if going to the Secretary of State, the courts have granted leave on such issues. These cases have all settled so far.

THE RECONSIDERATION

Problems have also emerged where the case succeeds but on recommendation is rejected. The decision of the local education authority reconsidering the matter must be in writing. In *R v Wiltshire Education Authority ex parte D* Judgement 28/1/92 Mr. Justice Potts unreported, CO/1393/91, held that on reconsideration a local education authority should:

(i) Obey the guidelines of the Court of Appeal as to the drafting of a statement and the insertion of provision and that to refuse to do so was unreasonable and unlawful.

(ii) That the failure to put before the panel reconsidering all the evidence including two items of essential evidence was unfair and unlawful; and

(iii) That although abandoned by the LEA, the appeal committee should never have considered a school not mentioned in the evidence or considered by a witness. Judicial review was granted.

The decision is important because it is an instance of the High Court interfering before an appeal to the Secretary of State where grave errors had been made by the LEA. It also imposed a general duty upon reconsideration to present the evidence fairly before the appropriate panel.

It must be emphasised in this case that there was no difference between the experts about need or provision if in a local school.

Equally, in our view, it follows that, if it is appropriate and fair, if a case is in writing, to place it all before the Panel reconsidering the written case, it must also be appropriate and fair, where the case was oral, to have it properly explained. There is certainly one decision of the Minister for Education on that issue where he so held.

Finally, the decision must also be a decision which explains itself adequately by way of giving proper reasons, as it is in writing and required as such by part of the appeal process. The judgement of the Court of Appeal in *R v The Civil Service Appeal Board ex parte Cunningham* 1991 4 AER p.310 is applicable in this situation.

THE MINISTER'S DECISION UPON APPEAL

There is no further appeal from the Minister, and judicial review is therefore the only remedy, and the appropriate one. Most important, the Court of Appeal in *R v The Secretary of State ex parte E* 1992 FLR p.377 has radically altered the approach to statements. In that case, the Court of Appeal quashed a decision on grounds of legal error. The Minister can also be challenged on unfairness or procedural error.

There are considerable grounds for alleging unfairness in practice against the Minister, as it has now emerged that in his appeals he refers the case for an opinion in evidence to an Inspector of Schools or a third party and never reveals the result. The referral has been shown to include the third party actually providing new evidence or, alternatively, disputing evidence which is not in dispute between the parties to the appeal, and there are a number of cases now challenging the Minister on this basis. The system used by the Secretary of State is very worrying.

CONCLUSION

Generally, LEAs have made and persist in making substantial errors in this field. It is significant that very few cases that go to the Court to seek judicial review actually come to a hearing and are settled. It is an effective remedy and much quicker than an appeal, as most children now cannot wait for the Minister to determine their case.

Chapter 8

The assessment and statement (legal requirements)

A statement is an individually tailored definition of a child's educational needs and the provision required to meet those needs. It is arrived at after detailed assessment and consultation. It is reviewed annually.

METHOD BY WHICH A STATEMENT IS MADE

The 1981 Act, (together with the 1983 Regulations made under it), provides for a very careful and detailed assessment of a child's needs and the provision required to meet those needs. The object of the assessment is first to decide what the child's needs are and second, to determine what provision is required. It is possible to appeal to an independent appeal committee and then to the Minister against the statement. There is also provision for appeal to the Minister but not to an independent tribunal against a decision when a local authority either does not make a statement after a child has been assessed or starts to assess but stops the process. The most likely circumstances in which such a decision would be made is where the authority accepts that there is a need for special educational provision but decides that the child can be dealt with by the school and its governors, (for example *R v. Secretary of State for Education and Science and another ex parte L* 1988 86 LGR p.13.)

However, the requirements of the statement are quite plainly that the child's needs and provision are thoroughly assessed and that a final decision is made upon it. The statement is an individualised document relating to the child. It must be reviewed annually[1] and has to be reconsidered where there is a need for a reassessment. If a statement has been made for the child prior to the child reaching the age of 13½ a reassessment is mandatory.[2] Regulation 9 requires such a reassessment for a child who is statemented and has not had his need assessed since before the age of 12½. Once the child has reached 13½, the authority is bound to reassess those needs during the following year.

The intention behind this regulation is to ensure that, at least once in his life, unless a statement is made after the age of 12½, the child's needs are looked at afresh. The intention is to ensure that the statement is amended or reassessed if a change is shown, or if, upon review, difficulties or problems are discovered – or if the child does much better. The Act intends that the whole child should be the subject of the statement, and that therefore the workings of the statement should be checked against the child on an annual basis.

It is therefore not surprising that the regulations require a very thorough investigation into the child's problems. The regulations made pursuant to the 1981 Act are the 1983 Education (Special Educational Needs) Regulations. They form the basis of assessment. In explaining to a lay person what a regulation is, the best description is that it is minor legislation, authorised by the provisions of the 1981 Education Act, which allows the Minister to direct LEAs as to how they will go about assessing a child's needs, and in what form they will make a statement of that child's needs if they decide to make a statement. These regulations must be obeyed and provide for a careful process of consultation which results in the reports of appropriate experts in order to assess, understand and clarify the child's problems, educational needs, and the provision required for the individual child.

Regulations 4–8 provide for the nature of advice to be sought by the LEA. The regulations themselves are self-explanatory in the main regarding the seeking of advice. Under the Act 'advice' means written advice.

The advice that must be sought specified by Regulation 4 of the 1983 Regulations and for the purpose of making an assessment must include

(a) educational advice[3]

(b) medical advice[4]

(c) psychological advice[5]

(d) Any other advice which the authority considers desirable in the case in question for the purpose of arriving at a satisfactory assessment.

Regulation 4(d) gives wide powers to the LEA. If, for example, the child has problems of a psychiatric nature, this empowers the LEA to seek reports from a consultant psychiatrist. Equally, it empowers the LEA to seek reports from other appropriate experts, for example speech therapists or physiotherapists.

The advice under Regulation 4(d) can obviously include parental representations or evidence; in any event, the LEA will have to consider such evidence. It does, however, give wide powers to seek appropriate expert reports which are not specified in the regulations where the need for such a report is revealed. In relation to parental representations and evidence, this must anyway be considered by the LEA under Regulation 8, when making a statement. However, if the LEA is aware of information that has not been obtained as a result of the other regulations, it is bound to obtain it under Regulation 4(d).

Before an assessment is made, Section 5 of the 1981 Act requires that the LEA must serve notice on a parent, but a parent has the right of appeal against the decision to assess. It is, of course, likely that such an appeal, which is to the Minister, will rarely be used. Further, if it is decided to discontinue the assessment or not to make a statement, again the LEA must serve notice of this on the parent and here again the parent has the right of appeal.

Regulation 8 requires the local authority to take into account the following:

(a) representations made by the child's parents;

(b) evidence submitted by or at the request of the parent;

(c) advice obtained in the case in pursuance of Regulation 4; this means the educational advice, medical advice and psychological advice; and

(d) information relating to the health or welfare of a child furnished by or on behalf of:

(i) any district health authority

(ii) any social services authority.

As regards categories of advice, it is important to note that the educational advice must be obtained from a qualified teacher, who is either the headteacher of the school which the child has attended at some time within the preceding 18 months or, if that advice cannot be obtained, a person whom the education authority are satisfied has experience of teaching children with special educational needs, or knowledge of the differing provision which may be called upon in different cases to meet those cases.

If advice is sought of the headteacher as specified in the regulations[6] and the headteacher has not taught the child himself or herself within the previous 18 months, the headteacher's advice must be given after consultation with a teacher who has taught the child.

Where the LEA knows or believes that a child is or may be deaf or partially deaf or blind or otherwise visually handicapped, then the advice sought must be from a person qualified to teach pupils with that type of disability.[7]

Psychological advice (Regulation 7)

In practice, advice under this regulation normally proves to be the most important. This advice is sought from an employed psychologist or from a person specifically engaged for that purpose. The importance of psychological advice cannot be underestimated in the majority of cases. In cases where there are difficult and complex medical problems the medical advice under Regulation 6 will obviously be very important; but in many cases the psychological advice is crucial.

If a parent has used an independent educational psychologist, regulations provide that if the LEA psychologist has reason to believe that another psychologist has relevant knowledge of, or information relating to, the child their advice must be given after consultation with the other psychologist.

If there is no disagreement between the educational psychologists there would seem to be little real need for consultation. However, this regulation makes it plain that the LEA's educational psychologist ought to consult if there is a difference in conclusion, especially if the reason is not apparent or clear to the LEA's psychologist. The obvious intention of this regulation is to avoid, if possible, a difference of opinion at a later stage and to see if agreement can be reached. When a parent has obtained independent help it is very important that they try and arrange for such a consultation if there is any difference of opinion.

It is important to note that the parent does have the right to attend the assessment by the LEA's educational psychologist. The Minister's Circular 22/89 provides a very useful checklist for assessing a child and finding out what is the problem. In Paragraphs 33–39 of this Circular the Minister carefully stresses the need for consultation in these cases and stresses that parents should be fully informed.

THE EDUCATION REFORM ACT 1988 (ITS APPLICATION TO ASSESSMENT – IN PRACTICE RARELY USED)

Section 18 of the 1988 Act, which deals with pupils with statements of special educational needs, allows the statement to exclude the child from the application of the provisions of the national curriculum or to have these provisions applied, with modifications which are specified in the statement.

Section 19 of the Act allows the headteacher of a maintained school, or such other person as the regulations specify, to direct that the national curriculum shall not apply to the child or shall apply with modifications.

Such a direction can only be made for a period not exceeding six months or for a determinable period not longer than six months from its beginning, although a new direction can be issued starting immediately afterwards. It will be necessary to consider the statutory provisions in more detail when considering the basis for making a statement. However, it is obvious that the national curriculum and its application must now be a factor considered when an assessment is made.

As Section 19 only gives power temporarily to exempt individual pupils, it is obviously not applicable if their condition is not just temporary, that is, if there is a permanent disability or a reasonably severe or complex problem such as dyslexia, which will need more than six months at least to bring the child up to standard. It is quite plain that the statute does not envisage the headteacher giving a temporary exemption in such a case where it would be assumed that it was a case for a statement. The regulations made under the 1988 Act only allow for an exemption in effect for one year (see regulations 4, 9 and 10) except for pupils with special needs. Both the statute and the regulations make it clear that the temporary exemption is not appropriate for more than mild or temporary difficulties. In the Minister's Circular 15/89 it is stated that Section 19 directions are not intended to provide long-term exemptions. The majority of pupils for whom a general direction concerning their special need is given will be able to resume the full national curriculum within six months. If, therefore, the child ought to be excluded from the national curriculum or partially excused from the national curriculum due to special educational needs, it is quite plain this is a factor which must be taken into account when an assessment is made, and when it is decided whether or not to make a statement. In effect, this means that a statement must now be made in cases where exemption is required. A case of complete exemption would probably be a rare one.

If it is clear that it will not be possible to make proposals to bring the child back into part of the national curriculum or all of it on the basis of the information available at the end of the first six month period, it is obvious that the LEA must consider the making of a statement as a result of the fact that the child will have to be exempted from the national curriculum or part of it. It would clearly be unreasonable to expect a child to cope with the national curriculum or part of it where, due to a learning difficulty, the child cannot do so, and in these cases his or her exemption requires the making of a statement. A common example of this is where older but severe dyslexics may not be able to cope with a foreign language.

Difficulties arise concerning the issue of exemption. First, a child may require complete exemption from a subject, for example from French for a severe dyslexic, or certain subjects for a severely disabled child. The need for this may only become clear once a child has gone to secondary school, in, for example, the case of severe dyslexics.

Every child has a right by law to the national curriculum. As will be considered in more detail later, the national curriculum includes various pass levels relating to ability which are referred to as attainment levels. Children with severe disabilities or limited abilities will, of course, be unable to achieve higher attainment levels. They have a right to the national curriculum and to the encouragement to aim for the maximum possible levels of attainment.

Equally, if one looks at children who are born with severe difficulties (which include brain damage) they will be primarily taught how to cope with life and to live a useful life in future. Such children obviously cannot cope with foreign languages, physics or chemistry. This sort of case will present little problem.

Where one gets a more difficult problem is, for example, with a child who is severely dyslexic or has a complex problem, but who has neither been statemented nor given provision until the problem is identified at a later age, for example 13. Such a child may have the reading and writing attainments of a six-year-old, but it is meaningless for that child to be classed with the attainment level of a six-year-old. What is needed for a child with these problems (or an older child) is to give them the ability to read and write properly and to cope with a job in future, or alternatively the ability to obtain examination passes at least at GCSE level. This will not be possible unless the child's problems are addressed by an intensive campaign because of the late identification of the needs. Speaking practically, the child may therefore need to be exempted from the national curriculum; the child's literacy, numeracy and learning problems must be addressed so that the child can read, write, comprehend and spell properly, and if necessary apply number skills. The child may then be brought back in to the national curriculum at a later stage in order to be able to obtain either examination passes or a better level of understanding of the national curriculum and get a reasonable chance in the job market.

It is obviously no use teaching a child history and geography at the level of an 11-year-old or 14-year-old if they can only perform at the level of a six- or seven-year-old. The practical needs of such a child have been stated above. These children will require exemption from the national curriculum; possibly all of it, but certainly much of it. The extent of any such exemption will clearly be the decision of the experts and is not a legal question.

It cannot, of course, be right that the child must be statemented if he or she needs to be exempted from French or a science subject or both at secondary level, but not if the child is of pre-secondary school age with, for example, severe learning difficulties in reading and writing and performance in these areas at six- or seven-year-old level.

Section 2 of the 1988 Act divides the national curriculum into core and foundation subjects. Section 2 (2) specifies the following

(a) The knowledge and skills and understanding which pupils of different abilities and maturity are expected to have by the end of each key stage (attainment targets).

(b) The matters and process which are required to be taught to pupils of different abilities and maturities during each key stage (called programmes of study).

(c) The arrangements for assessing pupils at or near the end of each key stage, for the purpose of ascertaining what they have achieved in relation to attainment targets for that stage.

The Act therefore uses exemption not only on the basis of an exemption from a particular subject, but on the basis that a child is subjected to certain programmes of study and attainment targets. Regulation 10, as amended, of the 1983 Statutory Instrument No. 29 includes a requirement that any modification to the provisions of the national curriculum in terms of attainment targets, programmes of study and assessment arrangements should be specified in a statement (see Regulation 10(i)(a)(i)(ii)). Provision which is substituted must also be specified, together with any full exclusion of the application from the national curriculum (see 10(i)(a)(i)(iv)).

In Circular 15/89 Temporary Exemptions from the National Curriculum [Paragraph 6], the Minister defines those pupils who should be the subject of exemption as including pupils who should be exempted from attainment targets, programmes, study or assessment arrangements.

In Paragraph 10 as the Minister states that headteachers may give directions in respect of an individual pupil only if they are of the opinion that it is for the time being inappropriate to offer the national curriculum as it currently applies to him or her; the Minister stresses the recognition of each child as an individual in relation to the targets, programme and arrangements. Attainment targets are an important factor. They may need exemption for a dyslexic but have application at a low but valuable level for the handicapped.

Clearly, it cannot be right to teach, for example, a child at the lowest level of the national curriculum when, although the child is of average or above average intelligence, he or she is aged 13 and reading and writing at the level of a six- or seven-year-old, and not exempt. Equally, to teach that child on the basis the child can attain the relevant level at 11 or any later assessment level is unrealistic.

Obviously, such a child needs a statement, specialist provision and exemption.

This is a clarification of the previous position whereby the local authority had, within the limits described by the Minister and previous case law, an area of discretion. In essence if a child should be exempted from all or part of the national curriculum then a statement must be made. In reaching such a decision the requirements of attainment, programme and assessment must be looked at.

This will be a crucial factor for parents to consider and to discuss with the LEA's officers. It is equally crucial that any independent experts make this point quite clearly and consult with the LEA's experts on it.

The legislation does not allow temporary exemption from the national curriculum to be used as an excuse not to make a statement. Obviously, with the slow learner or cases where there is some temporary problem or set-back due to illness or family problems, the need for temporary exemptions arise and it is these types of problem which represent a proper use of directions to exempt a child from part or all of the national curriculum.[8]

TEMPORARY PROVISION/PLACEMENT

Often parents will be advised that their child needs help, and that it would be best to start with this at once. A request for an assessment, and any assessment that follows will take time – at least six months, and probably a school year. The parent can in the meanwhile then obtain special teaching privately or from bodies such as The Dyslexia Institute. In some rare cases immediate measures are needed, or if the process takes too long there is a need to act. In those cases where an out of county placement is necessary, parents who can afford a temporary solution can place their child at a specialist school. What parents should say is considered below.

In other cases a request can be made for temporary interim provision. The LEA has a constant statutory duty in the absence of a statement to educate a child in accordance with its age, aptitude and ability and the child's special educational needs under Section 8 (2) (c) of the 1944 Education Act.

In Paragraph 64 of Circular 22/89 the Minister states that such placements can be made on a provisional basis as part of the assessment. The examples given relate to severe emotional or behavioural problems or instances where the assessment is likely to be protracted – they are only examples.

Another problem, in practice, is where a child under a statement attends the school and has to be withdrawn – most often because the school is not right for the child or, in some cases, the child has been excluded. In either case, the LEA is faced with a statemented child and the school named in the statement is not able to teach the child. The statement does not simply lapse – see *R v The Secretary of State for Education and Science ex parte E* No 3 Nolan J unreported, 27/6/91. Once a statement is made, there is only one statement. Therefore, the LEA must make provision for the child in accordance with the statement as soon as practicable, and either reassess, or amend the statement as appropriate to the case, having tried to make the best temporary provision possible until an appropriate school is found.

Effectively, the two situations are the same. One is where a statement has not yet been made, but it is clear that it will have to be made after which provision will be required. The other is where, for some reason, the statement becomes inoperative, due to the child not being able to continue at school. In both cases, there is a duty to make that provision which is obviously necessary, and which can be immediately provided for the child. It can either mean temporary tuition – namely, some form of home tuition, or temporary tuition at the minimum – or some extra provision in school. Where the statement requires very specialist provisions such as residential, and the reports agree on a necessity for such provision before a statement is finalised, there is an obligation upon the local education authority to make a temporary placement while matters are being resolved. It is therefore quite correct for the Minister to state that such additional placements should be made.

In cases where the parent, and not the LEA, place a child, it would be helpful if parents, in their dealings with the LEA, refer to the power to make a temporary placement under Paragraph 64 of Circular 22/89 and explain to the LEA that they are only making temporary provision because it is an emergency. It is also possible for parents to request the LEA, as part of the statementing process, to take over the provision, or make a provisional placement on a temporary basis.

MEETING THE LEA

The philosophy behind the 1981 Education Act, for all its defects, is a proper idea – namely, partnership between the LEA and parents. In this context, the provision under Section 7 for meetings with the parents and the LEA is a very good idea indeed. Although, in the first edition of this book, we placed great importance on these meetings, we would take the view that we understated the importance. Most cases are, in fact, resolved at this level, and even if they are not resolved, such meetings are helpful.

It is, however, important that LEAs actually listen properly and do not simply ignore what parents say. If the Act is to operate as a system of partnership, the LEA must accept that it can be wrong, and that parents have an equally important, if not in some cases a more accurate view of the child's problems. Parents representing themselves are often unable fully to explain their problems and the case, and they should remember that, if there are difficult problems at home, it is better to reveal the full position rather than to hide the truth because they feel ashamed of what is happening. There are, therefore, two problems which have emerged in practice. First, LEAs are prepared to hold meetings, but do not listen; this gives rise to grave resentment, litigation and unnecessary appeals. Second, parents are over-aggressive and abusive in meetings and do not make proper and accurate points. Those points that they do make have little to do with the case, and they do not explain the child's difficulties and problems accurately. With this in mind, we make the following points.

Where an LEA decides a statement is necessary, the LEA prepares a draft statement. By Section 7 (3)the LEA must serve a copy of the draft statement, and a notice of the parents' rights under subsection (4) on the parents.

The parents can then insist upon a meeting with an officer of the LEA or make representations on the draft statement. The parent has 15 days to inform the LEA of an intention to exercise this right.

If, after a meeting, the parents wish to arrange a further meeting they can arrange such further meetings under section 7 (5) if they disagree with any part of the assessment.

The LEA must consider any representations made orally or in writing and then serve a final statement in original or modified form, or decide not to make a statement (Section 7 (8)). They must notify the parent, in writing, of the statement, and of the parents' appeal rights. The statement must comply with the regulations and be signed and dated.

Meetings with LEA officers can be very beneficial and this right should be used where possible. It can be very useful if the parents have expert help at these meetings. The importance of the statutory meeting, particularly upon the draft statement, cannot be underestimated. Many cases between LEAs and parents are resolved at these meetings; they give the parents the opportunity to explain the full extent of the problem to the LEA officers, and often to the LEA educational psychologist as well.

For example, it is not unknown for some medical evidence to have been missed, or an emotional or behavioural problem not to have been brought to the attention of the LEA. Sometimes the parents may have thought it something to be ashamed of, or sometimes it has developed during the period of time after assessment is requested. Equally, where a parent has had to take action, the LEA might often think that the parent has deliberately made a judgement irrespective of the views of the LEA, and if the problems of the child, the family and the home which have resulted in this action are explained to the officers of the LEA, they often realise that the case is very different.

In those rare cases which are severe and complex and where there is a requirement for a placement in a specialist school or environment the parents are often helped considerably by the presence either of expert legal advice or of an educational psychologist who is well versed in the legal issues. Equally, any lawyer attending must be very knowledgeable in this field and know the special problems of children and their special educational needs.

These meetings have proved very important and are often a successful means of resolving the problem. The Act does not forbid legal or other representation at such meetings and assistance. In some ways the meeting has proved to be one of the most important parts of the statutory process. The interchange of views often leads to a reasonable solution.

It should be appreciated that parents may have severe pressure upon them, either emotionally or practically. They may not have been able to put forward the real problems with sufficient clarity in the past. Many parents of dyslexic children, for example, are themselves dyslexic, often inarticulate, and either uncomfortable with written matters or unable to follow them. Some of them may be reasonably successful people and be successful at disguising their problem. This emphasises the importance of having an experienced adviser in difficult cases at a meeting of this nature. Those who attend such meetings find it very helpful to provide a list from the parents' point of view of what are

(1) the child's needs

(2) the provision required to meet those needs for the child.

Equally, where some particular problem has been missed, reference should be made to omissions of problems or the development of new problems in such a list. Local education authorities will appreciate having such matters presented to them in a written, cogent form so that they can understand the case for the other side.

NOTES

1. Para 5 Schedule 1 Part II 1981 Act.
2. Regulation 9 1983 S1 No. 29.
3. Regulation 5.
4. Regulation 6.
5. Regulation 7.
6. Regulation 5 (1) (a).
7. Regulation 5 (3).
8. Circular 15/89 Paragraph 13 sets out the Minister's views. It is to be noted the Act and the Regulation No 1181 are not as restrictive as this paragraph.

Chapter 9

Basis for making a statement

In the previous chapter we considered assessment and looked at those matters that should be considered in making an assessment and done as a result.

Section 7(2) of the 1981 Education Act states that 'the LEA shall, if they are of the opinion that they should determine the special educational provision,' make a statement of a child's special educational needs. That discretion was defined both by the Minister and the Courts.[1] The Minister's old Circular 1/83 was in fact an accurate and good definition as to when a statement should be made, namely, when there was a severe or complex problem.[2] The new Circular 22/89 is, unfortunately, far less clear. The reason for this is that Paragraph 30 of Circular 22/89 deals in essence with the case of *R v The Secretary of State for Education and Science ex parte L* 1988 86 LGR 13. That case concerned the issue of whether, in all cases of children with special needs, irrespective of the severity or complexity of the problem, the need to make a statement was discretionary or a duty. Under the 1944 Act, before the 1981 Act, no statement had to be made but there was a duty to provide educational treatment in all cases.

The Court of Appeal in *ex parte L* decided there was a discretion, but not how it might be exercised. The guidance is not a clear guide as the Minister has not retracted his previous view that it should be adhered to in all cases.

The earlier Circular 1/83, in Paragraph 14, provided better guidance. This requires that a statement should be made in cases of severe or complex learning difficulties and in any case where an out of county placement or a specialist school placement is necessary.

A statement should be made where the LEA are making provision (other than temporary) with extra resources, with additional support or equipment centrally, or where it has delegated it to the school and is therefore making provision itself.

However, the making of a statement must be approached on the basis that it was the intention of Parliament to increase and not decrease the number of children who were protected by the provisions in the Education Act 1944 relating to special education. (Mr Justice Taylor in *R v Hampshire Education Authority ex parte J* 84 LGR p.547, made this point quite clearly at page 556.)

The basic criterion for the making of a statement is, in essence, has the child a severe or complex learning difficulty which makes it necessary for the authority itself to determine or make the appropriate provision? It should always be borne in mind that if the LEA makes provision it has determined it. The concept of LMS (Local Management of Schools, introduced by the 1988 Education Reform Act) means that the LEA may be forced to make provision (and a statement) if the school, using its best endeavours, fails for a good reason to do so. In Paragraph 30 of 22/89 the Minister states 'If the LEA decides, following an assessment under Section 5, that it will determine provision that should be made, eg by placing the child in a special school and prescribing the special education provision to be made for the child in that school, it will then be under a duty to make and maintain a statement.' However, if the LEA determines and makes provision in such cases it must make a statement. In short, the Minister now provides more opaque guidance than before, whilst the criteria laid down in Circular 1/83, the earlier Circular, provided, in general, a useful guide. Circular 22/89 is in general a greatly improved circular.

However, in Paragraph 9 of 1/83 the Minister did state that the requirement for a statement may vary from area to area, as the sort of provision available depends on the range of provision normally available in the authority's schools. This is an argument also made by Hereford and Worcester in exparte L. It has been suggested by some LEAs that, if you make better provision, there is less likelihood that you will need to make a statement in some cases. This suggestion was rejected by the Court of Appeal in *R v The Secretary of State for Education and Science ex parte L* 1988 86 LGR p.13. The leading judgment in that case was given by Lord Justice Dillon with whom the rest of the Court of Appeal agreed. This proposition was rejected at page 23: 'I find it difficult to accept that this was the intention of Parliament'.

It is not surprising that this proposition found little support in the Court of Appeal because the statute obviously is not in any way concerned with local conditions but is plainly concerned with a general standard throughout the country. The 1981 Act amends and extends the 1944 Act, Section 8 2c, and is concerned with a national system and a single statutory criterion. It must be stressed that a difficulty does not have to be both severe and complex but simply either severe or complex.

Further, there are a number of cases which have arisen in practice where, although children require the ordinary school, in order to protect the child a statement is necessary because they need close monitoring and close supervision. This is more appropriate for children who have been the subject of abuse or who have psychiatric problems – which may be in addition to other problems.

In general, therefore, a statement should be made in the following cases:

(i) Where a child has a severe or complex learning difficulty.

(ii) Where a child requires exemption from the national curriculum to any degree which is not temporary.

(iii) Where the ordinary school cannot or will not make provision for the child.

(iv) Where the child requires a statement for its own protection. While we outline this as a separate category, it really falls into the category of severe or complex learning difficulty, the facts of that particular child's case being severe or complex. It is worth noting that, as the Court of Appeal says in exparte E,[3] 'you look at the whole child', and this is part of the whole child approach. However, it is worth separating this point out as a reason to make a statement.

EXEMPTIONS UNDER 1988 ACT

The national curriculum and Sections 18 and 19 of the Education Reform Act 1988 bring into consideration further important factors. A statement must now be made if a child requires exemption from all or part of it.

In practice the new system operates in this way. Where a temporary direction, called a 'general direction', is given[4] the headteacher must provide information to the governing body or to the LEA and the parent of the pupil. That information must include the reasons for it, its date and its expiry date, details of provision being made for the pupil during that period and a description of the manner in which it is proposed to secure the implementation at the end of the period of the provisions of the national curriculum.[5]

Alternatively, the headteacher can make an indication that in his or her opinion the pupil has, or probably has, special educational needs by virtue of which the LEA should be required to determine special educational provision. This is called a 'special direction' by Regulation 4 (3) (b) made under the 1988 Act. The headteacher can only make a special direction if he or she consults the LEA, Regulation 3 (2). What therefore happens if the LEA opposes this initial opinion? For practical purposes this is a new task given to the headteacher, and it may be that the regulation gives the impression the LEA's view will be important, or decisive.

However, Section 19 of the 1988 Act gives the headteacher unfettered discretion. It is a requirement which, even if valid, has no effect on the headteacher's discretion under Section 19. It may, however, bring additional material to light in an individual case.

The Education Reform Act therefore firstly provides a means of having a child assessed if the child has a need which requires exemption. It is therefore an additional means of securing an assessment where neither the parent nor the LEA appreciate that there is a need.

What however is quite crucial about these provisions is that, plainly, by reason of Section 19 (4) (c) 1, a child can only be exempted under these regulations if either it is proposed to make an assessment under the 1981 Act or the headteacher can describe the manner in which he or she proposes to secure the implementation of the national curriculum at the end of this temporary period, which is limited to a period of 6 months.[6]

A statement has to be reviewed on a yearly basis and has to be reassessed, as we have seen, at a certain point. Temporary exemption can only be granted on a six monthly basis with two further three month extensions. Plainly, Parliament has distinguished between those children who have a problem that is considered to be a temporary problem and those who have a special educational need which calls for provision which means that the child cannot for at least a reasonably lengthy period cope with part or all of the national curriculum. Obviously, with, for example, dyslexic children, while they may be able to do 'A' levels and go to university they may not at any time in their education properly be able to deal with a part of the national curriculum. Therefore, if a child has such a special educational need and requires exemption from the national curriculum, a statement must be made. More importantly, perhaps, severely disabled pupils will need to concentrate on living rather than learning skills and may well be wholly or substantially outside the national curriculum. Equally, a child with a severe problem not picked up until he or she is quite old i.e. between 12 and 15, may well, for example, need to concentrate on learning simply to acquire the skills to read and write, and will need to be outside the curriculum.

The importance of Section 18 should not be underestimated or the fact that the temporary exemption provision in Section 19 is a temporary exemption and not a permanent exemption or a lengthy exemption. If a child is not entitled to a Section 19 exemption, and children with a difficult problem will not be, a statement should be made. In practice, these procedures are rarely used.

Unless it is expected that the child's special educational needs can be catered for within a short period of time, if there is a need for provision which includes exemption from the national curriculum or a modification, then a statement must be made. Not to do so would be an error of law and would operate to frustrate the objects of the 1981 Education Act and would be unlawful (per Lord Reid in *Padfield v The Minister of Agriculture and Fisheries* 1968 AC p.997). Further, it would be a wrongful exercise of discretion by the local authority (see *Council of Civil Service Unions v Minister for the Civil Service* 1985 1 AC p.374).

In the view of the authors, if one is justifying a statement on a complex argument under the national curriculum then one is on very weak ground. The issue is always whether or not the child has a severe or complex learning difficulty, and such matters are subsidiary to that point. At the end of the day, therefore, the authors consider that this is the issue which should involve all parties. It is also the issue which at the end of the day will interest any court, or the Minister on any appeal.

NOTES

1. DES Circular 1/83 *R v Secretary of State for Education and Science ex parte L* 86 LGR p.13.
2. Although it contained one error in the light of case law.
3. 1992 FLR p.377.
4. Regulation 4 (3).
5. Regulation 5.
6. Regulation 4 (3) b (i) and (ii).

Chapter 10

Children with special needs but without a statement

The 1981 Act creates two categories of children. The first concerns those with special educational needs which call for the LEA to determine their needs and make a statement. The second are those children with special educational needs for whom the LEA, the governors, or the headteacher of the relevant school must make provision. The ultimate duty is always upon the LEA to make provision as is set out in Section 2 of the 1981 Act and Section 8 (2) (c) of the 1944 Act. The duty of the LEA is absolute under the 1944 and 1981 Act, and that of the headteacher and governors qualified.

Section 2 requires first that the child be educated in an ordinary school, if in essence this is compatible with parental views, the receipt of provision, the efficient use of resources, and the provision of efficient education for the other children with whom the child is educated. The duty falls upon the LEA. The duty of the school, whether opted out or not, is to use its best endeavours to see that the child obtains provision, that the child's needs are known, and to ensure that the teachers are aware of the importance of identifying and providing for registered pupils with special educational needs (see Section 2 sub-section 5).

The case law (*R v The Secretary of State for Education and Science ex parte L* 1988 86 LGR p.13, the Court of Appeal) made it quite clear that the local authority did not have to make a statement in every case where special needs existed, irrespective of their severity. The duty on the school is to use its 'best endeavours'. This is a far less stringent duty, if it be a duty at all in the strict sense of the word. If the school has resources it must use them, but if there are none or they are inadequate then the LEA must make provision.

POSITION PRIOR TO THE EDUCATION REFORM ACT 1988

According to Section 8 of the 1944 Education Act the LEA must educate a child in accordance with its age, aptitude and ability. Section 8 (2) (c) requires the LEA to provide for a child's special educational needs, and normally make provision in ordinary schools by reason of Section 1 and 2 of the 1981 Act.

Prior to the 1988 Act the situation was that if a child had a special educational need which required provision then that child might either be identified by the school, the LEA or the parents. If identified, there were obviously two possibilities. Firstly, provision could simply be made after an assessment. Secondly, an assessment would be commenced under Section 5, and either a statement would not be made or the assessment would not culminate in a statement. The child would then be given provision in the local school where the duty is firstly on the headteacher and the governors,[1] then the LEA.[2]

The difficulty with this situation was that if the provision did not work, there was no right to challenge it as there is with a statement. Appeals in relation to statements are considered later in this book. No appeal right existed in the case of a child who had no statement and did have special educational need and had provision, but the parents considered it was not working and the LEA refused to adjust its provision.

The only means then available to the parent was a judicial review of the decision of the LEA, or complaint to the Minister. The situation has now substantially changed as a result of Section 19 of the Education Reform Act 1988. That Act permits the headteacher of a maintained school to direct in relation to a pupil registered at the school for a period specified in the direction, that the provisions of the national curriculum do not apply wholly or partially.[3]

SECTION 19

The format of the Section

Section 19 first sets out the conditions whereby the Minister may make regulations to enable the headteacher of any maintained school or grant maintained school to direct that the provisions of the national curriculum shall not apply or shall apply with modifications and to revoke or vary any such direction.[4] The Minister's power to make such regulations are severely restricted by Section

19 (2). The maximum period is of six months for a period determinable not later than six months from its beginning and to extend it for a further period of six months.[5] The Regulations specify directions for exemption as either *special* or *general*. It is special directions that cover children with special needs.

Second, the section describes both the method of giving such a direction[6] and the contents of the direction.[7] The headteacher must give a direction with the prescribed information contained therein to the governing body. Where the school is county, voluntary, or a maintained special school to the LEA the headteacher must take prescribed steps to give the information to the parent of the pupil.

The information in such a notice

The information to be contained in the notice is prescribed by Section 19(4) and Regulation 5 of the 1988 Regulations and is as follows:

(a) The fact that the headteacher has taken the action in question, its effect and his reasons for making it.

(b) The provision that is being or is to be made for the pupil's education during the operative period.

(c) Either

(i) A description of the manner in which he proposes to secure full implementation in relation to this pupil after the end of the period of the national curriculum or

(ii) An indication that, in his opinion, the pupil has or probably has special needs, by virtue of which the local education authority would be required to determine the special educational provision that should be made for him whether by way of an initial assessment, which would be under Section 5 of the Act of 1981, or, alternatively, by way of a review of any statement of his special educational needs that is being maintained at the time under Section 7 of the Act.[8]

(d) The reasons for and period of the direction.

The headteacher must therefore explain what action has been taken to effect this action and the reasons for taking it.[9] At the same time he or she must outline the provision to be made for the pupil's education during the operative period of the direction. A parent may also request such a direction under the Act and Regulations and may appeal in case of refusal. There is thereby created an avenue of appeal in cases of non-statemented children.

The requirement is that the headteacher must set out in the prescribed information either a description of the manner in which it is proposed to secure the full implementation of the national curriculum at the end of the period or indicate that the pupil probably has special needs or alternatively there is a need for a review of his statement.[10] This means that the child for whom a direction can be given to exempt from the national curriculum temporarily must be a child for whom the headteacher makes reasonable proposals so that the child can be brought back into the national curriculum at the end of the set period of six months. Although there is a power to extend exemption, if necessary, that power is limited to a six month period. The extension can only be made if it is reasonably foreseeable that the child can be brought back into the ambit of the national curriculum at the end of the original six months, although an extension can be contemplated when making the decision.[11] Those for whom exemption can be obtained on a temporary basis are children with mild problems which can be dealt with by means of remedial provision which redresses the problem so that the child can be brought within the terms of the national curriculum within a foreseeable period of six months. However, if progress is not as was expected, there can be one or more extensions of the six month period. Obviously, children who are ill for a long period, have fallen behind, or who have other similar problems causing a difficulty with their education are envisaged particularly by this provision in the Act. However, it is impossible to classify all potential situations in which this provision will apply.[12]

A headteacher is required by Section 19(4)(c) to describe the manner in which it is proposed to secure the full implementation after the end of the period of exemption and as it is only possible to issue direction for a six month period. This provision cannot be used to make constant extensions where, in fact, the truth is that the child should be exempted. Plainly, extensions are permissible. The headteacher must be in a position to propose that at the end of the six month period, or the extension period if all goes as planned, the child will be back within the national curriculum, even if the possibility of an extension or extensions are envisaged when the original decision is made. The Act does not contemplate continuous extensions for children with special needs who have a severe or a complex learning difficulty.

In cases of children with special needs, the headteacher of a grant-maintained school must give the information not only to the governing body but also to the local education authority (Section 19 (5)).

The duty of the LEA, where a special direction is given by the headteacher that the child has or probably has special needs or that there is a need to review the statement (by Section 19 (6)) is to consider, on receiving the information given to the authority under Section 19 by the headteacher, whether any action on their part is required under Section 5 of the 1981 Act, which requires assessment of a child's special educational needs.

If this situation arises, any parent would be well advised to couple it with a Section 9 request under the 1981 Act for an assessment. If the headteacher is giving such an indication, it must be on the basis that he or she does not consider that the temporary exemption provisions from the national curriculum under Section 19 do not apply. The headteacher will only make such direction if he and his staff are of that opinion that the child requires a statement or a change in a statement. In cases of special education the headteacher must consult the LEA (by Regulation 3 (2)). The duty is only to consult. It is therefore very difficult to conceive, on a practical basis, that a local authority could refuse to assess if such a direction was given. Indeed unless the decision of the headteacher is unreasonable, it would be unlawful for the local authority to refuse a Section 5 assessment. These powers limit, in practice, consideration of the local authority's discretion under Section 7 (2) of the 1981 Act as to whether or not to make a statement. If the headteacher of the child's school is of the opinion that the child must be exempted from the national curriculum, it is the headteacher who decides upon temporary exemptions under the Act, subject to the appeal powers. If it is the headteacher's view that the child cannot be subject to a temporary exemption, then, as the only other exemption available to the child from the national curriculum is that under Section 18, namely a statement, it is plain that unless he or she acts unreasonably the LEA ought then to make a statement.[13]

The power of the headteacher to issue a special direction under Section 19 (4) (c) (ii) is solely for the purpose of allowing the local authority to consider the recommendation that there should be an assessment or a review.[14] If such a review or assessment has taken place and those teaching the child are of the opinion that the child cannot cope with the national curriculum and should be exempted for a substantial and or lengthy period by means of a statement under Section 18 of the 1988 Act then the LEA in practice ought to make a statement. If the parents agree then clearly this is so. If, however, they disagree, the appeal procedure is of course available. Section 5 of the 1981 Act provides an appeal which would apply if an LEA assess and refuse a statement, in the face of the school's views.

Therefore the inability of the child to cope with parts or all of the national curriculum means that a statement should now be made in such a case.

The third element contained within Section 19 is the giving of a right of appeal to the parent of a child who is exempted from the national curriculum or to a parent who takes the view that the child should be exempted.

NOTES

1. Section 2 (5) 1981 Act.
2. Section 8 2c 1944 Act as amended by 1981 Act.
3. Regulation 3 16 (ii) 1988 Act Regs SI 1181.
4. Section 19 (1).
5. By regulation 9 1988 Regs this means two further three month extensions.
6. Section 19 (3).
7. Section 19 (4)
8. Section 19 4 C II.
9. Reg 5 1988 Regs.
10. Reg 5 f (i) and (ii).
11. See 1988 Circular 13/89 paras 13 to 18.
12. Similar examples are given in the Minister's Circular 15/89 1988 Act paras 13 and 17.
13. By unreasonably we mean the legal definition see *CCSU v Mind for Civil Service* 1985 AC374.
14. Regulation 3 b (ii).

Chapter 11

Appeals

INTRODUCTION

The Education Act 1981 creates rights of appeal against the refusal to assess a child's special educational needs and, once assessed, the needs and provision specified in the statement. The first appeal is provided for by Section 5 (6) of the Act, and the second under the provision of Section 6 of the Act. However, the Education Reform Act 1988 creates a second appeal system for children. Although this appeal is not strictly an appeal involving special educational needs and provision, because its concern is exemption from the national curriculum, in practice it is an appeal for those children with special educational needs. This is recognised by the 1988 Act itself, which makes express provision for the 1981 Act to be considered by the appeal system. The present proposals before Parliament, if passed, will change this system in April 1994.

APPEALS UNDER THE 1981 EDUCATION ACT (STATEMENTS AND CESSATION OF ASSESSMENTS AND REFUSALS TO STATEMENT AFTER STARTING TO ASSESS)

Section 8 subsection 1 of the 1981 Act provides for the local authority to make arrangements to enable a parent to appeal against the 'provision' in a statement. That appeal is expressed to be against the provision specified in the statement. The appeal is to an appeal committee constituted under the 1980 Education Act, with alterations in its make-up, introduced by the 1981 Act.

The extent of the appeal

The appeal is expressed to be against the special educational provision Section 8.[1] An appeal follows any statement that is the result of any assessment of a child's needs. If the needs are mis-stated in the assessment, the provision cannot be adequate. So the appeal relates not only to the extent of provision but also deals with the child's needs.[2] This can also include the school named in Part IV of the statement.[3]

The 1983 Special Needs regulations lay down a prescribed form for a statement. In Part IV of the statement the local authority is required to state the type of school or name a school if appropriate.[4] It may well be that the statement is correct in relation to the nature of provision and need but the only apparent disagreement is the school chosen. For example, the parents may contend that the school's approach is not right or it is not the right type of school. This was accepted by the Minister and the Divisional Court in *R v Secretary of State for Education and Science ex parte O* unreported. The parent's right to have a child educated in accordance with parental wishes given by sections 2(3) of the 1981 Act and 76 of 1944 Act is relevant to any issue, including choice of school.[5] The Education Reform Act 1988 amended Section 8 (1) of the Education Act 1981, and now provides for an appeal not only on the first or any subsequent assessment of the child's special educational needs under Section 5, but also where any amendment is made to the special educational provision specified in the statement, other than on assessment under Section 5. In *R v Clwyd County Council ex parte A, Times* 26/8/92 it was held that where a statement was amended after an appeal, the parent could either appeal again to the local committee or go to the Minister, according to the parent's wishes.[6]

This amendment was introduced by Paragraph 84 of Schedule 12 to the 1988 Education Reform Act. In practice, this means that an appeal will lie against amendments not only to needs, but also to provision, and this will also encompass the school in Part 4 of the statement, as the school is where the provision will be implemented.

Power to amend

Amendments to a statement are governed by paragraph 6 of Schedule 1 of the 1981 Act. An amendment is best described as a change to a statement which can be made without a reassessment. If the

LEA's actions are in effect a reassessment then the LEA should reassess. If the LEA wishes to amend a statement but has caused reports of the nature of some or all of the reports required by the regulations on assessment to be made,[7] then it should reassess. It can amend if:

1. It serves notice in writing of its proposal and of the parents' right to make representations. Paragraph 6 (1) Schedule 1.
2. The parent upon whom notice has been served makes representations within 15 days of service. Paragraph 6 (2) Schedule 1.
3. The LEA has considered the representations and on taking a decision informs the parent in writing of the decision (paragraph 6 (3) Schedule 1). Due to Paragraph 85 of Schedule 12 of the 1988 Act the LEA must also inform parents in writing of their right to appeal.

Where the school is the main subject of dispute it is likely that the needs and provisions are not adequately stated in the statement. If such a situation arises it is likely there is some need which requires provision, which ought to be considered on appeal and ought to be contained in the statement.

The extension of rights of appeal by the 1988 Act

The 1988 Education Reform Act in Schedule 12 paragraph 84 amends Section 8 (i) of the 1981 Act. It adds a right of appeal against:

(a) the first or any subsequent assessment of a child's special educational needs under Section 5.

(b) any amendment to the special educational provision specified in the statement otherwise than on the making of any such assessment by the authority, including one made after a local appeal.

The right of appeal is therefore extended to all amendments to the statement and paragraph 6 (3) of the 1981 Act is amended to provide that where the LEA propose to amend the statement and they make a decision, they are required to inform the parent in writing of the parent's rights of appeal under Section 8 (1) of the Act 1981. The rights of appeal therefore extend to all statements made on any assessment and any amendment made to the statement.

TIME FOR APPEAL TO AN APPEAL COMMITTEE

The time limit for appeal is determined by the LEA. However, it is normally said by LEAs to be 14 days but could be extended for good reason; this is a discretionary time limit set by LEAs and not statutory. The 1988 Act in fact sets no time limit.

NATURE OF APPEAL

The appeal is to an appeal committee. The constitution of that committee is governed by the provisions of the Education Act 1980 Schedule 2 as amended. The procedure at the appeal is governed by the 1980 Education Act, Schedule 2 Part 2. However the appeal committees are subject to the jurisdiction of the Council on appeal committees and are also covered by the provisions of the Tribunal's Inquiries Act 1971, particularly those duties relating to reasons.[8]

In general the appeal committees are conducted in a friendly and informal manner. The Chief Education Officer or a senior education official often presents the case on behalf of the LEA. The education authority will normally serve a written statement of the history and reasons for its decision in the matter and then present its case through the Education Officer. It does on occasion happen that the legal department is brought in to conduct the LEA case. However, in general somebody from the legal department will act as a clerk to the appeal committee. It may be that somebody with some experience, generally from the legal department, will attend to advise the clerk or the appeal committee on procedure.

The LEA will generally seek to have at least one educational psychologist in attendance and probably the special educational needs or statementing officer, if there is one, to explain their views. Otherwise, some other senior official might attend. The medical officer may well be asked to give evidence and sometimes the headteacher of the school thought to be the appropriate school. It also happens that where there is a special unit involved, it is possible that the head or a senior teacher in the special unit is also called to give evidence to the appeal committee. Where there is a detailed written case, it is unecessary to have a lot of witnesses. It is not unusual to have the education officer and educational psychologist for the LEA solely.

Although the manner of the appeal committee is informal, the issues are often complex and difficult. The issues involve not only the presentation of expert evidence, but the detailed questioning of expert witnesses. The LEA case is normally presented carefully and professionally by experienced professionals. Parents should make no mistake that the LEA professionals do have a mastery of this complex human and legal subject.

THE PARENTS' CASE

The parents' case will often have been made initially by way of letters written and reports. It is therefore possible for parents to act for themselves and rely upon the written evidence. Such is the complexity of these cases that, because no legal aid is available,[9] parents would not be advised to present such an appeal (unless they themselves are experienced professionals or have no choice) because of the nature and complexities of the issues considered upon appeal. In many cases, however, they have no choice due to lack of means. In these cases help should be sought from voluntary bodies such as Mencap, the BDA or Network for the Handicapped.

Where the appeal involves a dispute over substantial provision, which means expenditure, parents would be well advised to have an experienced educational psychologist in the independent sector, who will already have advised them and produced reports, attending the hearing. If medical advice favourable to the child is available, this evidence should be used to best effect. If an experienced doctor would find it difficult to attend a hearing, their reports must be clearly written and then can be used to good effect. The skills involved in the presentation of these cases, although this is an appeal committee, require a detailed understanding of the child's problems and the nature of the expert evidence. Few cases are simple. The parents are facing experienced officers and the resources of a complete department of the LEA. The officers will also probably have sought legal advice or help from other departments. In those circumstances, despite the absence of legal aid, whoever appears for the parents should be experienced in this field.

The authors take the view that, at the very least, the parent's educational psychologists, or at least one of them, are essential witnesses as they will know LEA officers throughout the country, if not in the area concerned, and be able to make professional points to the appeal committee and the LEA. This is a minimal requirement.

Because of the issues involved in these cases the parents are normally greatly assisted by experienced legal presentation of their case.

CONDUCT OF THE PARENTAL CASE

Having considered what is necessary for the preparation of the appeal case, and upon the assumption that representation by a lawyer, plus an expert to give evidence, is available to the parents, we consider further how cases should proceed. First, part of the dispute may involve the question of whether the local schools, or a local school has the provision required to meet the child's needs. The parents should ensure that, before the hearing, their expert educational psychologist (or at least they themselves) go to the school and discuss the provision available at that school for the child's needs, if this is at all possible. Most LEAs are happy to arrange this visit. It is obviously crucial that the parents satisfy themselves that the school nominated in the statement can do at least what is set out in the statement. The amendments to Circular 22/89 make it clear that LEAs should offer this facility to parents. If other provision is necessary than that in the statement, its availability should be checked. Some cases, of course, will not involve this issue because it will not be necessary to attend such a school, due to the fact that there are more basic disputes about needs and provision. If, however, such a check is made, it is important that parents have full details, and that these details are put in writing to present to the appeal committee. It is, equally, very important in complex cases that, if possible, some form of brief written synopsis of the parents' case should be put before the appeal committee. It may be very helpful for the parent simply to hand it in to the appeal committee at the hearing. The issues in these cases often involve complex psychological or medical matters, or a mixture of such matters. It is difficult for an appeal committee to follow the parents' case unless some structure is placed on it.

The LEA has the advantage of having their department represented, their case in writing, and, quite possibly, the advantage of being local people in front of a local appeal committee. The parents' case should, therefore, be properly formulated and it is suggested that the method used in any meeting under Section 7 should be used again – namely, that a list of defects in the statement should be compiled in short form, together with an alternative statement, or the changes required to the statement. Issues of law should also be identified.

It is to be emphasised that the object of the appeal is the child's needs and provision. The appeal is not, therefore, adversarial in the same manner as normal litigation in the English courts and appeal committees. The LEA case is often presented in writing, with some additional oral factors. It is not, therefore, necessary to cross examine in detail, unless some additional facts, surprising points or significant area of disagreement emerges or has emerged. It is often far more profitable simply to clarify these issues and ask no questions at all (or just a few pertinent ones), and then have the parents get on and present their case.

The presentation of the parents' case is particularly dependent upon a proper explanation, backed up (in our view) by a written commentary of the type described above. The parents' expert, having prepared a report, should assume that it has been read by the Committee, as should the parents and/or their representatives. It is far better if the expert talks to his report, and emphasises the child, the needs, and the points of dispute in the evidence to support his or her opinion. In these cases, because parents often consult experts, or ask for help after the statement is made, it is likely that there is much agreement between the experts about the child; this should be made clear.

While there may be agreement about evidence, this is often not apparent to the appeal committee. The areas of agreement should be explained and stressed and where there is either disagreement, or the LEA has simply not covered the issue, these points should be stressed by the evidence.

As regards the parents, a picture of the child and the child's problems is extremely important. The human history and story of the problems suffered by the family is often absolutely crucial to these cases. The parents would not be appealing unless they thought the LEA was wrong and that their child's problems were different from, or more severe than those contained in the statement. It is therefore terribly important that these issues are explained.

THE POWERS OF THE APPEAL COMMITTEE

The appeal committee under the 1981 Education Act has the power either to confirm the special educational provision or remit the case to the LEA for reconsideration. These powers are contained in Section 8 (3). The appeal committee does not have power to enforce its findings.[10]

The appeal committee is bound to give reasons[11] for its decision; these reasons must be sufficiently detailed for the parent to know the basis upon which the decision was reached, including what evidence was accepted and rejected, and the material facts or rulings of law found by the appeal committee.[12]

If the committee agrees that the statement is inadequate it does not have the power to enforce its findings. It can only remit a case to the local education authority for them to reconsider its decision in the light of the committee's observations Section 8 (5).

The committee's reasons for its decision are therefore crucial. It is crucial that the LEA knows why the appeal committee rejected the statement or thought it inadequate; alternatively, the parent are entitled to know why they lost the case.

If the committee does not give its decision adequately in writing and state its reasons, although there is an appeal to the Secretary of State, it is difficult to see how a parent faced with reasons which are not adequately expressed can properly make an appeal to the Secretary of State against a decision of the committee. In those circumstances the parent can apply for judicial review for an order to compel the committee to give its reasons.

If a parent succeeds, the LEA must reconsider its decision in the light of the observations of the committee. It is therefore open to the authority to disagree, but as Parliament gave the parents an appeal, plainly a successful appeal cannot be lightly rejected and the appeal committee's observations ignored. LEAs abide by the committee's decisions and only depart from them with good reason. The Act sets out a rigid set of procedures to be followed and if the LEA or the appeal committee is in breach, judicial review is available to enforce the duty.[13]

If the parents lose, or if the LEA does not follow the recommendations of the appeal committee or if, after the appeal committee's recommendations have been applied wholly or partially, the parents are unhappy, then the parents can appeal to the Secretary of State under Section 8 (6).

If, after an appeal, the LEA considers making a change in the statement it is under a duty to consult and act fairly.[14]

RE-CONSIDERATION OF THE PARENTAL CASE

Section 8(5) require the LEA to re-consider the statement in the light of the appeal committee's observations and imposes a duty to inform the appellant in writing of their decision. Considerable problems have arisen concerning the behaviour of some LEAs upon re-consideration. The Act is not clear on these issues.

In *R v The Wiltshire Education Authority ex parte D* CO/1393/91 28/1/92, Mr Justice Potts held that a local panel, considering the statement again under Section 8(5), acted unfairly when it failed to consider all the written reports before the appeal committee which formed the evidence upon which the appeal committee made its decision.

In that case, Mr Justice Potts pointed out that, on a general basis, in re-considering cases, LEAs should place all documents before the panel or body re-considering, that were before the appeal committee. It is obviously not possible to understand the appeal committee's findings unless the information is available to the LEA committee re-considering.

In that case, a crucial expert report and the mother's written statement were not sent, and the judge pointed out that the Court of Appeal in exparte I required the whole child to be considered, and that you could not consider the whole child unless you had the mother's written statement. Equally, as the case depended upon findings of fact in favour of one particular expert opinion, the fact that expert opinion was contained in two reports, the second being a later report, the fact that the report was not sent was fatal to the whole re-consideration.

The LEA, through its officers, must therefore fairly re-consider the case and re-consider it on the basis of the findings of fact by the appeal committee. It follows that, if parents are unrepresented and simply present their case orally, the LEA is under an obligation to present the case fairly upon reconsideration. There has been at least one decision by the Minister of Education along these lines. This logically follows from the decision of Mr Justice Potts.

However, it appears that some LEAs have attempted to dispute the finding of fact by the appeal committee. As they have lost the case, such findings of fact are as a matter of law *res judicata*. It is not, therefore, open to officers of the LEA that has lost the case simply to say that these findings of fact are wrong. There is a difference between the facts found and the observations. The LEA can reject observations.

During a re-consideration, the LEA often again consults parents. If it does so, it is under a duty to act fairly, as set out above (13). Further, if a radical change in provision, or a different provision is suggested as a result of the appeal committee's decision which has not been considered either by the appeal committee or by the LEA upon appeal, the LEA will be under a duty to consult and will be acting unlawfully and unfairly if it does not inform the parents of the change in plans.

APPEAL TO THE SECRETARY OF STATE

Section 8 of the Education Act 1981 provides for an appeal to the appeal committee. If the appeal committee refuses an appeal there lies the right to an appeal to the Minister.

In order to consider the Minister's powers it is right to consider the committee's powers. It can either

(a) confirm the special educational provision specified in the statement;[15] or

(b) remit the case to the local education authority for reconsideration in the light of the committee's observations.[16]

Where a case is remitted, the authority must reconsider it in the light of the appeal committee's observations and then inform the appellant in writing of the LEA's decision.

MINISTERIAL APPEAL

By Section 8 (6), a right of appeal to the Secretary of State exists. Section 8 (6) states that:

In any case where

(a) an appeal committee confirms the decision of a local education authority as to the special educational provision to be made for a child: or

(b) a local education authority inform an appellant of their decision in a case which has been remitted to them under subsection (4) (b).

the appellant may appeal in writing to the Secretary of State.

An appeal therefore arises if a parent wishes to appeal either against the decision of an appeal committee which upholds the statement or alternatively where the LEA has considered the committee's recommendations and either ignored them or having reconsidered the statement failed to reconsider it in a manner that satisfied the parents.

TIME LIMIT

There is no time limit provided in the Act for such appeals. Although statements have to be reviewed annually (a duty not always observed) there is normally no change on review.[17] One reason for an appeal is that the parent, having incurred expenditure, will want a refund on the basis that the LEA ought to have incurred it and it was the LEA's statutory duty to educate the child in accordance with the child's special educational needs. Unfortunately, according to the Divisional Court, there is a gap in the legislation in this respect in *R v The Secretary of State for Education and Science ex parte Davies*, 1992 2 FLR p.190 Divisional Court in which Mr. Justice Auld gave the lead judgment. It was held that the Secretary of State's powers were capable only of dealing with the present or future situations and not the past. So if a child has left school the Minister has no power to act in relation to those past issues.

This is an invidious position and a great defect in the Act. Indeed as there are no time limits on the making of a statement an LEA can act in bad faith and delay as long as possible. The parent is under a statutory duty, which is more stringent than that upon the LEA, to educate the child not only in accordance with the child's age, aptitude and ability but also in accordance with the child's special educational needs. If a child leaves school, then, because of the provisions in Section 4, there is no longer any jurisdiction in the Minister, because the LEA is not responsible for the child.[18] However, in an earlier case (*R v The Secretary of State for Education and Science ex parte O* unreported dated 10th November 1988) it was said that past expenditure could be dealt with, so there is conflict on this issue. Plainly, the Education Acts, as with many other statutes of protective nature dealing with children, are concerned with the benefit and welfare of children. However, past expenditure may possibly be recovered on the basis of breach of statutory duty, or by an action in negligence if a case can be made out in negligence.

So far as the 1981 Education Act is concerned, in cases of children with special needs who have, or ought to have statements, the Act owes an individual duty to the individual child to assess the needs, and make arrangements for the provision for the child. The statutory provisions of the 1981 Education Act are not the same as those considered in *R v ILEA ex parte Ali* CO/1499/89 Transcript 14/2/90 when the Divisional Court held that Section 8 of the 1944 Education Act did not give rise to damages because that was a general duty relating to the education provided in the local area.

The 1981 Education Act, in Section 5, Section 7 and Section 8, relates to an individual child who should be the subject of an assessment or statement. Statemented children are a special class under the Act, and under the normal test in law, an action for breach of statutory duty lies where somebody is damaged by failure to comply with statutory duty under the Act. The authors therefore consider that, where there has been a failure causing damage under the Act – and such a failure will almost certainly involve professional negligence – a parent probably can recover, on behalf of their child, expenditure or damages for negligence and breach of statutory duty in the circumstances.

The Minister's powers on appeal are:

(a) to confirm the special educational provision specified in the statement, or

(b) to amend the statement so far as it specifies a special educational provision (this also includes needs as a matter of law), and make other consequential amendments to the statement as the Minister considers appropriate, or

(c) to direct the local education authority to cease to maintain the statement.

These provisions are contained in Section 8 sub-section 7. Section 8 contains no provision or procedure other than the fact that the appeal must be in writing (Section 8 (6)). The Minister can therefore regulate his own procedure. He could, if a case required, hold a full oral hearing, at his discretion. This has never been done, but he will often hold a meeting with one or both sides to clarify a case.

Practice and procedure on appeal to the Minister

As the appeal is in writing the Minister deals with an appeal in written form. Once an appeal is lodged he seeks representations from the LEA on the appeal lodged by the appellant. The Minister has in the past not revealed what is said by the LEA. This is a breach of the rules of natural justice.

The Secretary of State is under a duty to give a fair hearing to allow each party to properly put its case. As this is an appeal, he is in fact acting in a judicial capacity and must act in accordance with the rules of natural justice. He must most certainly act fairly (see Re KH an infant 1967 QB page 617). Further, if the LEA provides information to the Secretary of State which is of a confidential nature and is unknown to the parents, they must at least give the parents the outline of this information in order that they may be able to answer it (see *R v The Gaming Board ex parte Benamin and Another* 1970 QB p.417).

Although the Secretary of State appeared in some cases not to be aware of some of the provision of the rules of natural justice; in the case of *R v The Secretary of State ex parte Davies* 1989 2 FLR p.190, the Secretary of State conceded that he acted unfairly in failing to give an appellant opportunity to answer the LEA's case put to the Secretary of State. The Secretary of State announced in that case to the court that he had amended his procedure accordingly. The Secretary of State's practice is now to allow the parents to know what is being said by the LEA.

Practical experience of appeals has also revealed that the Secretary of State, probably in all cases, takes private advice. No appellant is given access to it. This is an extraordinary situation. The view of the authors is that the case cited above on natural justice, together with the case of *Mahon v Air New Zealand* 1984 AC p.808, clearly requires that an appellant has the right to refute or make representations in relation to reports received by the Secretary of State which are adverse to their case. The practice is also dubious in that this is an appellate process and there is no provision in the appellate process for allowing the Secretary of State to take such advice. In any event the provisions of the European Convention of Human Rights, particularly Article 6, indicates that this practice is unlawful in the context of the European Convention of Human Rights in that it is in essence a secret trial.

The practice of the Minister considered above has produced some very odd results indeed. A number of cases are now before the courts on this issue and it will be interesting to see the outcome. It has now emerged in some cases that the Minister is seeking advice from other persons, when the evidence before the Minister is agreed by both parties. The third party consulted by the Minister has given a report or advice that disputes the evidence before the Minister. The Minister then made a decision based on this advice or report, and it is never disclosed. The authors cannot regard this system as one which is either just or proper.

Delay

In the first edition of this book we mentioned the issue of delay, but were not aware of the seriousness of this issue. The system has been criticised in open court in their judgements by Mr Justice Rose and Mr Justice Kennedy. This is not surprising. There are now examples of cases that have taken well over two years, and some more than three years. The delay in relation to Appeals under Section 5 is excessive, particularly bearing in mind the fact that the only issue is whether a statement should be issued. This means that a child with special educational needs has not been given adequate provision, and is therefore in need of considerable help. Delays of this sort are totally wrong.

Maladministration has been shown by those dealing with the appeals. One case is known about where the Minister promised to deal with the case within a few days when discussing the matter with parents. When the parent rang up six months later, the parent was told that, unfortunately, they had forgotten all about the case. It was unfortunate that these reports are not isolated examples – neither are they rumour or story. a new 'fast track' appeal team or arrangement is now in place. It is to be hoped that matters will improve.

The authors have no doubt that, on the basis of practical experience, the Secretary of State seems in at least some cases totally incapable of investigating alleged bias or deliberate obstruction by the local authority. Indeed, in practice, the Secretary of State has ignored such allegations in appeals and in some cases no satisfactory investigation has been carried out by the Secretary of State into the case. There is evidence that in some cases, happily rare, local authorities take an adverse view of the parents or their case and the officers act in a stubborn and undoubtedly improper manner to frustrate parental aims. Also in many cases the committee has allowed the appeal, yet their decision has been ignored and no satisfactory explanation ever produced. In some cases the investigation by the Secretary of State has proved both inadequate and, has, frankly, ignored this type of complaint. Nonetheless, it cannot be said that the system does not work at all, though it can certainly be said that it does not work satisfactorily. The main factor in achieving success in the committee is that the committee can hear the evidence. The Secretary of State has on very rare occasions permitted and does permit meetings between his officials and the appellant parents. This will include their representatives. The Secretary of State has not allowed cross-examination of witnesses and this is quite essential. Unfortunately, in many cases where the LEA has gone wrong, it has gone wrong due to the error, incompetence or wrong headedness of its officers, and it is difficult to expose this in writing in some cases, unless there is some manifest error or it is an obvious case. This is because it is impossible to expose the truth, thinking and motivation behind the decision without proper oral evidence, tested by cross examination, as is done before the committee.

The authors would anticipate that this appeal system will give rise to a considerable volume of complaints. The latest proposals, if passed, will address these issues.

APPEALS UNDER SECTION 5

Reference has been made earlier to the fact that where a local authority, having started to assess a child under Section 5, decides not to make a statement then parents may appeal to the Secretary of State. The actual terms of Section 5 (6) are that it is a decision not to assess a child's needs. This is in fact an appeal against a decision not to make a statement.

Such an appeal, by virtue of the provisions of Section 5 (6), must be in writing. The local authority is bound to notify the parents as to their right of appeal under this sub-section. The Secretary of State can either reject the appeal or order the local authority to reconsider their decision.

The procedure on appeal to the Secretary of State is exactly the same as that under Section 8, except that there is no appeal to an independent appeal committee. The defect in this appeal system, namely that if a local authority does not make a statement there is no real effective redress although the provision given to a child is not working, has now been rectified in a clumsy manner by the provisions of the Education Reform Act 1988 Section 19. The effect of these provisions have been considered previously. As the national curriculum is not fully in place, we repeat that these appeals will only fully apply when it is fully in force.

THE 1988 ACT

Appeals where there is no statement

The Education Reform Act 1988 allows for children to be exempted from all or part of the national curriculum (Section 19 (1)). These provisions apply to children with special educational needs and the mention in the section of the possibility of special educational needs being a consideration in exempting a child in Section 19 recognises this fact. As previously mentioned, the headteacher can exempt a child for a fixed period or a period to be determined or for a further period at the end of a fixed or determinable period.

Section 19 sub-section 7 provides the parents with right of appeal against a refusal by the headteacher to recommend a statement under Section 7 of the 1981 Act and is effectively an appeal, albeit exercisable in reality after a period of time, against an LEA decision not to statement. It can be used to request a statement if the school gives no statement or provision and there is no statement. Where a direction to exempt temporarily is given or revoked or varied, or where the headteacher refuses to give, revoke or vary a direction in response to a request made by a parent of a pupil registered at the school, a parent can appeal to the governors. It is the latter power that will interest parents of children with special needs. Further, an appeal is possible where the headteacher fails after a request is made to act at all, once the period prescribed by the regulations has expired.[19]

Appeal lies with the governing body, which has the power either to confirm the headteacher's action or direct the headteacher to take such action authorised by the regulation as they consider appropriate Section 19 (8). This obviously includes power to recommend exemption for assessment under the 1981 Act.

The governing body are bound to notify the appellant and the headteacher in writing of their decision on any such appeal.

In theory, due to the provisions of the 1981 Act and the assessment procedure, one would not expect the parent to be asking for an assessment under Section 5 of the 1981 Act or for the headteacher to recommend an initial assessment. Where a child has been accepted as having special needs obviously those needs will have been assessed, but a statement may not have been made. Section 19 provides effectively right of appeal from a decision not to statement on the basis that matters have become worse or are worse than was thought, or on the basis that the provision assessed has not worked in a case where no statement has been. If the parent believes a child has special educational needs, then the correct course is to request an assessment under the 1981 Act which, by reason of Section 9, cannot be refused unless it is an unreasonable request. Therefore, if the child has not yet come to the notice of the LEA, the 1988 Act should be used together with the 1981 Act. In all such cases, the parents should request an assessment under Section 9 of the 1981 Act.

Further, if the headteacher takes the view that the child has needs but has not been assessed or has developed new or more needs, he or she has the power under Section 19 4 (c) (ii) to indicate to the LEA this opinion. Nonetheless, this again should mean that the LEA ought to apply Section 5 of the 1981 Act.

So children with special needs can use the appeal system. This is very useful where provision is being made for the child but no statement has been made and the parent believes the provision is inadequate or not working. Secondly, the parent could use the appeal system where an assessment has been made followed by no statement. In such cases, it should be used together with Sections 5 and 9 of the 1981 Act.

In those circumstances the real issue is whether a statement ought to be made under the 1981 Act, or, at least, whether provision is adequate, which will involve the question of what are the child's needs. The parent ought therefore to present to the governors, and initially to the headteacher, proper expert reports as described earlier. There is no reason why an expert cannot attend and explain to the governors his or her views and the parent's position. We would strongly recommend that this be done. There is also no reason why the parents cannot be legally represented at such an appeal, should they so wish.

Further appeal

Section 23 of the 1988 Act provides further appeal in the form of an appeal from the governing body. It is a widely worded section covering many issues under the 1988 Act.

The legislation covers a wider area of issues under the first part of the 1988 Act, but includes Section 19 appeals. There is no set procedure, bar the fact that the appeal must be in writing. In fact, the guidelines issued treat these appeals as appeals similar to those under Sections 6 and 7 of the 1980 Act (appeals against school placements.) There may be an oral hearing, if necessary.

The statutory provision is similar in terms to Section 68 of the 1944 Act, which is a judicial review power. However, this will not be so in Section 19 appeals as one has to look at that Section to see how the appeal arises. As this is a factual issue, an appeal on the facts would obviously be contemplated, on the basis of Section 19 and the exemption regulations. This section is badly drafted as it is really at once both a complaint power about the curriculum and an appeal section.

The Minister has a further power to consider the issue under Section 66, and plainly states in the circular that he will not consider such a complaint until this appeal procedure has been used.

As the Act itself provides an appeal system it seems that Section 23 can be regarded as a final appeal for the purposes of judicial review. In any event, if the issue is a procedural one, a judicial review is potentially available.[20]

NOTES

1. *R v Secretary of State for Education & Science ex parte O* Transcript CO/896/88 10th November, 1988.
2. *R v Secretary of State for Education & Science ex parte O* Transcript CO/896/88 10th November, 1988.
3. *R v Secretary of State for Education & Science ex parte O* Transcript CO/896/88 10th November, 1988.
4. 1983 SI No. 29 Reg 10.
5. Paragraph 61 and 62 Circular 22/89.
6. *R v Clwyd County Council ex parte A* CO/0569/62 22/7/92 *Times* 26/8/92.

7. 1983 SI No. 29 Regs 4 to 8 (ii) Para 69 Circular 22/89

8. *R v Surrey Education Committee ex parte H* 83 LGR p.219

9. Expert reports could be obtained through Legal Aid Green form.

10. Section 8 (5)

11. See Education Act 1980 Schedule 2 Part II para 9 and Section 7 (6) read together with Section II 1971 tribunal and Inquiries Act.

12. *R v Surrey Education Committee ex parte H* 83 LGR p.219 Court of Appeal.

13. *R v Somerset County Council ex parte Hamon*, see Transcript. 10.7.89 CO/47989.

14. *Per Lord Justice Carr ex parte Jackson*, see transcript. 10.7.89 Court of Appeal. Transcript CO/490189.

15. Section 8.4 (a).

16. Section 8.4 (b).

17. If a revision takes place it gives rise to a fresh right of appeal by amendment.

18. See section 4 (2).

19. Reg 14 (9) 1988 Regs.

20 Court of Appeal *R v Somerset LEA ex parte Hamon* Court of Appeal 10/7/89 Transcript CO/470/89. Court of Appeal *R v Kirklees Metropolitan Council ex parte Jackson* Court of Appeal 10/7/89 Transcript C/490/89.

Chapter 12

Education, provision and cost

In this chapter we shall consider the statutory nature of the education to be provided to children, the obligation to provide provision and the issue of cost. It is perhaps appropriate to deal with the third issue, ie cost, first.

As mentioned in Chapter 9, the 1981 Education Act created two categories of children. The first are those who can be educated in an ordinary school with provision for their needs without detailed and/or complex provision. The second is the rarer case of a child with severe or complex learning difficulties who requires a statement. Obviously, to make provision for a child individually is in normal circumstances likely to cost more than educating a normal child. For children who are the subject of a statement, however, provision will be more expensive, whether they are educated in an ordinary school, a local authority special school, or a specialist school not within the LEA sector.

It is easily forgotten that all children with special needs (who include children with severe disabilities and very rare conditions) are the responsibility of the local education authority for those needs which are educational. Some needs, such as speech therapy, can be both educational and medical, but in an individual case they are educational and should be treated as such.

The 1981 Education Act therefore recognises that it will cost more, sometimes considerably more, to deal with children with individual problems. For example, the authors have experience of a case considered in court of a child who, being over 13, was very serious; he was disabled in various other ways and required very specialist provision, including medical input. The total provision cost in excess of £60,000 a year. This was a very rare case indeed, but it illustrates the fact that in dealing with these individual problems, as required by law, cost is not a factor, save that resources must always be used efficiently (see below). However, the Children Act 1989 has by amending Section 3 of the Education Act 1981 empowered local authorities to pay the fees of any child who attends an establishment outside England and Wales which specialises in providing for children with special needs. This includes paying travelling fees and paying for a person to accompany the child. This section came into force on the 16th January 1990 as a result of Section 108(4) of the Children Act 1989. This was so that local authorities could permit children to attend very specialised establishments outside the United Kingdom.

Obviously, cost remains a factor in that local authorities are required not to waste money. However, while expanding the power of placement to institutes and schools outside the United Kingdom (so long as a child has a genuine but rare need), Parliament has made it quite clear that the Act is only cost-related in the requirement for efficiency.

THE STANDARD AND COST OF EDUCATION OR PROVISION

By Section 8 of the 1944 Education Act there is a general duty to educate pupils in accordance with age, aptitude and ability. Section 8 2 (c) of the 1944 Act requires the LEA to provide education suitable to age, aptitude and ability, and to have regard to the need for securing that special educational provision be made for a pupil with special educational needs. In the case of the headteacher or governors of a voluntary or county school (or now of a grant maintained school) they must use their best endeavours to ensure that the child's special educational needs are met by the appropriate provision. Where a statement is made, Section 7 (2) requires the local authority to make arrangements.

Section 2 (3) of the 1981 Education Act requires the LEA to make provision if the required conditions are met in an ordinary school. This section is considered later, but it adopts the recommendations of the Warnock Report that children with special needs should be integrated, if possible, and if it is in their interests, into normal schools. It should, however, be remembered that not all children are in fact suited to an ordinary school, and that certain provision needs a specialist school.

Section 2 (3) (a) states that this duty can only be applied if it is compatible with the child's receiving the special educational provision he or she requires. In the rare cases of children with severe complex problems, provision in an ordinary school will plainly not be compatible with their requirement. If, for example, a child needs small classes throughout the day, classes of 25–35 will not be compatible with his or her needs. Also, children with severe memory difficulties will not be able to cope with a normal curriculum in an ordinary school because the class will have no facilities to access or understand the ordinary curriculum, be too big, and have insufficient special aids. Children with less severe or less complex difficulties will obviously find a unit in an ordinary school compatible with their needs. There is presently a tendency to integrate without thought: more thought must be given to this issue.

Where a child has special needs and a statement is decided upon, the local authority must make and maintain a statement and arrange the special educational provision in the statement, unless the parent has made suitable arrangements by reason of Section 7(2). Cost is irrelevant where the Education Act 1981 is concerned but must be efficiently used.[1] This is hardly surprising, because children who have a severe disability or disablement are going to cost a great deal more to educate than children who are normal. In many cases it may in fact be cheaper to pay for a place at a special school, than to make expensive provision in the area for a few or a limited number of children. The efficient use of resources should be related to skills gains. In the less sensational cases this is a real practical problem. If an LEA go for cheap provision, it will take longer to help the child. This is more expensive long term. More expensive short term provision, which is cheaper in the long terms will therefore be lawful, and effective. More attention is needed on results and cost rather than cost alone.

In dealing with children who are not obviously rare cases, but who do have severe and complex difficulties, provision might currently be offered which is not going to bring about substantial progress and will take a long period of time to achieve any real progress. For example, administrators could see it as expensive to place a child in a specialist school for two to three years in order that the child can re-enter school with support at secondary level and achieve passes at a good rate in GCSE or, if the child is sufficiently able, 'A' Levels. They have concentrated on immediate cost, not realising that their provision will be required until the child leaves school at either 16 or 18. Costed out over the long term, and forgetting inflation, it is in fact far more expensive. In the case of a child with the dyslexic type of specific learning difficulty, therefore, the practical and lawful course is an urgent and more costly attack on the child's problem early on, resulting in a child who is not going to require a lot of specialist help or continued significant help throughout his or her school career and who is able to cope in an ordinary school with support. The need for long term provision is eliminated, or significantly reduced.

In practice, too little thought is given at the time of making a statement to considering placement, particularly at primary level. It is not enough to say that the child can cope in an ordinary system; the child's rate of progress and the relative results if more costly action is taken for a short time, as against what appears to be less costly action initially, ought to be considered much more carefully. These factors are not presently considered as frequently as they should be.

The words 'efficient use of resources', in both the Education Acts 1944 and 1981, do not always mean 'take the cheapest option'. They most certainly do not mean 'take second best if it is cheaper.'

However, for parents reading this book, the authors should make it quite clear that only a limited number of children with severe and complex problems require a specialist non-LEA placement.

Standard of education

The LEA is not under an obligation to provide the best education possible or a Utopian system, as Lord Justice Slade commented in *R v Surrey Education Committee ex parte H* 83 LGR p.219. Cost is therefore indirectly relevant in that the parent cannot simply insist on the best. The education must be that suitable to age, aptitude and ability and where provision is specified in a statement, the Local Education Authority must make that provision, irrespective of the issue of cost.[2]

If the local authority does not have within its maintained sector the required provision, it is bound under Section 7 (2) to make arrangements by reason of Section 6 of the Education (Miscellaneous Provisions) 1953 as amended by the 1981 Act. It has the power in appropriate circumstances to pay for a child either to go to an appropriate specialist independent school or to obtain appropriate provision, which is not available in its maintained schools. The amendment of Section 3 of the 1981 Education Act by the insertion of Section 3(A) has extended this power to include institutions outside the United Kingdom. It now includes placement outside England and Wales, but its primary intention was to allow payment of fees, travel, and the expenses of an accompanying parent for very specialised educational institutions abroad. This addition was considered in the introduction and was inserted by Section 108(4) of Schedule 12 paragraph 36 of the Children's Act 1989. This section is now in force.

WHAT HAPPENS IF A CHILD LEAVES SCHOOL?

The duty to make provision for children with a statement under Section 7, as well as the duty to make provision for children who do not have a statement, is a duty to make provision for children who are in school by virtue of the provisions of Section 4 of the 1981 Education Act.

Section 4(2) extends to children at school. A school is defined in Section 114 of the Education Act 1944 as being any institution for providing primary or secondary education, or both, whether maintained by the local authority or independent, and whether a special school or otherwise. The duty to educate by reason of the definition of senior pupil in Section 114 of the Education Act 1944 extends to the age of 19. However, the duty under the 1944 Education Act is to educate children attending school. In this context, therefore, it should be remembered that most or all sixth form colleges would constitute a school as defined by the Education Act 1944. The new further and higher education sector now has a clear duty to help young persons with special needs. It comes into force from April 1994.

FURTHER EDUCATION OR COLLEGES WHICH DO NOT CONSTITUTE SCHOOLS

The Education Reform Act 1988 by Section 120(2) amended Section 41 of the Education Act 1944 with effect from the 1st April 1989 and plugged a major gap in the law. If a student attends a college which is not a school, or leaves school for college, the previous duty to deal with the student's special educational needs was minimal. It would therefore be a matter of luck or judgement as to whether a child over 16 had a statement and provision, or provision in an ordinary school, or whether a child went to college and there was a duty to do virtually nothing. Sub-section 10 of Section 41 of the Education Act 1944 requires a local authority to have regard for the requirements of persons over compulsory school age who have learning difficulties, and under sub-section 1 the local authority must provide adequate facilities for further education. Section 41 sub-sections 1 and 2 place the same duty upon a local education authority in relation to Institutes of Further Education and provision that is placed upon them in relation to schools by Section 8 of the Education Act 1944.

THE NATURE OF THE DUTY UNDER SECTIONS 8 AND 41 OF THE EDUCATION ACT 1944

The duty provided for by Sections 8 and 41 is a general duty to provide facilities for education to children and students of all ranges of ability and to comply with the general requirements of the area. This duty therefore varies with the requirements from area to area. This is opposed to a duty owed to the individual pupil or student because of their special educational needs, which requires individual provision. In the recent case of *R v ILEA ex parte Ali* CO/1499/89 Transcript 14/2/90, the Divisional Court considered that this was a general duty that could not give rise to an individual right to damages or to redress. However, in contrast to the decision of the Court of Appeal in *Meade v Haringey London Borough* 1979 1 Weekly Law Reports p.637 the Court of Appeal, particularly Lord Denning, took a different view. The law in this area may therefore be described as presently uncertain, but for the purpose of the child with a special educational need or a student with a special educational need there is plainly an individual duty owed, whether or not there is a statement. It therefore does not matter what the extent of the general duty constitutes, as there is an individually owed duty.

Duty to those not at school but at college

The duty under Section 41 is to have regard to persons with learning difficulties over school age and is very similar to the duty under Section 8 of the 1944 Act. Sub-section 11 of Section 41 provides for a specific definition of learning difficulty which follows exactly that specific definition of learning difficulty which follows exactly that of Section 1(2) of the Education Act 1981; namely, that there is greater difficulty in learning than for the majority of persons of the child's age, or that there is a disability which prevents or hinders the child from making use of the facilities of the kind generally provided by the local education authority concerned in pursuance of their duty to provide education at college or otherwise. The limitation that language problems due to home or origin are not a learning difficulty excludes this problem from the definition.

Under Section 41 (13), the local authority has power to do anything which appears to them necessary or expedient for the purpose of or in connection with the exercise of their functions under this section. They therefore have a very wide power to provide for persons with learning difficulties. That power extends under Section 41(8) to become a duty to secure provision in further education for persons living outside their area. It is therefore stated in wider terms than the area-based duty under Section 4 of the 1981 Act, as further education will not be limited to the local area.

In exercising their power by reason of sub-section 9 the local authority must have regard to other bodies which provide further education in their area, such as universities or other institutions, and are not therefore required to duplicate necessary provision.

However, although the concept of statementing is not continued into further education the local authority must clearly have regard to the requirements of those with learning difficulties and provide what is necessary and expedient. Although the sub-section uses the words 'which appears to them' to be necessary or expedient it is not a mandate to do nothing. Unless, therefore, other institutions are able to provide the facilities required, the local authority is now under a duty to provide for learning difficulties of students over compulsory school age. There are now very similar powers to help students, but not so individual as under the 1981 Act. The new Act now redresses this problem.

PARENTAL WISHES

The LEA is bound by Section 76 of the Education Act 1944 (which must be read together with Section 2 (3) of the 1981 Act) to exercise all its powers and duties with regard to the general principle that, so far as is compatible with the provision of efficient instruction and to be educated in accordance with the wishes of their parents. It must be remembered that Section 76 is a general provision and not a specific provision under the 1981 Education Act.[3] In those circumstances it will be of use to parents, rather than LEAs. The LEA must take into account the parent's wishes and it can only reject them if it decides that the expenditure is unreasonable or incompatible with the factors outlined in the section. It cannot therefore ignore the parents' wishes. There are, moreover, obligations under Protocol 1 of the European Convention of Human Rights which extends this obligation further in favour of the parents.[4]

The issue of expenditure is not relevant to making and maintaining a statement. If the LEA were to refuse to make provision in a statement because it was too expensive that would be unlawful.[5] Neither could the LEA use Section 76, because it is only the parent's views that are capable of being rejected on the grounds of unreasonable expenditure. If the parents can show that the child needs a certain form of expensive provision and that the LEA cannot provide it, or that the provision suggested by the LEA is not adequate to meet a child's needs, then cost is an irrelevant factor. This was made clear in *R v Secretary of State for Education and Science ex parte Davies* 1989 2 FLR p.190.

EDUCATION IN AN ORDINARY SCHOOL

Where a child has special needs it is the duty of the LEA to ensure that the child's needs are met in an ordinary school. The intention of the Act therefore is to encourage, where possible, the integration of children with special needs with those who are normal. However, before a child can be educated in an ordinary school the LEA has to take into account the following factors:

1. The views of the child's parents.
2. That special educational provision is compatible with placement in an ordinary school.
3. That placing a child in an ordinary school will not interfere with the education of other children in the school.
4. That the placement represents an efficient use of the LEA's resources.[6]

By Section 8 (2) (c) of the 1944 Act the education must be appropriate to age, aptitude and ability and the child's special educational needs. Although, as Lord Justice Slade pointed out, the system is not Utopian,[7] plainly, the education must be adequate and reasonable. It must be capable of meeting a child's needs as well as being an education appropriate to the child's age, aptitude and ability. The issue of a refund of fees is different from the agreement by an LEA to take on the fees at an independent specialist school in rare severe and complex cases. In such cases, quite plainly LEAs are able to accept that a refund of fees would be proper in an appropriate case, up to a certain time. Exactly how far this duty goes is considered later.

No refund of fees can be made at least until a request is made for an assessment of the child's special educational need. Any parent would also be wise also to request grant help under Section 81 of the 1944 Act. However, the mere fact that a request has been made would not normally mean that the local education authority has a duty to consider refunding. Such duty would only normally arise upon the making of a draft statement, and upon the basis that the eventual statement nominates a specialist school outside the LEA sector. An LEA must normally be allowed a reasonable time to assess a child's needs, which is considered to be six months by Circular 22/89. Once it has established the position, which should normally be before the making of the final statement, the LEA will be bound (at its discretion) to consider refunding school fees, because it is from the point when a statement is actually made, at least in draft form, that the LEA acknowledges that it has a responsibility for the child, rather than the school and its headteacher.

Nonetheless, the whole process can take some considerable time. The parents are bound to act in the child's best interests and secure education in accordance with the child's special educational needs and suitable to the child's age, aptitude and ability (see Section 36 of the Education Act 1944). This is the parents' statutory duty in these circumstances, as well as the obvious desire of any parent who wishes to see their child properly educated. Where a parent is forced to act rapidly and make a provisional placement it would be wise for the parent to write to the local education authority and explain that it is a provisional placement. Where a parent cannot afford to take such action, there is power to make a temporary provisional placement. Circular 22/89 recognises that such power exists, although obviously such a power is only temporary and cannot predict the outcome of the statement. It would only be used in rare and difficult cases.

EDUCATION OUTSIDE OF SCHOOL

Section 3 of the 1981 Act allows an LEA to arrange for the special educational provision required for a child, or part of that provision, to be made for the child otherwise than in a school so long as the parents are consulted. So, if a child needs to attend a special unit elsewhere or obtain some other assistance outside school, there is ample power for the LEA to provide that provision elsewhere than in school.

NATURE OF PROVISION

In order to consider the nature of provision which is covered by the 1981 Act one must first see what is a special educational need as defined by statute. Section 1 sub-section 2 of the Act defines special educational needs as follows:

(2) Subject to subsection (4) below, a child has a 'learning difficulty' if:

(a) he has a significantly greater difficulty in learning than the majority of children of his age; or

(b) he has a disability which either prevents or hinders him from making use of educational facilities of a kind generally provided in schools within the area of the local authority concerned, for children of his age; or

(c) he is under the age of five years and is, or would be if special educational provision were not made for him, likely to fall within paragraph (*a*) or (*b*) when over that age.

The two main categories are Subsections 2(a) and (b) of Section 1 of the 1981 Act. These are extremely wide categories and so long as a child has a learning difficulty he will fall either within one or the other. The regulations made under the 1944 Act in 1959 set out a number of specific categories of children. The 1981 Education Act has simply widened the definition of learning difficulties so that all children with special educational needs now fall within the Act.

Definition is extremely wide (*R v Hampshire Education Authority exparte J*[8] at page 556).

SPECIAL EDUCATIONAL PROVISION

The Act defines special educational provision in Section 1 (3). It also qualifies provision by excluding children who speak a foreign language at home.

Provision is therefore something which is educational and is different in the sense of being additional to or in some way otherwise separate from educational provision made generally for children of the same age and in schools maintained by the LEA concerned.

In *R v Hampshire Education Authority ex parte J* 84 LGR p.547[9] the LEA attempted to argue that, as the child concerned was dyslexic and as they had a unit in one of their schools to cope with dyslexics, this was not special educational provision within the Act because it was not different from that provided by the LEA in their schools. This argument was rejected by Mr. Justice Taylor because, as he pointed out, the provision that must be considered is that made generally for children of the child's age in the schools maintained by the LEA and that therefore special education for dyslexics was different from, for example, Greek tuition, which also was not normally provided for children in their schools. The provision made for a child with special needs must be related to the learning difficulty which calls for special educational provision to be made. So that although Greek tuition was otherwise different from provision made generally and was educational, it was in no way related to a child's special educational needs. Provision made by the Act must be *special educational provision, not special provision or merely educational provision*. This is an important distinction because a child may need provision to be educated. For example, a child with speech difficulty may need speech therapy which may be either educational or medical. If it is essential to the child's education it will be a special educational need (see *R v Lancaster County Council ex parte CM* 10/3/89 Court of Appeal 133 *Solicitors Journal* p.484). The Court of Appeal held in exparte CM that speech therapy, which was essential to the child's need, was a special educational provision, although now provided normally by health authorities. The Court of Appeal held that if a health authority cannot help then an LEA should go to other health authorities or to the private sector, or employ a therapist.

A social or background factor could be a special educational need which required provision.[10] In *R v Secretary of State for Education and Science ex parte Goldblatt* Transcript COD/1990 p.65 the Minister conceded and the Court accepted that a religious background giving rise to a need for education in a school of a certain type of religion was capable of being a need that required provision, within the meaning of that Act. Circular 22/89 adopts this approach.

The regulations provide for a statement to specify other provision; the appropriate panel in the statement is normally Part 5, additional non-educational provision.

By Section 7(2)(b) the LEA may now clearly arrange non-educational provision although there was some doubt before. In *R v Oxford Education Authority ex parte W Times* 22/11/86,the Divisional Court decided that an education authority could reasonably decide that speech therapy was not educational provision. However, that case is now very probably bad law because in the Court of Appeal the LEA settled the case, giving the child the provision required before placing the child at a special school. The decision of the Divisional Court and the Court of Appeal in the Lancashire case now governs the issue. The Court of Appeal in the Lancashire case stated that they doubted that the Oxfordshire decision was correct. They are right. It is to be noted that what happened in Oxfordshire case appears not to have been brought to their attention. The Oxfordshire case should therefore no longer be relied upon.

Under the provisions of the Education Reform Act 1988 the LEA may now arrange non-educational provision (Paragraph 83 of Schedule 12). The LEA, under regulation 10 (2) (c), should only specify non-educational provision, if in their opinion, it will help the child properly to benefit from the special educational provision specified in the statement. In effect, this is very nearly a mandatory duty because it can only be placed in the statement if the LEA are of the opinion that the child needs it if he or she is to benefit properly from the special educational provision. In such a case that the expenditure upon the child's education specified in the statement will be frustrated unless the non-educational provision is made. If such provision is placed in the statement, because it is needed to help a child properly to benefit from the special educational provision, then not to do so would be to frustrate the objects of the Act; it would also be unlawful.[11] Further, it would appear that it is unlawful and unreasonable to refuse to make such provision if it is specified in Part V of the statement as being a provision which the LEA was of the opinion would assist the child to benefit from the special educational provision, and is not available if not provided by the LEA. Care should be taken to separate non-educational provision, eg. wheelchair or spectacles, from educational provision, eg. speech therapy.

If it is in fact, educational provision it should be in Part IV of the statement, not Part V. We shall not consider the powers for LEAs to recoup or share expenditure with health authorities. This does, however, happen.

DUTY OF PARENTS

Under Section 36 of the 1944 Act, as amended, parents must ensure a child with special needs is educated in accordance with the child's age, aptitude and ability, and the child's special needs. This is a very strict duty, and it constitutes a criminal offence to breach it.

DIFFERENCES IN AREA

Differences can arise from authority to authority. One area's provision maybe much better for children with special needs or children with special needs in a particular category, than another. In those circumstances it has been argued by some that a LEA may not have to make a statement because its provision is better in its particular area. This issue was considered by the Court of Appeal in *R v The Secretary of State for Education and Science ex parte L* 1988 86 LGR p.13. The Court of Appeal rejected this argument; the leading judgment on this issue being that of Lord Justice Dillon. The statutes themselves make no mention of the issue of area. The statutory test is the child's need which dictates the special educational provision. It is therefore not surprising that the Court of Appeal was not impressed by this argument.

GRANTS

The LEA has power under Section 81 to make a grant towards the whole or part of the costs of a placement at a specialist school (see Section 81 (6) 1944 Education Act). This allows an LEA to assist a placement where there is a strong but not a clear-cut case for placement at a specialist school, or in any emergency before a statement is made. The LEA can operate, but not impose, a policy that eliminates its discretion (*R v Hampshire Education Committee ex parte J* 84 LGR p.547). As there is a mandatory duty to place the child at a specialist school if a statement requires it, the policy must not in fact solely adhere to that duty or it will be no policy. There must be individual consideration of each case, even if there is a policy, and an LEA always retains the right to go outside its own policy. The right to apply for a grant should not be forgotten by parents.

NOTES

1. *R v Secretary of State for Education ex parte Davies Times* 6/11/89.
2. *R v Secretary of State for Education and Science ex parte Davies Times* 6/1/89, *R v Hampshire Education Committee ex parte J* 84 LGR p.547.
3. *R v ILEA ex parte F Times* May 1988.
4. *Belgium Linguistic ase Kjeldsen et al v Belgium European Court of Human Rights* 1976 judgement.
5. Section 6 1953 Education Miscellaneous Provisions Act.
6. Section 2 (3) of the 1981 Act.
7. *R v Surrey Education Committee ex parte H* 83 LGR p.219.
8. 84 LGR p.547.
9. 2. Supra.
10. These factors are expressly accepted in Circular 22/89.
11. *Padfield v the Minister of Agriculture and Fisheries* 1968 AC 1968 AC 997.

Chapter 13

The form and content of statements

The 1981 Education Act requires that a statement be in the prescribed form and that it should contain prescribed information (Paragraph 3 of Part 2 of Schedule 1 of the Act). The information required to be in the statement must, in particular, contain the following:

(a) Details of the authority's assessment of the special educational needs of the child, and

(b) Specification of the educational provision to be made for the purpose of meeting those needs.

It is the duty of the LEA, under Section 7 (1) of the 1981 Act, in statement cases, to determine special educational provision and to make a statement of the child's special educational needs. It follows from the above provisions that the LEA must have determined the provision and properly assessed the needs.

The analysis of needs must be careful and detailed. In Paragraphs 18, 60 and 61 of Circular 22/89 the Minister currently stresses this point. The provision should be specified in detail. In Paragraph 60 of Circular 22/89 the Minister makes it quite clear that vague guidance which does not specify the needs or provision to parents, the school and teachers is of no use. If the parents or teachers do not know what is required to meet the child's needs or what the child's needs actually are then the statement is of no practical use. A statement must therefore accurately and adequately define a child's needs and the provision to meet those needs. In the case of *R v Secretary of State for Education ex parte E, Times* 17/1/91, 1992 FLR p.377, Mr Justice Nolan said 'The statement was no ordinary form. Part II might be compared to a medical diagnosis and Part III to a prescription for the needs diagnosed. It was axiomatic that Part III must deal fully with Part II.'[1] The provision must be sufficiently detailed to give clear guidance to teachers, the school and parents. Equally, the statement must be sufficiently individualised to distinguish the child who is the subject of the statement, and that child's individual needs, from children of a general type who require special educational provision. It is worth quoting from Paragraph 61 of Circular 22/89 the following:

> 'It is important that this information should easily be understood by all those involved in the child's education including parents, so that they know exactly what is required. Statements that fail to specify in detail what provision the particular child requires are of little use to parents and professionals who are to act upon them.'

It must be a clear list of the child's needs and the required provision.

NATURE OF THE DOCUMENT

All local authorities must follow the form of statement specified in the Schedule to the 1983 Regulations. That form in the schedule is divided into five parts headed by Roman numerals. The important categories are:

(ii) Special educational needs.

(iii) Special educational provision.

(iv) Appropriate school or other arrangements.

(v) Additional non-educational provision.

The advice and representations received are attached in each separate category of advice as a separate appendix of the statement itself.[2] These appendices are not, it is to be stressed, the statement itself.

HOW A STATEMENT SHOULD BE COMPILED

A statement is, in essence, an individual list of the child's needs and the provision required to meet them. Regulation 10 of the 1983 regulations provides that a statement of a child's special educational needs shall include and set out the following:

(a) The special educational provision (in terms of facilities and equipment, staffing arrangements, curriculum or otherwise), which the education authority considered appropriate to meet those needs. In other words, educational provision has to be specified in sufficient detail to be identified and identified as relating to that child.

The Divisional Court in *R v The Secretary of State and Education ex parte O*, Transcript CO/896/99 10/11/88[3] made the point that one should not be too legalistic in the interpretation of these regulations. Nonetheless, the regulation makes it quite clear that provision should be made in considerable detail, as does Circular 22/89.

However, the regulations do require such detail to be specified if it is necessary to do so. Where a child's provision requires special staffing arrangements or special equipment or alternatively a special curriculum, the regulation makes it clear that this should be specified in the statement itself in Part III. These are, as it were, extra items. The provision itself must be clearly defined.

The regulation has now been considerably amended and the statement must not only now deal with exclusions from the national curriculum, but set out the relevant attainment levels, and proposals to cover the change in the national curriculum and the change in attainment levels. The Court of Appeal considered issues concerning the contents of needs and provision in *R v The Secretary of State for Education and Science ex parte E*, 1992 FLR p.377. The case has already been mentioned in some detail earlier. The Court of Appeal made the following points:

(i) All the needs assessed should be set out in the statement. It follows, also, that if on appeal further needs are discovered, they must be included in the statement.

(ii) That the provision to meet each and every need should be set out in the statement and that the LEA must go through the exercise of establishing what provision is available to meet each and every need, checking that it is available in the ordinary school and making sure that, if it is not, it will be supplied by the LEA.

(iii) That the statement must deal with the whole child and not with part of the child (Woolf and Balcombe LJ).

The Court of Appeal went on to state that the provision set out in the statement should be in sufficient detail to comply with the regulations. In that case, the Dorset statement considered was set out in detail, down to expressing the hours of provision to be made. This was obviously considered sufficient. In *R v Clwyd County Council ex parte A, Times* 26/8/92[4] when considering a 22 paragraph statement of provision which followed the Dorset approach, Mr Justice S. Brown said that a statement must not be 'too prescriptive. It must not use lack of detail as a disguise for a failure to make provision.'

In *R v Wiltshire Education Authority ex parte D* 28/1/92, CO/1393/91 unreported, Mr Justice Potts decided that the LEA's panel re-considering the case acted unreasonably in failing to agree to amend the statement so that it included provision to meet the needs which had been accepted by all the expert educational psychologists for both the parent and the LEA. In his judgement, he cited with approval the expert report by the co-author of this book, Dr Chasty, assessing the child's needs in the manner set out in the draft psychological report in Appendix 4. The judge regarded a breakdown of the various hours required to help the child as necessary in that case, in compliance with the regulations and statute.

(b) The type of school which they consider would be appropriate for the child or, if they consider a particular school would be appropriate, they must name that school (*R v ILEA ex parte F Times*, May 1988).[5]

On this issue, if the school is an independent specialist school, and if it is not approved under Section 12 and 13 of the 1981 Act, the approval of the Minister will have to be obtained for a placement. Many specialist schools do not have or want ministerial approval. In the case of individual children such approval is normally a formality, where one is dealing with a respected established school. In practice, the Minister often gives permission in this manner.

EDUCATION OTHER THAN AT SCHOOL

If education otherwise than at school is considered necessary to meet a child's needs, it must be specified. The most common example of this will be attendance at an outside unit.

NON-EDUCATIONAL PROVISION

In cases of children with severe disabilities the existence of non-educational provision may be quite crucial to an effective education.

The LEA can only specify provision which they will make available, or they are satisfied will be made available by the district health authority, a social services authority or some other body (see Regulation 10(i)(c)(1)). Such provision must be a provision which, in their opinion, must be made if the child is to benefit properly from the special educational provision specified in the statement (Regulation 10(i)(c)(2)).

The LEA can only specify such provision if, in their opinion, advantage should be taken of it for the child to benefit properly from the special educational provision and such provision would be essential or beneficial to education (These matters have already been considered). The regulation empowers an LEA to make such provision available or it would not say 'unless proposed to be made available by the Education Authority'. The amendment already mentioned to Section 7(2) of the 1981 Act, made by Paragraph 85 of Schedule 12 to the Education Reform Act 1988, plainly gives the LEA power in express terms to make such provision available. If such provision is essential to a child's education so that a child could not benefit or properly benefit from the special educational provision without it, the LEA ought to make such provision available.[6]

SIGNATURE OF THE STATEMENT

The statement must be in the prescribed form or in a similar form as that set out in schedule to the regulations. It must also be signed by a duly authorised officer of the education authority concerned and if it is not so signed it is not properly signed and authenticated (see Regulation 10 (2)).

THE RESTRICTION ON DISCLOSURE OF THE STATEMENT

The Act and Regulations restrict the disclosure of a statement. As they concern the welfare of children they are confidential documents. The general rule is that a statement cannot be disclosed without the parent's consent. These are exceptions laid down by Regulation 11 (1) of the 1983 Regulations. The duty of confidentiality not only includes the actual statement itself but also any representations, evidence, advice or information which is set out in the statement in pursuance of Regulation 10(1) see Regulation 11(3).

The following are exceptions to those provisions:

(a) Persons to whom the LEA are of the opinion that the statement should be disclosed in the educational interests of the child.[7]

(b) For the purpose of any appeal under Section 8 of the 1981 Act.[8]

(c) For the purposes of educational research that, in the opinion of the LEA, may advance the education of children with special educational needs. This is only if the person engaged in research undertakes not to publish anything contained in, or derived from a statement otherwise than in a form which does not identify any individual concerned, including in particular the child concerned and his parents.[9]

REVIEW OF THE STATEMENT

Statements must be reviewed on a yearly basis for the period beginning at the making of the statement or the previous review.[10] The LEA conducting a review should inform the parents of the existence of the review. A failure to do so will obviously invalidate the review, as the object of the review is to check that the statement is working properly and that the child's needs have been properly assessed. In practice, most LEAs do this, although some are not aware of their duty to inform parents.

No problems will arise if the parents and the school are satisfied that the child's needs are being properly addressed. Where, however, the parents are not satisfied, they should certainly comment in detail about the defects in the provision. It is important in such circumstances that, if possible, the parents obtain the help of the school.

In practice, many schools are very sympathetic, and they themselves will agree that the child needs more help. The parents should arrange to meet either the headteacher, or the teacher who will be the person who will deal with the review. If possible, the parents and the school should agree to inform the LEA, on review, of the exact position, and identify where more help is needed. It may well be that it can only be agreed that the child has other needs which require investigation, but this, at least, is an important factor to establish.

If the parents believe that the statement is not working, they should list why, and prepare their case, if possible before the LEA actually conducts the review. Some LEAs conduct the review by way of a meeting with the parents present. If that is the practice, it is even more important that the parents and the school agree where they can upon the issues. This particular method of consultation is considered the best way of conducting a review.

If the parents do not agree that the statement is working, and the school is not either helpful, or cannot comment, the parents should compile a list of areas where provision is not working, or where new needs have been established, and present it to the LEA. If these are important issues, after about a year a parent would be well advised to obtain an expert report on these points. It is never advisable to over-test children. However, after a year it is perfectly proper to check the operation of a statement or provision in this manner.

If there is reasonable evidence that the statement is not working, a parent is entitled to request a review, or an amendment of a statement, or a re-assessment. If this has been done, it must be put in writing. If the LEA does not review a statement, it will be in breach of statutory duty.

In *R v The London Borough of Hounslow ex parte W* 20/12/91 unreported CO/1452/91, Mr Justice Rose held that the LEA, who had failed to review the statement, could not rely on the statement and say that it continued to make valid provision for the child when there had been a change of circumstance (see the transcript, p.9(c) to 11(g) CO/1452/91 Friday 20th December 1991).

In that case, the child had changed from primary to secondary school and his condition was accepted by all parties as having improved in some areas, but in other areas problems still remained and were severe.

If there had been no change, the LEA could have been entitled to rely on the statement, but as, in that case, it was obvious that there had been a change in the child's needs, the LEA's decision was flawed as being unreasonable, because it was in breach of statutory duty at the time.

REASSESSMENT

As previously set out in Section 9 of the 1981 Act, a parent can ask for a reassessment and that cannot be refused unless the LEA is satisfied that the assessment is inappropriate. A parent who is dissatisfied with their child's provision and progress may request a reassessment on that basis. As previously set out, any parent who does so ought to do so with the support of an expert report or the LEA's staff making the provision.

MANDATORY REASSESSMENT

All children who are the subject of a statement must be reassessed between the age of 13½ and 14½ if the child has not been assessed after the age of 12. Regulation 9 of the 1983 regulations makes this a mandatory requirement. It is obvious that there should be a reassessment if the child is about to transfer from primary to secondary school. This should be done before transfer.

Obviously, where the provision for a child changes substantially, there is a need for a reassessment. So where the provision available to a child in a statement requires a substantial element of reassessment, then the proper course for an LEA to take is to reassess the child's needs under Section 5.

AMENDMENT

The LEA has power to amend a statement by reason of Paragraph 6 Part II of Schedule 1 of the 1981 Act. Where an amendment is proposed, they must serve on the parent, in writing, the proposal together with notice of the parent's right to make representation. The parent then has 15 days beginning upon the date on which the notice is served to make representations. From there the local authority must consider any representations made to them and, when making a decision, inform the parent in writing of their decision. These provisions do not apply where the statement is no longer necessary.[11]

MOVING HOUSE TO A DIFFERENT AREA

If a child moves house to a different area, obviously the LEA is under the same general obligations as the former LEA. Where there is a statement, the old authority can transfer the statement to the new authority and must do so if the old authority requests it.[12] The LEA which made the statement is entitled to transfer if it thinks fit. If a statement has been transferred, it is valid until it is replaced. The obligation is therefore now upon the new authority. The transfer involves a limited reassessment if the parent consents (see Regulation 12(3)). If the parent wants a complete reassessment, then the parent does not have to give consent, and a reassessment must take place. All the old reports, and the old statement, will be considered, together with the new assessments, or representations and evidence if any. The new authority can therefore either reassess or, alternatively, if the statement is less than three years old and the parents agree, the reports that formed the basis of the old assessment can be used.[13]

Where a statement is not transferred, the old authority is plainly under an obligation until the statement is replaced to make the provision specified in the statement. This is a plain incentive to transfer in any cases involving expense. Section 7 of the Education Act 1981 makes no reference to the issue of the pupil being registered at one of their schools or being in the local area. The provisions for the assessment of children who are the subject of a statement are plainly those that relate to a child residing in the area. However, the obligation to maintain the statement and the provision is not dependent on residence. If the new LEA wishes to reassess, then it has power to do so, but the old statement remains the valid statement until the reassessment takes place. If not transferred the obligation remains with the former LEA which has made the provision. Once a statement is made it is a statement, not residence, which determines the LEA's obligation, subject to Section 4 of the 1981 Act.

NOTES

1. Cited with approval by the Court of Appeal 1992 FLR p.377.
2. Reg 9 1981 SI No. 29.
3. Supra.
4. *Times* May 1988 (Transcript more useful).
5. Transcript CO/0569/62 22.7/92 reported *Times* 26/8/92.
6. *Padfield v The Minister of Agriculture and Fisheries* 1968 AC p.997.
7. Regulation 11 (1) A.
8. Regulation 11 (1) B.
9. Regulation 11 (1) C.
10. Paragraph 5 of Schedule 1 Part II of the 1981 Act.

11. Paragraph 7 Part II of Schedule 1 of the 1981 Education Act 12.
12. Regulation 12 1983 SI No. 29.
13. Regulation 12 (3) 1983 SI No. 81.

Chapter 14

The Children Act and its effect on the Education Act 1981

While there are interlinks between the Acts, we deal only with the educational issues. In considering the assessment provisions under the 1981 Act, Section 43 of the Children Act must be considered. In the case of children with special needs it is likely to be important because it means that, if a child has educational needs but also other needs which require, for example, residential placement due to problems at home or an inability to cope at home, the local education authority can, under Section 43, be compelled to assess the need. Section 43 reads as follows:

PART V PROTECTION OF CHILDREN

Child assessment orders

43 (1) On the application of a local authority or authorised person for an order to be made under this section with respect to a child, the court may make the order if, but only if, it is satisfied that

(a) the applicant has reasonable cause to suspect that the child is suffering, or is likely to suffer, significant harm;

(b) an assessment of the state of the child's health or development, or of the way in which he has been treated, is required to enable the applicant to determine whether or not the child is suffering or is likely to suffer, significant harm; and

(c) it is unlikely that such an assessment will be made, or be satisfactory, in the absence of an order under this section.

(2) In this Act 'a child assessment order' means an order under this section.

(3) A court may treat an application under this section as an application for an emergency protection order.

(4) No court shall make a child assessment order if it is satisfied –

(a) that there are grounds for making an emergency protection order with respect to the child; and

(b) that it ought to make such an order rather than a child assessment order.

(5) A child assessment order shall –

(a) specify the date by which the assessment is to begin; and

(b) have effect for such period, not exceeding 7 days beginning with that date, as may be specified in the order.

(6) Where a child assessment order is in force with respect to a child it shall be the duty of any person who is in a position to produce the child –

(a) to produce him to such person as may be named in the order; and

(b) to comply with such directions relating to the assessment of the child as the court thinks fit to specify in the order.

(7) A child assessment order authorises any person carrying out the assessment, or any part of the assessment , to do so in accordance with the terms of the order.

(8) Regardless of subsection (7), if the child is of sufficient understanding to make an informed decision he may refuse to submit to a medical or psychiatric examination or other assessment.

(9) The child may only be kept away from home –

(a) in accordance with directions specified in the order;

(b) if it is necessary for the purposes of the assessment; and

(c) for such period or periods as may be specified in the order.

(10) where the child is to be kept away from home, the order shall contain such directions as the court thinks fit with regard to the contact that he must be allowed to have with persons while away from home.

(11) Any person making an application for a child assessment order shall take such steps as are reasonably practicable to ensure that notice of the application is given to –

(a) the child's parents;

(b) any person who is not a parent of his but who has parental responsibility for him;

(c) any other person caring for the child;

(d) any person in whose favour a contact order is in force with respect to the child;

(e) any person who is allowed to have contact with the child by virtue of an order under Section 34; and

(f) the child,

before the hearing of the application.

(12) Rules of court may make provision as to the circumstances in which –

(a) any of the persons mentioned in subsection (11); or

(b) such other person as may be specified in the rules,

may apply to the court for a child assessment order to be varied or discharged.

(13) In this section 'authorised person' means a person who is an authorised person for the purposes of Section 31.

This section can be used where a child has a need which the local education authority denies as an educational need. The parent can now compel the LEA or the appropriate person, as defined under the Act, to assess the child's need. In cases where children are being subjected to harassment at school or have a sense of failure, which results in severe emotional or behavioural problems, such an assessment can be very useful to compel appropriate specialist help.

Section 17 of the Act provides that it shall be the general duty of every local education authority to:

(a) Safeguard and protect the welfare of children within their area who are in need and;

(b) So far as consistent with that duty to promote the upbringing of such children by their families by providing a range in level of services appropriate to meet those children's needs.

The remainder of this section is set out in Appendix 8.

Schedule 2 Part 1 of the Act obliges local authorities to take reasonable steps to identify the extent to which there are children in the area in need and to publish information about services provided under Sections 17, 18, 20 and 24.

Paragraph 3 of Part 1 of Schedule 2 provides that, where it appears to a local authority that a child within their area is in need, the authority shall assesses needs for the purposes of the Act at the same time as any assessment of his needs made under:

(a) The Chronically Sick and Disabled Person's Act 1970.

(b) The Education Act 1981.

(c) Disabled Persons (Services, Consultations and Representation) Act 1986 or,

(d) Any other enactment.

It is important, therefore, for parents to remember that, where there is a need and an assessment is taking place under the 1981 Act, they ensure that the powers to assess a non-educational need are used. Where a local educational authority refuse to assess the need, and the request to assess the need under the Children Act is made upon a reasonable basis, judicial review is the remedy to compel such an assessment.

Few LEAs will realise at present that it is their responsibility as a local authority to assess the need if it is under the Children Act and the LEA involved. A good reason to request an assessment is needed for an assessment to be made.

This is, therefore, an additional help for parents where the child has severe or complex difficulties and where some of those difficulties are not being shown at school – for example where the child is one who psychologically turns in on him or herself.

Chapter 15

The circumstances in which a statement can be discontinued

In practice problems have arisen where local education authorities have discontinued statements in circumstances where they are not entitled to do so.

Section 5 of the Education Act 1981 provides for the LEA to assess a child's special educational needs. Section 5(6) provides for an appeal against the decision that the LEA is not required to determine the child's special educational provision.

In those circumstances when a local education authority proceeds to the draft statement under Section 7 having determined the special educational provision to be made for the child under Section 7 (3), it must serve a copy of the proposed statement. In *R v Isle of Wight County Council ex parte AS Times* 22/4/92 Schiemann J. held that an LEA did not need to make a final decision until it issued a final statement. A draft statement can be withdrawn.

Sections 7(4) and (6) of the Act provide for a series of meetings whereby the parents can make representations. In practice a parent will always be saying that the statement should be continued but that the local education authority has not in fact made proper provision for the child's needs in the statement.

In those circumstances it will be rare indeed that the parent will be saying that there should be no statement. Section 7(8) provides that a local education authority, after considering representations can:

(i) Make a statement in the original form

(ii) Make a statement in a modified form or

(iii) Determine not to make a statement

Section 7(8) provides for the local education authority to notify the parent in writing of their decision. It is considered that this obligation means that the written decision must provide proper logical reasons.

However, in order to decide not to make a statement, something substantial must happen over and above the LEA disagreeing with the parent's representations. Once an LEA assesses a child's needs under Section 5, Section 5(6) requires the LEA to take stock and decide whether or not to determine the child's needs. It is only if they decide that they should determine the child's needs that they then make a statement.

In order to decide not to continue the draft statement, it appears fairly clear that the LEA will have had some new development in mind.

CESSATION BY AMENDMENT

The other situation whereby a statement can be discontinued is by amendment. Powers of amendment are contained in Section 6 of Schedule 1 to the Act.

If an LEA proposes to amend or cease to maintain a statement, by Paragraph 6(1) they must serve on the parents a notice containing the right to make representations under this paragraph. The parents then have 15 days to make representations. The LEA must consider them and inform the parent of their decision in writing.

A statement can therefore be discontinued by amendment. Again, this power is very restricted. The LEA cannot simply decide to amend. It must do so on information and they must have clear information on which to discontinue a statement. Obviously, any child with a statement would be expected to improve. The fact that the child improves does not mean that a statement is not required, because the child may not continue to improve or may fall back unless the child still gets specialist help.

It would only be in rare cases, therefore, that this power will have any application. An LEA can certainly not conduct a reassessment and call it an amendment as that would be unlawful, but it is possible that power can be used as the Act contemplates it. It is significant that there is no right of appeal against this decision. Judicial review would apply in the circumstances. The power should only therefore be used in very clear and obvious cases, most likely where a child was made the subject of a statement because of an illness which had cleared up, and after a period of help the child had been brought back to normal. A specific learning difficulty or a disability is always there, even if the help brings the child up to normality; the child often needs the help in order to continue to be normal.

Bibliography

Adams, F., (1986), *Special Education*, Councils and Education Press, Harlow: Longman.

Baddeley, A., Grant, S., Wight, E. and Thomson, N., (1974), 'Imagery and visual working memory', in Rabbit, P. and Dominic S. (Eds), *Attention and Performance*, V, New York: Academic Press.

Baddeley, A., (1976), *The Psychology of Memory*, New York: Basic Books.

Baddeley, A., (1978), 'The trouble with levels: re-examination of Craik and Lockhart's framework for memory research' *Psychological Review*, 85, 139–152.

Baddeley, A. and Hitch, G., (1974), 'Working memory', in Bower, G. (Ed), *The Psychology of Learning and Motivation*, Volume 8, New York: Academic Press.

Baddeley, A. and Lieberman, K., (1980), 'Spatial working memory' in Nicherson, R. (Ed), *Attention and Performance*, VIII, Hillsdale, NJ: Lawrence Erlbaum.

Cermak, L. and Craik, F. (Eds), (1979), *Levels of Processing in Human Memory*, Hillsdale, NJ: Lawrence Erlbaum.

Chasty, H. T., (1989), 'The Challenge of Specific Learning Difficulties', Proceedings of Conference Meeting Points 1989. Reading: British Dyslexic Association.

Chasty, H. T., (1990), 'Meeting the Challenges of Specific Learning Difficulties' in *Children's Difficulties in Reading, Spelling & Writing*, Pumfrey, P. D., and Elliott, C. D., London: Falmer.

Chasty, H. and Zdzienski, D., (1986). 'Working memory and comprehension', paper given to British Psychological Society Cognitive Section 1986.

Colle, H., and Welsh, A., (1976), 'Acoustic masking in primary memory', *Journal of Verbal Learning and Verbal Behaviour*, 15, 17–32.

Colle, H., (1980), 'Auditory encoding in visual short term recall: effects of noise intensity and spatial location', *Journal of Verbal Learning and Verbal Behaviour*, 19, 722–735.

Craik, F., and Lockhart, R., (1972), 'Levels of processing: a framework for memory research'. *Journal of Verbal Learning and Verbal Behaviour*. 11, 671–684.

Craik, F., and Levy, B., (1976), 'The concept of primary memory'. In Estes, W. K. (Ed), *Handbook of Learning and Cognitive Processes*. Vol.4 P.119. Hillsdale NJ: Lawrence Erlbaum.

Crowder, R., (1982), 'The demise of short term memory', *Acta Psychologica*, 50, 291–323

Cornwall, K., Hedderly, R., and Pumfrey, P. D., (1983), 'Specific learning difficulties: the "Specific reading difficulties" versus "dyslexia" controversy resolved.' *Occasional Papers of the Division of Educational & Child Psychology of the British Psychological Society* 7, 3, 1–121.

Dunn, L. M., (1968), 'Special education for the mildly retarded – is much of it justifiable'? *Exceptional Children* 35, 5–22.

Elliott, C. D., (1989), 'Cognitive profiles of learning disabled children'. *British Journal of Developmental Psychology*.

Feuerstein, R., Rand, Y., and Hoffman, M. B., (1979), *The dynamic assessment of retarded performers*. Baltimore: University Park Press.

Groden, (1969): 'Lateral preferences in normal children'. *Perceptual and Motor Skills*, 28, 213–214.

Hayakawa, S., (1965), *Language in thought and action*. London: Allen and Unwin.

Howe, J. A., (1989), 'Separate skills and general intelligence, the autonomy of human abilities'. *British Journal of Educational Psychology*, 59, 3.

Kolers, P., and Smythe, I., (1979), 'Images, symbols and skills'. *Canadian Journal of Psychology*. 33, 158–184.

Macmillan, D. L., Jones, R. L., and Aloia, G. F., (1975), 'The mentally retarded label: A theoretical analysis and review of research'. *American Journal of Mental Deficiency* 79, 241–261.

McDonald Critchley, (1970), The Neurological approach in assessment and teaching of dyslexic children'. in White, Franklin, A., and Naidoo, S., (eds), *Assessment and teaching of dyslexic children*, London: ICAA.

Perfetti, C. A., and Lesgold, A. M., (1977), 'Discourse comprehension and individual differences'. In Carpenter, P., and Just, M., (Eds), *Process in comprehension*. Hillsdale, NJ: Lawrence Erlbaum.

Reisberg, D., Rappaport, I. and O'Shaugnessy, M., (1984), 'Limits of working memory: The digit digit span'. *Journal of Experimental Psychology: Learning, Memory and Cognition*, 10, 2, 203–221.

Salame, P., and Baddeley, A., (1982), 'Disruption of short term memory by unattended speech: Implications for the structure of working memory'. *Journal of Verbal Learning and Verbal Behaviour*. 21, 150–164.

Stobart G., (1986), 'Is integrating the handicapped psychologically defensible?' *Bulletin of British Psychological Society* 39, 1–3.

Tizard, J., (1972), *Children with specific reading difficulties*. London: HMSO.

Tyler, S., and Elliott, C. D., (1988), 'Cognitive profiles of groups of poor readers and dyslexic children on the British Ability Scales'. *British Journal of Psychology* 79.

Vincent, D., Green, L., Francis, J. and Powney, J., (1983), *A review of reading tests*, London: NFER Nelson.

Warnock Report, (1978), *Special educational needs report of the Committee of Enquiry into the education of handicapped children and young people*. London: HMSO.

Appendix 1

The parent's checklist

Questions to ask to indicate *suitability* of LEA mainstream school provision.

1. Preliminary Research

(a) Ask LEA for a copy of its policy on educating Spld children. If it hasn't one: why not?

(b) Every school is required to produce a prospectus: obtain and read the one for your named school. This gives an idea of ethos, background, aims and academic practice.

(c) Ask for copies of school's handouts and circulars to parent on special needs arrangements and provision.

(d) Who are the parent governors? Do they carry out their duty to see that statemented children are taught as outlined in the statement? Contact them and ask.

(e) How many schools like this does the LEA maintain? How special is it? What extra resources are available to it?

(f) From *Education Year Book*, or LEA statistics, ascertain size of school and number of teachers. Calculate average class size. Check this later from the head and by your own observation.

(g) Although Warnock suggests 20 per cent of school population at sometime have special needs, calculate 1⁄10 of enrolment in suburban areas, 1⁄7 of enrolment in inner city areas to have special needs. This indicates crudely the size of school's special educational needs problem. Note and relate to facts on resources and staffing gleaned on school visit.

2. Visit School

(a) *Talk to head:* What is attitude to special needs children? Supportive? Disinterested?

(b) What is attitude to Spld / dyslexia?

(c) What does *head* consider is the major problem faced by school's special needs staff?

(d) What is head's calculation of average size of class? (remember groups in excess of 20 will provide very difficult learning conditions for students with serious Spld).

(e) How many statemented children attend the school? How many with Spld?

(f) What is school's INSET policy for (i) class teachers (ii) special needs staff.

3. Enquire about national curriculum

(a) How broad? Flexibility is more important than breadth. Problems of implementation of national curriculum.

(b) What facilities are available for practical subjects work; art, craft, design etc?

(c) What is preferred teaching approach, if any? Formal, informal, multi sensory?

(d) What individual arrangements are made to help those weak in fundamentals?

(f) What arrangements can be made to make up teaching missed by late entry or Spld?

(g) Do students have regular access to typewriter, computer, word processor, tape recorder?

(h) Ask to see some standard text books for that age group. Calculate text difficulty using Fog index. Relate to student's reading ability. Wide discrepancy indicates degree of difficulty student will experience on curriculum.

4. Talk to head of Special Needs

(a) What is attitude to special needs children?

(b) What is attitude to Spld/dyslexia?

(c) What is major problem faced by special needs department? Check whether this is:

(i) containing broadly based literacy difficulties in children from a range of backgrounds.

(ii) teaching basic skills competence to slower learning students.

(iii) dealing with social emotional and motivational problems.

(iv) meeting individual special needs.

(d) Does the special needs department have its own accommodation, or does it use the classrooms of other departments, or other *ad hoc* arrangements.

(e) What resources and equipment are available?

(f) What structured multi-sensory programmes are used?

(g) If teaching is 'objectives' based,

(i) how realistic are objectives?

(ii) how well do objectives integrate to make a coherent language programme which is different from what child has been given previously?

5. Visit a class *(try to go to one which contains a statemented pupil)*

(a) Check class size, note the sense of purpose or otherwise in the ongoing activity.

(b) Look at teaching methods. Try to assess the way in which information is presented. How much reading, note taking, copying, essay writing would be necessary for survival in that class?

(c) Note any special arrangements in operation for individual children.

(d) At end of lesson, try to talk briefly to class teacher. Was class teacher aware of the special needs of the statemented child? How sympathetic and knowledgeable is that class teacher towards the problems of the Spld/dyslexic student?

6. Summing Up

You should now be able to answer these key questions:

(a) How sympathetic are the staff?

(b) How knowledgeable and well trained in this special educational need?

(c) How suitable is the general curriculum?

(d) How detailed and individually appropriate is the special provision?

(e) How appropriate are the buildings and resources?

(f) Is this school conversant with the particular special needs of my child, can it make and maintain the required provision?

(g) Does this provision offered by LEA take due account of the efficient use of all resources, including my child?

(h) Will this provision result in fast gains, and good morale or slow gains, low curriculum success and falling morale.

(i) Can it competently meet my child's special educational needs?

Accept or reject the provision.

Appendix 2

History notes written by Pearse, aged 8 years 0 months

WISC (R) Verbal Scale 136. Performance Scale 120
Dotting speed: R 30.2
L 31.4
Slow times show motor difficulty. Similar times indicate ambidexterity.
Vernon Graded Word Spelling Test: score 7y 6m

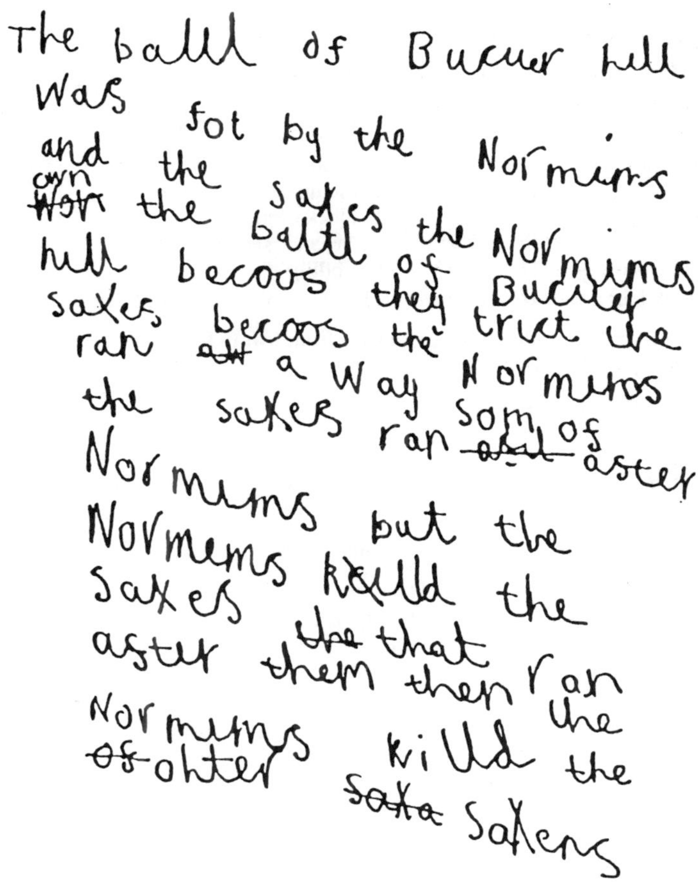
The balll of Bucner hill
Was fot by the
and the Normums
own ~~Won~~ the saxes the
balltl the Normums
hill becoos of
saxes becoos they Bucner
ran ~~all~~ trict the
a Way Normums
the saxes som of ran ~~all~~
Normums aster
Normums but the
saxes killd the
aster ~~the~~ that them then ran
Normums the
~~of~~ ohter killd the
~~saxa~~ saxens

Appendix 3

Sample report

Name:

Address:

Date seen:

Date of Birth: 3 July
Age: 11 years 4 months

Test Results

Ability

WISC(R) (Wechsler Intelligence Scale for Children (Revised))

Standard: verbal: average
visual: very high

Ability : Centile Rank = 80%

Full Scale IQ = *not quoted*

Verbal Scale IQ =	*96*	*Performance Scale IQ =*	*131*
Information	6	Picture completion	12
Similarities	11	Picture arrangement	15
Arithmetic	9	Block design	18
Vocabulary	10	Object assembly	17
Comprehension	11	Coding	10
Digit span	(7)		

Average range 8–12: Individual scores vary from 1 to 19 for these tests.

Further Diagnostic Testing

Laterality
Handedness: for writing – Right. Dotting Speed: Right 21.2 seconds
Left 21.8 seconds

Fine motor control: slow, and close to ambidexterity

Eyedness:	Telescope:	Left	confusions & uncertainties in binocular control
	Aperture:	Middle & left, then right	
	Cone:	Right	

Left/right awareness:	confused	
Memory		
	WISC(R) Digit Span test	7 year 6 months
	British Ability Scales Recall of Digits Subtest	8 year 2 months. Centile 26. T44 below average auditory short term recall
	British Ability Scales Immediate Visual Recall	7 year 8 months. Centile 10. T37 Weak visual short term recall
	British Ability Scales Recall of Designs	9 year 8 months. Centile 28. T44 below average visuo-motor memory competence. Difficulties with orientation of designs on the page.

Abilities in:	*Difficulties in:*
Visual sequencing	Auditory short term recall
Visual perception	Fine motor control
Constructive visual thinking	

Attainment in Basic Skills

Reading
SINGLE WORD RECOGNITION

British Ability Scales Word Reading Test (A)	Reading age 7 years 3 months: Centile 4, T32 Very slow average response time of 4 secs per word. Accuracy rate 62% is low. Very weak word recognition skills	
CONTINUOUS PROSE		
Neale Analysis of Reading	Reading accuracy:	Age 7 years 6 months
Ability (Form C)	Reading comprehension:	Age 8 years 5 months
	Reading speed 54 wpm	Age 8 years 5 months

Spelling
Vernon Graded Word Spelling Test Spelling age 6 years 8 months. Centile 2. Serious difficulties in spelling.

Writing Skill
Pen grip: angular right hand: page twisted through 90 degrees to write down to up

Fluency/speed: slow at 10 words per minute

Writing style: poorly controlled unjoined print script which lacks flexibility

Punctuation: omitted

Spelling: limited word choice and high error rate of 30%, indicate spelling difficulties

Sentence structure: adequate

Expression of ideas: restricted and immature

Tests of Number

British Ability Scales Basic Number Skills Test (C)	Number age 8 years 8 months: Centile 11. T38 Weak written calculation skills

Referral Details

was referred for assessment at chronological age 11 years 4 months by his parents, Mr and Mrs . has special educational needs requiring a special provision to be made. The has produced a revised draft Statement on 18th September Mr and Mrs seek guidance on 's level of intellectual ability, his information processing competence in auditory and visual short term memory and fine motor skills, and his attainments in the basic curriculum skills of reading, spelling, writing and numeracy, so that they may be advised further on the nature and extent of 's difficulties in learning, and an appropriate provision which can be made for him in the school.

General Background

Prior to assessment, Mrs confirmed that had enjoyed a normal childhood, with developmental stages occurring at the expected time. No untreated difficulties remain in his vision or hearing which might restrict his literacy learning. enjoys good health and does not take medication which might retard his learning competences.

The early development of his physical skills was normal, with the usual stages occurring as expected, culminating in the establishment of right hand preference, which appears to be somewhat inconsistent. The early development of speech was normal, with making speech sounds accurately, and later expressing his ideas competently in words.

It is noted that can be forgetful, and he experiences concentration and attention difficulties. His working memory skills will be investigated and commented on in this report.

shows signs of anxiety and stress, which appear to relate to his difficulties in learning. He has shown both temper tantrums and behavioural difficulties in school, and his sleep patterns are not particularly regular. Despite these signs of stress, he gets on effectively with other children outside the family, but has some difficulties with his brother at home and with older children in school. It is evident that experiences difficulties in cognitive skills development and some social difficulty which will be investigated and commented on in this report.

General Level of Intellectual Ability

The Wechsler Intelligence Scale for Children (Form R) was administered to . This enables his problem solving to be assessed on two dimensions, the Verbal using words and the Performance using hand and eye skills. On the Verbal scale, had an IQ of 96 in the average ability range. In this section of the test, his subtest scores fluctuated from the high side of average to below average. Score variations like this are usually observed in the test profile of students with specific learning difficulties.

Use of Language in Thinking

In the Verbal subtests, where direct application of speech to problem solving is necessary, achieved an average standard. In Similarities, where he had to use abstract verbal reasoning skills to perceive the relationship between ideas, his score is average. He achieved the same standard in Vocabulary, where he had to define words in common English use, and also in Comprehension, where he had to use receptive language skills to process complex speech about social situations. scores on these three subtests confirm that he used speech adequately in verbal problem solving.

Auditory Short Term Memory in Verbal Problem Solving

In Digit Span, which indicates the development of 's auditory short term memory, his score of 7 is much below average and he shows marked difficulty in this important information processing skill. He shows some limitation in auditory short term memory capacity, and has poor ability to apply sequencing skills to material held in short term memory.

In Arithmetic, where had to use working memory skills to extract the sense of the question and apply to it his knowledge of tables, his score of 9 is in the average range. He achieved a lower standard in Information, where he had to recall and use his general knowledge.

's scores on these three subtests indicate that his ability to apply working memory skills to verbal problem solving is limited.

Visual Thinking Competence

On the Performance Scale had an IQ of 131, in the very high intellectual category. In this section of the test, his subtest scores fluctuated from maximum to average.

In Picture Completion, where had to perceive the omissions in pictures, his score of 12 is on the high side of average and he shows competent visual analysis. In Picture Arrangement, where he had to place into a left to right order sets of pictures which tell stories, his score of 15 is much above average and he shows well developed visual sequencing skill.

In Block Design, where had to build patterns using blocks, his score of 18 is close to test maximum and he shows excellent visual perceptual skills. In Object Assembly, where he had to build jigsaw puzzle type pictures from parts, his score of 17 again approaches test maximum and he shows excellent constructive visual thinking skill.

's scores on these subtests are at a very much above average standard, and indicate that this aspect of his problem solving is a considerable cognitive strength for him.

In Coding subtest, where had to use visual short term memory and fine motor manipulation on a number coding task, his score of 10 is average. He shows some inefficiency in the application of both these skills to the copying process.

General Ability Level

It is undesirable to quote a full scale IQ score for as this would conceal the disparity between his verbal problem solving which is average, and his visual problem solving which is in the very high intellectual category. He shows a pattern of high visual problem solving capability and average verbal problem solving capability with widely scattered test scores, the balance of which is adequately reflected by his above average ability centile ranking of 80. 's difficulties in learning require further investigation and comment in the next section of this report.

Further Diagnostic Testing

Tests of Laterality

HAND SKILLS

writes with his right hand. On a test of dotting speed which enables a comparison to be made between the speed, accuracy and control of one hand with the other, he returned a right hand time of 21.2 seconds and a left hand time of 21.8 seconds for the test. These times are very similar and indicate that is properly regarded as being ambidextrous. The times are some 6–8% slow and indicate that he has a degree of fine motor manipulative difficulty.

EYE SKILLS & SPATIAL AWARENESS

shows quite marked uncertainty in monocular and binocular control skills, and these confusions and uncertainties were reflected by later inadequacies in his line tracking in reading. is advised that the family doctor, Dr should be asked to consider referring to the Department of Ophthalmology at his local hospital, or to the Royal Berkshire Hospital, Reading, for administration of the Dunlop Test.

's sense of left/right awareness is confused, and this adds to his difficulties in line tracking.

It is evident that experiences fine motor and eye control difficulties which will have affects upon his attainments in literacy skills.

Tests of Memory

AUDITORY/VERBAL

's score on the Digit Span subtest of WISC(R) was translated into an age score using the appropriate table on page 189 of the WISC manual. He achieved a 7 year 6 month level and shows marked retardations in auditory short term recall.

As a check on this, the British Ability Scales Recall of Digits Subtest was administered. On this test achieved an 8 year 2 month level, on the 26th centile rank, and shows below average auditory short term recall. These results are consistent and indicate that 's auditory short term memory skills are below average.

VISUAL
The British Ability Scales Subtest of Immediate Visual Recall was administered. On this test, achieved a 7 year 8 month level, on the 10th centile rank, and shows weak visual short term recall.

The British Ability Scales Recall of Designs Subtest was administered. On this test, achieved a 9 year 8 month level, on the 28th centile rank, and shows below average visuo-motor memory competence. shows particular difficulties with the orientation of designs on the page and was somewhat confused by his own habit of twisting the page when writing or drawing.

RESULTS ON COGNITIVE TESTS
On the tests of cognitive ability administered, shows skills in learning in visual sequencing, visual perception, and constructive visual thinking. He shows difficulties in learning in auditory short term recall and fine motor skills which will lead to some limitations in his attainments in the basic curriculum skills.

Attainment in the Basic Skills

Reading

SINGLE WORD RECOGNITION
The British Ability Scales Word Reading Test A was administered. On this test, had to recognise and name single words presented out of context. He achieved a 7 year 3 month standard, on the 4th centile rank, and shows weak word recognition skills. He shows a very slow response time, at an average of 4 seconds per word. It is noted that his accuracy of word recognition is extremely low with a 62% accuracy level. 's word recognition skills are very weak.

CONTINUOUS PROSE
The Neale Analysis of Reading Ability (Form C) was administered. On this test had to read continuous passages of English prose of increasing difficulty; when reading accuracy, comprehension and speed are monitored. On word accuracy, he achieved a 7 year 6 month level, his comprehension was at an 8 year 5 month standard, and his reading speed at 54 words per minute was at a similar standard. These subtest scores confirm that 's continuous reading skills are inefficient.

Spelling

The Vernon Graded Word Spelling Test was administered. On this test, had to write down words which were dictated. He achieved a 6 year 8 month standard, on the 2nd centile rank, and his spelling skills show very significant difficulty.

Writing

A test of 's continuous writing skill was administered and analysed. He holds his pen in an angular right hand grip, with the page twisted through 90 degrees, so that he writes from down to up rather than from left to right. His speed of writing production is slow at 10 words per minute. uses a poorly controlled unjoined print script which lacks flexibility. In this work, punctuation marks are omitted and appears not to understand basic punctuation rules. His spelling in writing is very weak, with a limited word choice being evident and an extremely high error rate of 30% indicating his serious spelling difficulties. 's sentence structure is adequate, but his expression of ideas in writing is limited and immature.

Tests of Number

The British Ability Scales Basic Number Skills Test (C) was administered. On this test had to carry out simple addition, subtraction, multiplication, division, fractions and decimals calculations. He achieved an 8 year 8 month level, on the 11th centile rank, and his calculation skills are very weak.

Conclusions

On the tests of cognitive and literacy skills administered, shows average verbal ability, very high visual ability, but has difficulties in learning in aspects of auditory and visual short term recall and fine motor control, which lead to restrictions and retardations in his reading, spelling, writing and numeracy, consistent with specific learning difficulty or dyslexia.

Personality

The CPQ Child Personality Questionnaire (Form A) by Catell and Porter was administered to . This enables the personality of the student to be assessed on fourteen major dimensions. 's personality profile is attached as an appendix to this report. Key points in his profile are that is reserved, lacks stability, is shy, shrewd and tense. Calculation of the optional second order factors in this test show him to be rather introverted, independent and anxious. It is therefore evident that has quite marked behavioural difficulties which affect his personality to some extent, and these exceed those normally encountered in students with specific learning difficulties/dyslexia. Therefore, 's behavioural difficulties must be considered in the provision to be made for him, and should be written into his Statement as an area which contributes to his difficulties in learning.

Comments on the Statement of Special Educational Needs

Mr and Mrs are advised that the Statement of Special Educational Needs produced by the is lacking in some essential details which would enable an appropriate provision to be made for .

In section 2, Special Educational Needs, no reference is made to 's quite marked difficulties in learning in aspects of auditory short term recall, visual short term recall and fine motor skills. It is agreed that the social/behavioural difficulties which experiences have been mentioned, but the management of these difficulties is made much more difficult by the Authority's insistence that these needs should be met totally in the ordinary classroom of local school.

The special educational provision does not refer to 's difficulties in memory and motor skills which are amenable to teaching and should have been included as part of the programme. 's literacy skills problems have been mentioned and some reference is made to developing competence in the establishment of better peer relationships, but this is going to be an unnecessarily complex task if it is attempted within the large classroom of the local school.

Educational Provision

The provision to be made for should cover five major areas. In section one, his clearly evident difficulties in learning need to be addressed. One hour per week should be spent on the development of appropriate standards in fine motor control and working memory skills. The Somerset Thinking Skills Development Programme by Blagg, Ballinger and Gardiner, or the Instrumental Enrichment Programme by Professor Reuven Feuerstein will be relevant.

The second section of 's programme should deal with his obvious difficulties in literacy skills. He should be taught by means of a structured multi-sensory language programme, with *Dyslexia: A Language Training Course for Learners and Teachers* by Kathleen Hickey, being appropriate, as is *Alpha to Omega* by Hornsby and Shear, published by Heinemann, or the Lucy Cowdens Course available from Kingston Polytechnic. requires some three hours per week on this work.

The third section of 's programme should address his difficulties in numeracy, with assistance being given to enable him to manipulate tables and number facts more accurately, and to handle the written aspects of numeracy much more efficiently. One hour per week should be given to this work.

The fourth section of 's programme should address his serious behaviour and personality difficulties, looking at his behavioural skills and improving these in the small group setting, so that he develops social competences which may be transferred into the larger class group.

The final section of 's programme should take account of his very marked curriculum skill deficiencies. Until these have been dealt with by appropriate specialist teaching, he will need some five hours support per week on the curriculum, to enable him to have access to the learning experiences provided in school.

Mr and Mrs should note that the special provision to be made for is detailed, and his local school may find it difficult to make and maintain the required provision.

They may find that independent specialist boarding schools can offer appropriate specialist support. It may be a more efficient use of the local Authority's resources to place in a suitable specialist 'out county' school.

Appendix 4

The Psychological Assessment Report

These matters should be considered in depth in the assessment report. The Institute's format is standard throughout the country and should be adhered to.

First page	test scores
Then page two and following:	Referred by parents, school/LEA/ other sources

Outline the student's abilities and problems leading to failure. Does family think child is clever? Is there a family incidence of similar in school work?

Background

1. *Early history – general milestones*

   Physical, visual, aural, speech development

2. *School history:*

   How fragmented? How helpful?

3. *Personal details:*

   Child's attitude, behavioural background. Concentration and attention, working memory competence. Is there an a priori emotional disturbance, or a consequent behavioural difficulty?

4. *Intellectual ability*

   Discuss subtests strengths WISC-R or BAS to highlight key abilities and difficulties in learning.

5. *Look at the extent and impact of the difficulties in learning*

   (a) Fine motor skills, left/right awareness, directions. Comment on motor skill development in relation to literacy.

   (b) Perception

Auditory:	Wepman
Visual:	Bender

   (c) Working memory skills

Tests	Testing
BAS	Immediate/delayed visual recall.

		Recall of digits. Recall of designs
or	Aston Index	Auditory & visual sequential memory
or	Benton	Appropriate subtests
or	Koppitz VADS	Oral/aural, oral written visual oral, visual written
or	ITPA	Auditory and visual sequential memory

Basic curriculum skills

6. Language skills

Speech, reading, spelling, writing, to comment in individual attainments in the basic curriculum skills to reach conclusion about effectiveness of student language skills when judged by the standards of others of this age, ability and background.

7. Assess numeracy skills

by British Ability Scales, Vernon/Gillham and Hesse if WISC-R arithmetic subtest score or parent/school reports suggest this is needed.

8. Personality and social skills

Using Eysenck Personality Questionnaire, or Child Personality Questionnaire by Cattell and Porter or 16PF by Cattell, looking particularly at sociability, dominance, impulsivity, sensitivity, insecurity, tension and anxiety, to relate the student's social and personality skills to the circumstances in which he learns, and consider the need to provide counselling and personality skills development as part of the student's programme.

9. Conclusion

Subject is of below/average/high/very high intellectual ability; has (marked) weaknesses in fine motor skills/working memory skills and behavioural/social/personality difficulty related to retardations in reading spelling, written language, and or numeracy. His difficulties are/are not in keeping with specific learning disability/dyslexia.

10. Teaching provisions

The range of teaching provisions to be made for students with specific learning difficulties will be wide and varied. The provision made must be individual and relate to the abilities and difficulties in learning experienced by the student. The provision should cover (a) learning skills, (b) (i) language skills, (ii) numeracy skills, (c) study/thinking skills, and (d) behavioural skills, and (e) link effectively to the school curriculum.

(a) learning skills

(i) Fine motor skill development (train the hand)

(ii) Laterality-sequencing training (where do I start?)

(iii) Working memory training: develop deliberate control of available capacity, extend capacity, teach discarding of irrelevant information, choose time for learning, switch modalities frequently, multi-sensory is best.

(iv) Visual perceptual training: skill in recongising shapes consistently.

(v) Auditory perceptual training: skill in recognising sounds consistently.

(b) (i) language skill

(vi) Language development through talk:

(i) getting sounds and words right

(ii) getting sentences right

(iii) concept/idea/labelling

(iv) creating an organisation for talk.

(vii) Structured multi-sensory training to develop simultaneous skills in reading, spelling and writing and making most effective use of deficient memory skills.

(b) (ii) numeracy skills

(viii) Number language training: using structured multi-sensory methods.

(c) study/thinking skills

(ix) Extraction, representation, storage and recall of ideas.

(x) Expression of ideas in writing.

(xi) Development of active control of the learning/thinking process in 'metacognition'.

(d) behavioural skills

Developing the competences to enable the learner to operate effectively in a range of social and learning groups with varying purposes, structures, climates.

11. Special educational needs

To be discussed – teaching help needed in some or all of the above.

(i) Specify extent of programme required (1) learning, (2) literacy, (3) numeracy, (4) social development, (5) curriculum support in terms of hours per week.

(ii) If exam concessions certificate appropriate, please issue.

(iii) Refer parents to headteacher or remedial advisor for help. Advise on rights under Education ACT 1981, if necessary.

(iv) If in independent sector, the schools listed in Appendix 5 can help. Fees range from £8,000 to £12,000+. It is unlikely that LEAs or charities will pay.

Appendix 5

List of special needs schools

Specialist day

Fairley House, London

Specialist boarding – age 9–13

East Court, Ramsgate, Kent	co ed.
Edington, Bridgwater, Somerset	co ed.
Old Rectory, Brettenham, Nr Ipswich	co ed.

Specialist boarding – age 11–16+

Kinloss School, Martley, Worcs	boys
Mark College, Highbridge, Somerset	boys
Nunnykirk Hall, Northumberland	co ed.
Ravenscroft, Farleigh Castle, Nr. Bath	co ed.
Shapwick Senior School, Bridgwater, Somerset	boys

Prep schools

These schools will select dyslexic applicants, in keeping with the demands of their curriculum and dyslexic provision.

Appleford School, Salisbury	co ed.
Brighton College (Hawkhurst Court)	co ed.
Bruern Abbey, Oxon.	boys
Edgarley Hall, Glastonbury, Somerset	co ed.
Long Close School, Slough	boys
Westbrook Hay School, Hemel Hempstead, Herts	boys

Senior – age 11–16+

These schools will select dyslexic applicants, in keeping with the demands of their curriculum and dyslexic provision.

Co-educational

Claysmore School, Iwerne Minster, Dorset
Millfield, Street, Somerset
Sibford School, Sibford Ferris, Banbury
Stanbridge Earls, Romsey, Hants
Stoke College, Sudbury, Suffolk

Wrekin College, Telford, Shopshire
Ravenscroft School, Farleigh Castle, Nr Bath
(accepts students placed by LEAs)

Boys only

Bethany School, Goudhurst, Kent
Bloxham School, Banbury, Oxon
Brickwall House, Northiam, Nr Rye, East Sussex
Cawston College, Cawston, Norwich
Eccles Hall, Norwich, Norfolk
Ellesmere College, Shropshire
Grenville College, Bideford, N. Devon
Northease Manor, Lewes, East Sussex
St David's College, Llandudno, N. Wales

Girls only

Bedgebury School, Goudhurst, Kent
Micklefield School, East Sussex
St Mary's School, Wantage, Oxon
Woldingham School, Woldingham, Surrey

For children with more serious difficulties

Brickwall House, Northiam, Rye, East Sussex
Keffolds Farm, Haslemere, Surrey
Mark College, Highbridge, Somerset
Knowle House School, Pirbright, Surrey
Nunnykirk Hall, Northumberland
Northease Manor, Lewes, E. Sussex
Ravenscroft School, Farleigh Castle, Nr Bath
Reeves Hall, Diss, Norfolk

This is not a complete list of schools offering education for dyslexics, but gives some indication of possibilities.

Also known to have support, and to have dealt with relatively unusual or severe cases, is Development Centre, London.

Further enquiries can be made with ISIS (Independent Schools Information Service). Parents should note that a number of independent schools have support in varying degrees, but have had not statemented children. Parents should look at schools which have had statemented pupils rather than simply schools that offer support. As a child who is statemented has by definition a severe or complex problem, many schools suggested by ISIS will not be suitable.

H. T. Chasty
John Friel

Appendix 6

Statutory extracts

EDUCATION ACT 1944

8 Duty of local education authorities to secure provision of primary and secondary schools

(1) It shall be the duty of every local education authority to secure that there shall be available for their area sufficient schools –

(a) for providing [primary education, that is to say, full-time education suitable to the requirements of junior pupils who have not attained the age of ten years and six months, and full-time education suitable to the requirements of junior pupils who have attained that age and whom it is expedient to educate together with junior pupils who have not attained that age]; and

(*b*) for providing secondary education, that is to say, full-time education suitable to the requirements of senior pupils, other than such full-time education as may be provided for senior pupils in pursuance of a scheme made under the provisions of this Act relating to further education [and full-time education suitable to the requirements of junior pupils who have attained the age of ten years and six months and whom it is expedient to educate together with senior pupils];

and the schools available for an area shall not be deemed to be sufficient unless they are sufficient in number, character, and equipment to afford for all pupils opportunities for education offering such variety of instruction and training as may be desirable in view of their different ages, abilities, and aptitudes, and of the different periods for which they may be expected to remain at school, including practical instruction and training appropriate to their respective needs.

(2) In fulfilling their duties under this section, a local education authority shall, in particular, have regard –

(*a*) to the need for securing that primary and secondary education are provided in separate schools;

(*b*) ...

[(*c*) to the need for securing that special educational provision is made for pupils who have special educational needs; and]

(*d*) to the expediency of securing the provision of boarding accommodation, either in boarding schools or otherwise, for pupils for whom education as boarders is considered by their parents and by the authority to be desirable:

Provided that paragraph (*a*) of this subsection shall not have effect with respect to special schools.

76 Pupils to be educated in accordance with the wishes of their parents

In the exercise and performance of all powers and duties conferred and imposed on them by this Act [the Secretary of State] and local education authorities shall have regard to the general principle that, so far as is compatible with the provision of efficient instruction and training and the avoidance of unreasonable public expenditure, pupils are to be educated in accordance with the wishes of their parents.

81 Power of local education authorities to give assistance by means of scholarships and otherwise

Regulations shall be made by [the Secretary of State] empowering local education authorities, for the purpose of enabling pupils to take advantage without hardship to themselves or their parents of any educational facilities available to them –

(*a*) to defray such expenses of children attending county schools, voluntary schools, or special schools, as may be necessary to enable them to take part in any school activities:

(*b*) to pay the whole or any part of the fees and expenses payable in respect of children attending schools at which fees are payable:

(*c*) to grant scholarships, exhibitions, bursaries, and other allowances in respect of pupils over compulsory school age, including pupils undergoing training as teachers:

(*d*) to grant allowances in respect of any child in respect of whom any scholarship exhibition bursary or other allowance has been granted by a former authority before the date of the commencement of this Part of this Act.

EDUCATION ACT 1981

1. Meaning of 'special educational needs' and 'special education provision'

(1) For the purposes of this Act a child has 'special educational needs' if he has a learning difficulty which calls for special educational provision to be made for him.

(2) Subject to subsection (4) below, a child has a 'learning difficulty' if –

(*a*) he has a significantly greater difficulty in learning than the majority of children of his age; or

(*b*) he has a disability which either prevents or hinders him from making use of educational facilities of a kind generally provided in schools, within the area of the local authority concerned, for children of his age; or

(*c*) he is under the age of five years and is, or would be if special educational provision were not made for him, likely to fall within paragraph (*a*) or (*b*) when over that age.

(3) 'Special educational provision' means –

(*a*) in relation to a child who has attained the age of two years, educational provision which is additional to, or otherwise different from, the educational provision made generally for children of his age in schools maintained by the local education authority concerned; and

(*b*) in relation to any child under that age, educational provision of any kind.

(4) A child is not to be taken as having a learning difficulty solely because the language (or form of the language) in which he is, or will be, taught is different

from a language (or form of a language) which has at any time been spoken in his home.

2 Provision of special education: duties of local education authorities etc

(1) …

(2) Where a local education authority arrange special educational provision for a child for whom they maintain a statement under section 7 of this Act it shall be the duty of the authority, if the conditions mentioned in subsection (3) below are satisfied, to secure that he is educated in an ordinary school.

(3)The conditions are that account has been taken, in accordance with section 7, of the views of the child's parent and that educating the child in an ordinary school is compatible with –

(*a*) his receiving the special educational provision that he requires;

(*b*) the provision of efficient education for the children with whom he will be educated; and

(*c*) the efficient use of resources.

(4) It shall be the duty of every local education authority to keep under review the arrangements made by them for special educational provision.

(5) It shall be the duty of the governors, in the case of a county or voluntary school, and of the local education authority by whom the school is maintained, in the case of a maintained nursery school –

(*a*) to use their best endeavours, in exercising their functions in relation to the school, to secure that if any registered pupil has special educational needs the special educational provision that is required for him is made;

(*b*) to secure that, where the responsible person has been informed by the local education authority that a registered pupil has special educational needs, those needs are made known to all who are likely to teach him; and

(*c*) to secure that the teachers in the school are aware of the importance of identifying, and providing for, those registered pupils who have special educational needs.

(6) In subsection (5)(*b*) above 'responsible person' means –

(*a*) in the case of a county or voluntary school, the head teacher or the appropriate governor (that is to say the chairman of the governors, or, where the governors have designated another governor for the purposes of this paragraph, that other governor); and

(*b*) in the case of a nursery school, the head teacher.

(7) Where a child who has special educational needs is being educated in an ordinary school maintained by a local education authority it shall be the duty of those concerned with making special educational provision for that child to secure, so far as is both compatible with the objectives mentioned in paragraphs (*a*) to (*c*) of subsection (3) above and reasonably practicable, that the child engages in the activities of the school together with children who do not have special educational needs.

4 General duty of local education authority towards children for whom they are responsible

(1) It shall be the duty of every local education authority to exercise their powers under this Act with a view to securing that, of the children for whom they are responsible, those with special educational needs which call for the local

education authority to determine the special educational provision that should be made for them are identified by the authority.

(2) For the purposes of this Act a local education authority are responsible for a child if he is in their area and –

(*a*) he is registered as a pupil at a school maintained by them or is registered as a pupil in pursuance of arrangements made by them by virtue of section 6 of the Education (Miscellaneous Provisions) Act 1953 at a school which is not maintained by them or another local education authority; or

(*b*) he has been brought to their attention as having, or as probably having, special educational needs and –

(i) is registered as a pupil at a school but does not fall within paragraph (*a*) above; or

(ii) is not registered as a pupil at a school and is not under the age of two years or over compulsory school age.

5 Assessment of special educational needs

(1) Where, in the case of a child for whom a local education authority are responsible, the authority are of the opinion –

(*a*) that he has special educational needs which call for the authority to determine the special educational provision that should be made for him; or

(*b*) that he probably has such special educational needs;

they shall make an assessment of his educational needs under this section.

(2) Assessments under this section shall be made in accordance with the following provisions of this Act.

(3) If a local education authority propose to make an assessment of the educational needs of a child under this section they shall, before doing so, serve notice on the child's parent informing him –

(*a*) that they propose to make an assessment;

(*b*) of the procedure to be followed in making it;

(*c*) of the name of the officer of the authority from whom further information may be obtained; and

(*d*) of his right to make representations, and submit written evidence, to the authority within such period (which shall not be less than 29 days beginning with the date on which the notice is served) as may be specified in the notice.

(4) When a local education authority have served a notice under subsection (3) above and the period specified in the notice in accordance with paragraph (*d*) has expired, the authority shall, if they consider it appropriate after taking into account any representations made and any evidence submitted to them in response to the notice, assess the educational needs of the child concerned.

(5) Where a local education authority decide to make an assessment under this section they shall notify the child's parent in writing of their decision and of their reasons for making it.

(6) If, after making an assessment of the educational needs of a child under this section, the local education authority decide that they are not required to determine the special educational provision that should be made for him the parent may appeal in writing to the Secretary of State.

(7) In a case falling within subsection (6) above the local education authority shall notify the parent in writing of his right of appeal under that subsection.

(8) On an appeal under subsection (6) above the Secretary of State may, if he thinks fit, direct the local education authority to reconsider their decision.

(9) The provisions of Part I of Schedule 1 to this Act have effect in relation to assessments under this section.

(10) Where, at any time after serving a notice under subsection (3) above, a local education authority decide not to assess the educational needs of the child concerned they shall notify his parent in writing of their decision.

7 Statement of child's special educational needs

(1) Where an assessment has been made in respect of a child under section 5, the local education authority who are responsible for the child shall, if they are of the opinion that they should determine the special educational provision that should be made for him, make a statement of his special educational needs and maintain that statement in accordance with the following provisions of this Act.

(2) In any case where a local education authority maintain a statement under this section in respect of a child, it shall be the duty of the authority to arrange that the special educational provision specified in the statement is made for him unless his parent has made suitable arrangements.

(3) Before making such a statement a local education authority shall serve on the parent of the child concerned –

(*a*) a copy of the proposed statement; and

(*b*) a written explanation of the effect of subsections (4) to (7) below.

(4) If the parent on whom a copy of a proposed statement has been served under subsection (3)(*a*) above disagrees with any part of the proposed statement he may, before the expiry of the appropriate period –

(*a*) make representations (or further representations to the authority about the content of the proposed statement;

(*b*) require the authority to arrange a meeting between him and an officer of the authority at which the proposed statement can be discussed.

(5) Where a parent, having attended a meeting arranged by a local education authority under subsection (4)(*b*) above, disagrees with any part of the assessment in question he may, before the expiry of the appropriate period, require the authority to arrange one or more meetings under subsection (6) below.

(6) Where a local education authority receive a request duly made under subsection (5) above they shall arrange such meeting or meetings as they consider will enable the parent to discuss the relevant advice with the appropriate person or persons.

In this subsection –

'relevant advice' means such of the advice given to the authority in connection with the assessment as they consider to be relevant to that part of the assessment with which the parent disagrees; and

'appropriate person' means the person who gave the relevant advice or any other person who, in the opinion of the authority, is the appropriate person to discuss it with the parent.

(7) In this section 'appropriate period' means the period of 15 days beginning –

(*a*) in the case of a request under subsection (4)(*b*) above, with the date on which the statement mentioned in subsection (3)(*b*) above was served on the parent;

(*b*) in the case of a request under subsection (5) above, with the date fixed for the meeting arranged under subsection (4)(*b*) above; and

(*c*) in the case of representations, or further representations, under subsection (4)(*a*) above –

(i) with the date mentioned in paragraph (*a*) above; or

(ii) if one or more meetings have been arranged under the preceding provision of this section, with the date fixed for the last of those meetings.

(8) Where any such representations are made to a local education authority the authority may, after considering those representations –

(*a*) make a statement in the form originally proposed;

(*b*) make a statement in a modified form; or

(*c*) determine not to make a statement;

and shall notify the parent in writing of their decision.

(9) On making a statement under this section a local education authority shall serve on the parent of the child concerned –

(*a*) a copy of the statement;

(*b*) notice in writing of his right under section 8(1) of this Act to appeal against the special educational provision specified in the statement; and

(*c*) notice in writing of the name of the person to whom he may apply for information and advice about the child's special educational needs.

(10) The Secretary of State may by regulations prescribe the frequency with which assessments are to be repeated in respect of children for whom statements are maintained under this section.

(11) The provisions of Part II of Schedule 1 to this Act have effect in relation to statements made under this section.

8 Appeals against statements

(1) Every local education authority* shall make arrangements for enabling the parent* of a child* for whom they maintain a statement under section 7 to appeal, [against the special educational provision* specified in the statement.

(a) following the first or any subsequent assessment of the child's special educational needs under section 5, and

(b) where the authority makes any amendment to the special educational provision specified in the statement otherwise than on making of any such assessment.]

(2) Any appeal by virtue of this section shall be to an appeal committee constituted in accordance with paragraph 1 of Part I of Schedule 2 to the Education Act 1980.

(3) Part II of that Schedule shall have effect in relation to the procedure in any such appeal but with the following modifications –

(*a*) paragraph 7 (matters to be taken into account by appeal committee) shall have effect as if for paragraphs (*a*) and (*b*) there were substituted the words 'any representations made by the appellant under section 7 of the Education Act 1981';

(*b*) paragraph 9(*b*) (decision to be communicated to school governors) shall not apply; and (*c*) for any reference to section 7 of the 1980 Act there shall be substituted a reference to this section.

(4) An appeal committee hearing an appeal by virtue of this section may –

(*a*) confirm the special educational provision specified in the statement; or

(*b*) remit the case to the local education authority for reconsideration in the light of the committee's observations.

(5) When an appeal committee remit a case to a local education authority the authority shall reconsider it in the light of the committee's observations and shall inform the appellant in writing of their decision.

(6) In any case where –

(*a*) an appeal committee confirm the decision of a local education authority as to the special educational provision to be made for a child; or

(*b*) a local education authority inform an appellant of their decision in a case which has been remitted to them under subsection (4)(*b*) above;

the appellant may appeal in writing to the Secretary of State.

(7) On an appeal under subsection (6) above the Secretary of State may, after consulting the local education authority concerned –

(*a*) confirm the special educational provision specified in the statement;

(*b*) amend the statement so far as it specifies the special educational provision and make such other consequential amendments to the statement as he considers appropriate; or

(*c*) direct the local education authority to cease to maintain the statement.

9 Requests for assessments

(1) If the parent of a child for whom a local education authority are responsible but for whom no statement is maintained by the authority under section 7 asks the authority to arrange for an assessment to be made of the child's educational needs the authority shall comply with the request unless it is in their opinion unreasonable.

(2) If the parent of a child for whom a local education authority maintain a statement under section 7 asks the authority to arrange for an assessment of his educational needs under section 5 and such an assessment has not been made within the period of 6 months ending with the date on which the request is made, the authority shall comply with the request unless they are satisfied that an assessment would be inappropriate.

EDUCATION REFORM ACT 1988 NATIONAL CURRICULUM EXCEPTIONS

Exceptions by regulations

17. The Secretary of State may by regulations provide that the provisions of the National Curriculum, or such of those provisions as may be specified in the regulations –

(a) shall not apply; or

(b) shall apply with such modifications as may be so specified;

in such cases or circumstances as may be so specified.

Pupils with statements

18. The special educational provision for any pupil specified in a statement under section 7 of the 1981 Act of his special educational needs may include provision–

(a) excluding the application of the provisions of the National Curriculum; or

(b) applying those provisions with such modifications as may be specified in the statement.

Temporary exceptions for individual pupils

19. (1) The Secretary of State may make regulations enabling the head teacher of any maintained school, in such cases or circumstances and subject to such conditions as may be prescribed –

(a) to direct as respects a registered pupil at the school that, for such period as may be specified in the direction (the 'operative period' of the direction), the provisions of the National Curriculum –

(i) shall not apply; or

(ii) shall apply with such modifications as may be so specified; and

(b) to revoke any direction given by him under the regulations and to vary any such direction except so as to extend its operative period.

(2) The conditions prescribed by the regulations shall, in particular, limit the period that may be specified in any direction given under the regulations to a maximum period specified in the regulations; and any maximum period specified in the regulations in relation to directions given under the regulations or in relation to directions so given in any circumstances so specified –

(a) shall be either –

(i) a fixed period not exceeding six months; or

(ii) a period determinable (in such manner as may be specified in the regulations) not later than six months from its beginning; and

(b) may (without prejudice to section 232(5) of this Act) differ according to whether or not the direction in question is given in respect of a period beginning immediately after the end of the operative period of a previous direction or within such period after the end of the operative period of a previous direction as may be specified in the regulations.

(3) Where a head teacher gives a direction under regulations made under this section in the case of any pupil or varies any direction so given, he shall give the information mentioned in subsection (4) below, in such manner as may be prescribed –

(a) to the governing body; and

(b) where the school is a county, voluntary or maintained special school, to the local education authority;

and shall take such steps as may be prescribed to give that information also to a parent of the pupil.

(4) That information is the following –

(a) the fact that he has taken the action in question, its effect and his reasons for taking it;

(b) the provision that is being or is to be made for the pupil's education during the operative period of the direction; and

(c) either –

(i) a description of the manner in which he proposes to secure the full implementation in relation to the pupil after the end of that period of the provisions of the National Curriculum; or

(ii) an indication of his opinion that the pupil has or probably has special educational needs by virtue of which the local education authority would be required to determine the special educational provision that should be made for him (whether initially or on a review of any statement of his special educational needs the authority are for the time being required under section 7 of the 1981 Act to maintain).

(5) Where the head teacher of a grant maintained school includes such an indication of opinion as is mentioned in subsection (4)(c)(ii) above in information given to the governing body under subsection (3) above, he shall also give that information, in such manner as may be prescribed, to the local education authority.

(6) It shall be the duty of a local education authority, on receiving information given to the authority under this section by the head teacher of any maintained school which includes such an indication of opinion with respect to a pupil, to consider whether any action on their part is required in the case of that pupil under section 5 of the 1981 Act (assessment of special educational needs).

(7) Where the head teacher of a maintained school –

(a) gives, revokes or varies any direction with respect to a pupil under regulations made under this section;

(b) refuses to give, revoke or vary such a direction in response to a request made, in such manner and circumstances as may be prescribed, by the parent of a registered pupil at the school; or

(c) fails within such period as may be prescribed following the making of such a request to give, revoke or vary such a direction in accordance with the request;

the parent of the pupil concerned may appeal to the governing body.

(8) On any such appeal the governing body may –

(a) confirm the head teacher's action' or

(b) direct the head teacher to take such action authorised by the regulations as they consider appropriate in the circumstances;

and it shall be the duty of the head teacher to comply with any directions of the governing body under paragraph (b) above.

(9) The governing body shall notify the appellant and the head teacher in writing of their decision an any such appeal.

(10) Before making any regulations under this section, the Secretary of State shall consult with any persons with whom consultation appears to him to be desirable.

EDUCATION (SPECIAL EDUCATIONAL NEEDS) REGULATIONS 1983

1. These Regulations may be cited as the Education (Special Education Needs) Regulations 1983 and shall come into operation on 1 April 1983.

Interpretation

2. (1) In these Regulations a reference to representations made, or evidence submitted, by a child's parent is a reference to representations made, or written evidence submitted, in pursuance of section 5(3)(*d*) of the Act of 1981 except that, where such representations have been made orally, any reference thereto is a reference to a written summary of those representations which the parent has accepted as accurate.

(2) In these Regulations any reference to the district health authority or the social services authority is, in relation to a particular child, a reference to the district health authority or social services authority in whose area that child lives.

(3) In these Regulations, except where the context otherwise requires, any reference to a Regulation is a reference to a Regulation contained therein and any reference in a Regulation to a paragraph is a reference to a paragraph of that Regulation.

(4) In these Regulations

'the Act of 1981' means the Education Act 1981;

'the Act of 1986' means the Disabled Persons (Services, Consultation and Representation) Act 1986;

'district health authority' has the same meaning as in the National Health Service Act 1977;

'education authority' means a local education authority;

'social services authority' means a local authority for the purposes of the local Authority Social Services Act 1970 acting in the discharge of such functions as are referred to in section 2(1) of that Act;

Notice of decision to make an assessment

3. Where in pursuance of section 5(5) of the Act of 1981 an education authority notify the parent of a child of their decision to make an assessment they shall send copies of the notification to the social services authority and the district health authority.

Advice generally

4. (1) For the purpose of making an assessment an education authority shall, in the case of the child concerned, seek –

(a) educational advice as provided in Regulation 5;

(b) medical advice as provided in Regulation 6;

(c) psychological advice as provided in Regulation 7, and

(d) any other advice which the authority consider desirable in the case in question for the purpose of arriving at a satisfactory assessment,

subject, however, to Regulation 12.

(2) The advice sought in pursuance of paragraph (1) shall be written advice relating to –

(a) the educational, medical, psychological or other features of the case (according to the nature of the advice sought) which appears to be relevant to the child's educational needs (including his likely future needs);

(b) how those features could affect the child's educational needs, and

(c) the provision rendered requisite by those features of the child's case, whether by way of special educational provision or non-educational provision additional thereto requisite if the child is properly to benefit therefrom.

(3) A person from whom advice is sought in pursuance of paragraph (1) may in connection therewith consult such persons as it appears to him expedient to consult; and he shall consult such persons, if any, as are specified in the particular case by the education authority as persons who have relevant knowledge of, or information relating to, the child.

(4) When seeking a person's advice in pursuance of paragraph (1) an education authority shall furnish him with copies of

(a) any representations made by the parent, and

(b) any evidence submitted by, or at the request of, the parent.

Educational advice

5. (1) The educational advice referred to in Regulation 4(1)(a) shall, subject to paragraphs (2) and (3), be sought from a qualified teacher being –

(a) the head-teacher of a school which the child has attended at some time within the preceding 18 months, or

(b) if advice cannot be obtained as aforesaid (because the child has not attended school or otherwise), a person whom the education authority are satisfied has experience of teaching children with special educational needs or knowledge of the differing provision which may be called for in different cases to meet those needs.

(2) The advice sought of a head-teacher as provided in paragraph (1)(a) shall, if the head-teacher has not himself taught the child within the preceding 18 months, be advice given after consultation with a teacher who has so taught the child.

(3) Where it appears to the education authority, in consequence of medical advice or otherwise, that the child in question –

(a) is deaf or partially hearing, or

(b) blind or otherwise visually handicapped,

and the person from whom advice is sought as provided in paragraph (1)(a), or

(b) is not qualified to teach deaf or, as the case may be, blind pupils, then the advice sought shall be advice given after consultation with a person who is so qualified.

(4) In this Regulation –

(a) the expression 'qualified teacher' means a person who, in pursuance of the regulations relating to the employment of teachers from time to time in force under section 27 of the Education Act 1980, is qualified to be employed as a teacher at a school to which that section applies;

(b) any reference to a person qualified to teach deaf or blind pupils is a reference to a person who is so qualified to be employed at such a school as a teacher of a class for deaf or, as the case may be, blind pupils (otherwise than to give instruction in a craft, trade, or domestic subject);

and the provisions as to consultation contained in paragraphs (2) and (3) are without prejudice to each other or those of Regulation 4(3).

Medical advice

6. The medical advice referred to in Regulation 4(1)(b) shall be sought from a fully registered medical practitioner who is either designated for the purposes of this

Regulation by the district health authority or is nominated by them in the case in question.

Psychological advice

7. (1) The psychological advice referred to in Regulation 4(1)(c) shall be sought –

(a) from a person regularly employed by the education authority as an educational psychologist, or

(b) from a person, in the case in question, engaged by the education authority as an educational psychologist.

(2) The advice sought of a person as provided in paragraph (1) shall, if that person has reason to believe that another psychologist has relevant knowledge of, or information relating to, the child, be advice given after consultation with that other psychologist.

(3) The provision as to consultation contained in paragraph (2) are without prejudice to those of Regulation 4(3).

Matters to be taken into account in making an assessment

8. When making an assessment in the case of a child an education authority shall take into consideration –

(a) any representations made by the child's parent;

(b) any evidence submitted by, or at the request of, that parent;

(c) the advice obtained in the case of pursuance of Regulation 4, and

(d) any information relating to the health or welfare of the child furnished by or on behalf of –

(i) any district health authority, or

(ii) any social services authority.

Mandatory re-assessment

9. Where an education authority maintain a statement in respect of a child whose educational needs have not been assessed since before he attained the age of 12 years and 6 months then, during the period of 12 months beginning with the day on which he attains the age of 13 years and 6 months, the authority shall re-assess those needs.

Provision on Statements

10. (1) A statement of a child's special educational needs, made in pursuance of section 7(1) of the Act of 1981, shall also –

(a) specify the special educational provision (in terms of facilities and equipment, staffing arrangements, curriculum or otherwise) which the education authority consider appropriate to meet those needs;

(b) without prejudice to the generality of sub-paragraph (a) specify either –

(i) the type of school which the education authority consider would be appropriate for the child and, if they consider that a particular school would be so appropriate, the name of that school, or

(ii) if they consider it appropriate that the child should be provided with education otherwise than at a school, particulars of the provision which they consider would be appropriate;

(c) specify any additional non-educational provision –

(i) which, unless proposed to be made available by the education authority, they are satisfied will be made available by a district health authority, a social services authority or some other body, and

(ii) of which, in their opinion, advantage should be taken if the child is properly to benefit from the special educational provision specified in pursuance of sub-paragraphs (a) and (b) above, and

(d) set out the representations, evidence, advice and information taken into consideration in pursuance of Regulation 8.

(2) A statement shall be in the form set out in the Schedule hereto or a form to the like effect and shall be authenticated by the signature of a duly authorised officer of the education authority concerned.

Restriction on disclosure of statements

11. (1) Subject to the provisions of the Act 1981 and of these Regulations, a statement in respect of a child shall not be disclosed without the parent's consent except –

(a) to persons to whom, in the opinion of the education authority concerned, the statement should be disclosed in the educational interests of the child;

(b) for the purposes of any appeal under section 8 of the Act of 1981;

(c) for the purposes of educational research which, in the opinion of the education authority concerned, may advance the education of children with special educational needs, if, but only if, the person engaged in that research undertakes not to publish anything contained in, or derived from, a statement otherwise than in a form which does not identify any individual concerned including, in particular, the child concerned and his parent;

(d) on the order of any court or for the purposes of any criminal proceedings;

(e) for the purposes of any investigation under Part III of the Local Government Act 1974 (investigation of maladministration), or

(f) for the purposes of an assessment of the needs of the child with respect to the provision of any statutory services for him being carried out by officers of a social services authority by virtue of arrangements made under section 5(5) of the Act of 1986.

(2) The arrangement for keeping statements shall be such as to ensure, so far as is reasonable practicable, that unauthorised persons do not have access to them.

(3) In this Regulation any reference to a statement included a reference to any representations, evidence, advice or information which is set out therein in pursuance of Regulation 10(1)(d).

Children moving from one education area into another

12. (1) This Regulation shall apply where a child in respect of whom a statement is maintained moves from the area of one education authority ('the old authority') into that of another ('the new authority').

(2) The old authority shall transfer the Statement to the new authority.

(2A) Where the Statement has been transferred as aforesaid and the old authority had received an opinion in pursuance of section 5(1) or (2) of the Act of 1981 or had given notification for the purposes of section 5(5) of that Act, they shall so inform the new authority.

(3) Where the statement has been transferred as aforesaid and –

(a) the new authority, being of the opinion mentioned in section 5(1) of the Act of 1981, in pursuance of section 5(3) thereof, serve notice on the child's parent that they propose to make an assessment, and

(b) the transferred statement was made within the period of 3 years immediately preceding the date of the notice,

then, with the written agreement of the parent, the educational, medical or psychological advice which the new authority are required to seek by Regulation 4(1) may be sought from the old authority instead of as provided in Regulation 5, 6 or 7 and accordingly, in such case, any reference in Regulation 4(3) or (4) to a person from whom advice is sought shall be construed as a reference to the old authority.

(4) Where the statement has been transferred as aforesaid but the new authority are not of the opinion mentioned in section 5(1) of the Act of 1981 then they shall notify the child's parent that they are not of the opinion and, accordingly, do not propose to make an assessment.

ASSESSMENTS AND STATEMENTS OF SPECIAL EDUCATIONAL NEEDS: PROCEDURES WITHIN THE EDUCATION, HEALTH AND SOCIAL SERVICES

INTRODUCTION: DUTY OF LOCAL EDUCATION AUTHORITIES

1. The Education Act 1981 (the 1981 Act) made important changes to the law on the provision of education to children with special educational needs (SEN). It gives duties to local education authorities (LEAs), District Health Authorities (DHAs) and school governing bodies. Its provisions require the involvement of parents in assessment procedures and give scope for the involvement of voluntary bodies. Under Section 5(1) of the Act LEAs have a duty to make an assessment of those children in their area with special educational needs which require or may require the LEA to determine the appropriate special educational provision. Section 7(2) of the Act requires LEAs to arrange that the special education provision specified in a statement is made for the child unless the parent has made suitable arrangements. Section 2(4) of the Act places LEAs under a duty to keep under review their arrangements for special education provision.

PURPOSE OF CIRCULAR

2. The purpose of this Circular is to review the implementation of the provisions in the 1981 Act relating to the making of assessments and statements of special educational needs in the light of experience since 1981; of the report of the House of Commons Education, Science and Arts Select committee 'Implementation of the Education Act 1981'; and of the provisions in the Education Reform Act 1988 (the 1988 Act) concerning the introduction of the Nation Curriculum, local management of schools and the establishment of grant maintained schools. Its purpose is to offer advice to LEAs, working in conjunction with DHAs and Social Services Departments (SSDs), in reviewing their procedures concerned with the making of assessments and statements. The new elements in the circular are not intended to require additional expenditure. This circular replaces DES Circular 1/83, Health Circular HC(83)(3) and Local Authority Circular LAC(83)2. A separate Circular is being issued in Wales. Circular 8/81 remains in force.

DEFINITIONS UNDER THE EDUCATION ACT 1981

3. Under Section 1 of the 1981 Act children have *special educational needs* if they have a leaning difficulty which calls for special educational provision to be made for them. *Learning difficulty* is defined in terms of children who have a significantly greater difficulty in leaning than the majority of children of their age; and/or have a disability which either prevents or hinders them from making effective use of educational facilities of a kind generally provided in schools in their LEA area for children of their age; or who are under the age of 5 years and are, or would if special educational provision were not made for them, be likely when over that age to fall within the terms above.

4. *Special educational provision* in relation to a child over 2 means educational provision which is additional to, or otherwise different from, the educational provision made generally for children of the same age in schools maintained by the LEA concerned. For children under 2 it covers educational provision of any kind (see para 78).

5. Gifted children without special educational needs as defined under Section 1(1) of the Act are excluded from the Act's provisions. For a pupil whose mother tongue is not English, the child's lack of competence in English must not be equated with leaning difficulties under this Act.

6. *Medical advice.* For the purpose of this Act, medical advice is to be taken in its widest sense and includes coordinated information from all the doctors concerned in the assessment of the child's special educational needs, together with the advice, in full, from other non-medical specialists. The latter might include speech therapists, physiotherapists, occupational therapists, school nurses and health visitors.

DEVELOPMENTS SINCE 1981

(1) SELECT COMMITTEE REPORT AND OTHER FINDINGS

7. The House of Commons Select Committee on Education, Science and the Arts in its report of May 1987[1] made recommendations following evidence from a wide range of organisations. Statutory and voluntary bodies, and others concerned with the rights of children with special educational needs, have made representations. Parents and children and their representatives have also revealed problems and sought remedies through complaints, appeals and through recourse to legal action. Results of research projects and surveys, both local and national, have highlighted a number of difficulties and proposed improvements in procedures, many of which have been adopted in this Circular.

(2) THE NATIONAL CURRICULUM

8. The 1988 Act lays down new requirements for the school curriculum. It requires all maintained schools, including special schools, but not hospital schools or Children's Homes with Education, to provide a balanced and broadly based curriculum which promotes the spiritual, moral, cultural, mental and physical development of pupils at the school and of society, and prepares pupils for the opportunities, responsibilities and experiences of adult life. The curriculum is to be relevant to the full range of pupils' needs. It requires every maintained school to provide for each pupil of statutory school age, as part of his or her curriculum, 10 foundation subjects (9 from age 5 to 11), each with nationally specified

[1] 'Special Education Needs: Implementation of the Education Act 1981' HC 201–1 (ISBN 0 10 293487 8) and HC 201–2 (ISBN 0 10 294187 4).

objectives – attainment targets – and programmes of study. Pupils' progress compared with the attainment targets will be monitored and formally assessed and recorded by prescribed methods throughout compulsory schooling and must be reported at the end of each of the four key stages – ie for most pupils at the ages of 7, 11, 14 and 16. External qualifications offered to pupils of compulsory school age must be those approved by the Secretary of State for Education and Science, and the syllabuses associated with them must be those approved by the School Examinations and Assessment Council. Information about pupils' programmes and about their attainments as individuals and collectively must be made available to parents and others, and local arrangements established for the consideration of complaints. In advance of full implementation of the National Curriculum, pupils will be required to be taught each foundation subject for a reasonable period of time. The Act requires provision to be made for religious education and collective worship for all registered pupils at maintained schools, except maintained special schools. Separate arrangements for religious education and worship in special schools are made through Section 12(4) of the 1981 Act as amended by paragraph 9 of Schedule 1 to the 1988 Act.

9. The National Curriculum will be introduced progressively from the start of the Autumn Term 1989. Detailed guidance is set out in the Department of Education and Science (DES) Circular 5/89 and in the booklet 'From Policy to Practice'. The Secretary of State for Education and Science believes that all pupils, including those with SEN, should follow the National Curriculum to the maximum extent possible. The level of attainment defined will cover a wide spread of achievement and will enable pupils of very different abilities to demonstrate progress in relation to the same curriculum. The National Curriculum framework, and specific provisions within it, provide wide scope for teachers to deal with the full range of individual pupils' needs.

10. The basis for this is Sections 17–19 of the 1988 Act. These, and the powers to make Orders under Section 4 prescribing attainment targets, programmes of study and assessment arrangements, offer three main ways of taking account of SEN:

(i.) by Orders or regulations under Sections 4 and 17 respectively which allow the Secretary of State for Education and Science to modify or disapply parts of the National Curriculum and related assessment arrangements in specified general cases or circumstances. The attainment targets, programmes of study, assessment arrangements, or the requirement to study foundation subject(s) may all be modified or disapplied as necessary. For example, where the National Curriculum requirements would involve certain kinds of physical or practical work, alternative arrangements might be allowed for those whose physical disabilities could put at risk their own safety or that of others. Such arrangements might apply to pupils with or without statements;

(ii.) for individual pupils, by a statement of special educational needs. Section 18 of the 1988 Act provides that such a statement may modify or disapply any or all of the requirements of the Nation Curriculum if they are inappropriate for the individual pupil concerned. This ensures that any departure from the National Curriculum will be decided only after a full assessment of the pupil's needs and in the light of all the evidence available, including the views of the parents. The statement should indicate in Section 3 any modifications to the National Curriculum necessary to meet the child's special educational needs, in terms of programmes of study, attainment targets and assessment and testing arrangements similarly, where it is considered essential exempt the child from one or more foundation subjects, details should be stated. Whether modification or disapplication is involved, the foundation subject(s) affected should be identified clearly so as to ensure that unambiguous information is available to any school the child attends.

(iii.) by regulations under Section 19 as detailed in DES Circular 15/89. These regulations enable a headteacher to give a general or special direction to modify or disapply the National Curriculum for an individual pupil on a temporary basis and for a period of no longer than 6 months in the first instance. The regulations specify the cases and circumstances in which general and special directions will apply. *General directions* may apply to any pupil including a pupil with a statement at an ordinary or special school who develops temporary problems which it would not be appropriate to reflect in the statement. What distinguishes a general direction from a special direction is the expectation that, after expiry of the specified period, the pupil may expect to return to the National Curriculum or whatever aspects of it applied to him or her before the general direction came into force. *Special directions* have a much more limited application and may be used by a head teacher to modify or disapply the National Curriculum for up to 6 months where the head is of the opinion that an individual pupil has special educational needs which require the LEA to assess the pupil with a view to a statement. A temporary exception will not always be necessary when a headteacher refers a pupil for assessment. Head teachers should consider in each case if there is a clear case for a short-term exception, and should not assume that this will be the case or prejudge the outcome of the 1981 Act assessment procedures. It will remain for the LEA to determine whether there are sufficient grounds for assessment.

(3) LOCAL MANAGEMENT OF SCHOOLS

11. The 1988 Act requires every LEA to prepare a scheme for local management of schools (LMS). The Department of Education and Science Circular 7/88 offers detailed guidance on the implementation of this part of the Act and sets out criteria for the approval of such schemes by the Secretary of State. To secure approval, schemes must be consistent with the continuing statutory responsibilities of LEAs and Governing Bodies, including the requirements of the 1981 Act.

12. Under local management schemes LEAs will have discretion as to whether or not they delegate provision for pupils with statements of SEN in ordinary schools and special units organised as a part of ordinary schools. Where such provision is delegated the formula for allocating resources to schools must take account of the need to channel resources to meet the particular needs of pupils in such schools. The LEA will retain its duty under the 1981 Act to ensure that the special educational provision specified in the statement is made for pupils with statements, and will be expected to reflect this in the conditions of the scheme. It will be for the school to consider how best to deploy its overall resources in order to offer the necessary provision, but it will be obliged to offer what is specified in the statement.

13. Where the costs of pupils with statements are delegated, the LEA will retain responsibility for identifying, assessing and determining the provision required

for individual pupils with statements, and will be able to allocate additional resources as additional children are so identified. The LEA remains responsible for annual reviews and mandatory re-assessments and for ensuring, through inspection if necessary, that appropriate provision is made and maintained. Since reviews may also lead to adjustments of provision the LMS scheme should be flexible enough to enable any necessary additional resources to be made available without delay, both in-year and between years.

CHILDREN WITH SEN, BUT WITHOUT STATEMENTS

14. The 1981 Act followed the 1978 Warnock Report[1] and embodied a number of the recommendations in that report. The Warnock Report proposed that for educational purposes the concepts of 'handicapped pupils' and special educational treatment', which were incorporated in the 1944 Act, should be replaced by the concept of 'children with special educational needs'. The report estimated that nationally as many as 20% of children had special educational needs for which some additional provision might need to be made at some time in their school career from within or outside the resources of the ordinary school. That proportion will vary between individual schools. Section 8 (2) (c) of the 1944 Act was therefore amended by the 1981 Act to place a duty on LEAs 'to have regard to the need for securing that special educational provision is made for pupils who have special educational needs'.

15. Since the implementation of the 1981 Act, attention has tended to focus on the 2% of the school population who have statements and the statutory procedures to be followed for this. This emphasis has in some areas drawn attention away from the larger group, for whom nonetheless LEAs and school governors have duties under the Act. For these children many schools have made special provision, whether on their own initiative or as part of a range of developments organised centrally by various LEAs.

16. There remains a need for LEAs and governors to take steps to satisfy parents of children without statements that appropriate educational provision will be available in schools to meet their particular needs. Schools should publish information for parents indicating their special support provision for children with SEN, but with no statements. Parents will need an explanation of the way in which the introduction of the National Curriculum applies to the education of their children. LEAs will look to health authorities for provision of services for children with medical problems and for those requiring professional nursing or paramedical help in ordinary schools; and for advice and guidance for those children who require drugs or other medication or care.

FOCUS ON THE CHILD

17. When it is thought that a child may need special educational provision, the positive and constructive approach is to focus on his or her needs rather than on disabilities. The feelings and perceptions of the child concerned should be taken into account, and older children and young persons should be able to share in discussions on their needs and any proposed provision. The extent to which a learning difficulty hinders a child's development does not depend solely on the nature and severity of that difficulty. Other significant factors include the personal resources and attributes of the child as well as the help and support provided at home, and the provision made by the school and the LEA and other statutory and

---

[1] Report of the Committee into the Education of Handicapped Children and Young People: Cmnd 7212: ISBN 0 10 172120 X

voluntary agencies. A child's special educational needs are thus related both to abilities and disabilities, and so the nature and extent of the interaction of these with his or her environment.

MONITORING AND ASSESSMENT UNDER THE 1981 ACT

18. The assessment of SENs is not an end in itself; it is the first step towards a better understanding of a child's learning difficulties for the practical purpose of providing guidance to the education needed and establishing a basis upon which to monitor the child's progress. When carrying out assessments, the LEA should ensure that clear distinctions are made between:

(i.) the child's relevant past and present levels of functioning, emotional states and interests and how these represent resources and deficiencies in relation to the educational demands which will be made on the child.

(ii.) the analysis of the child's consequent learning difficulties;

(iii.) the specification of goals for change in the child and environment (including school, home and the wider community);

(iv.) the specification of the child's requirement for different kinds of approaches, facilities or resources, in order to facilitate access to the National Curriculum, with any modifications that are considered essential;

(v.) the perceptions and wishes of the parent and child;

(vi.) the special educational provision and services required to meet the identified needs.

19. The monitoring and assessment of each child's progress are continuous processes. They begin around birth and continue in the home and with the health and social services before the child becomes known to the LEA. The procedures followed as part of that process should provide a useful background to understand the child's educational needs. For the child under 5, paras 78 to 81 of this Circular refer. For the child of or approaching compulsory school age, it will, in most cases, be for the school or a suitably qualified teacher under the guidance of the LEA to decide how that individual child's needs should be assessed and met. Where the support provided by the school does not seem to meet the child's needs, the school will need to refer the child for assessment. Where it seems that a child's difficulties might justify making a statement under section 7 of the 1981 Act, section 5 of that Act and the Education (Special Educational Needs) Regulations 1983 SI 1983/29 specify the procedures to be followed . The statutory assessment procedures may result from school-based assessment,from a recommendation by the LEA psychological service, or through referral from another source. Parents may request assessment under Section 9(1) of the 1981 Act and LEAs must comply with such requests unless they are unreasonable in the LEA's opinion. Not every child who may have SEN and is assessed will need a statement in order to determine provision, except in the case of children of Service parents where their frequent moves between authorities can cause developmental delay if no statement is available to facilitate effective placement and provision within the new authority's schools.

PARENTS AND PARENT ADVOCATES

20. Sections 5, 7 and 8 of the 1981 Act lay down the procedures under which parents may make representations and submit evidence to the LEA as part of the process of determining their child's SEN. To encourage the cooperation and involvements of parents, LEAs should provide them with written information about their rights and duties as parents, and the duties of LEAs together with

details of the special educational provision available. Cooperation is likely to be improved if parents have written guidelines to assist them in their contribution to the assessment. LEAs should recognise, however, that premature references in their information to the 1981 Act enforcement powers can be regarded by parents as threatening and coercive. The published information should use straightforward, plain language and should include the names, addresses and telephone numbers of the various staff with whom discussions can be held during the assessment process. A check list of the main points to be covered is at Annex 4. LEAs, as many have already done, should make guidance leaflets available in other languages for ethnic groups. Special arrangements may be needed for parents with hearing, sight, reading and other difficulties, and occasionally for translation.

21. Parents, and the child, where practicable, should be helped and encouraged to participate in the assessment of the child's SEN as the 1981 Act envisaged. Frankness and openness between the parents and the providers will help the process significantly. The feelings and perceptions of the child should be taken into account, and the concept of partnership should wherever possible be extended to older children and young persons. Some parents may wish to bring an adviser or friend and translators for support at meetings where their child is being discussed. LEAs should welcome and encourage this and include appropriate information in their published guidance to parents.

INTEGRATION

22. The 1981 Act placed LEAs under a duty to secure that, subject to conditions specified in Section 2(3), children with statements should be educated in ordinary schools. This obliges LEAs to consider on its merits a parent's request for a place in an ordinary school. The Act also requires under Section 2(7) that the child with a statement should share in the activities of the school together with pupils without special educational needs. Many parents want their children with statements to be accepted by and remain within ordinary schools, and they also seek to obtain the best quality and balance of educational, social, health and other provision for their children. Parents need objective information about the range of suitable provision for their children. Situations and perceptions vary from one LEA area to another and thus different patterns of provision have resulted. Valuable developments include the increasing incidence of trained special needs support services, resourced provision in ordinary schools and extensive links between special and ordinary schools. The 1988 Act aims to raise expectations of all pupils, including those with statements. Its provisions are intended to ensure that these expectations are appropriate, so that all children, including those with SEN, can benefit to the best of their ability. In their schemes for the local management of schools, either (LMS) LEAs will have scope to target resources on pupils with statements in ordinary schools, either by excepting the relevant funds from delegation or by delegating resources through a specific factor. Whatever the way an LEA chooses to provide for children with statements, appropriateness and quality of provision are vital.

ASSESSMENT UNDER THE 1981 ACT

23. Whether or not a statement follows an assessment, all children who may have SEN stand the best chance of receiving the quality of education they require if their needs are identified in their first years at school, assessed thoroughly, and provided for promptly and appropriately. This calls for close cooperation

between parents and all the statutory services, and a thorough understanding by each of the participants of the part which they and others play in this process. Where a child is kept out of school, the child's education is not disrupted during the process of assessment and statementing. Where a parent absents a child with SEN from school without the LEA's prior agreement, the LEA should be mindful of their duty concerning such attendance under Section 37 of the Education Act 1944. Authorities may need to give thought to arrangements which assist families from an early stage to establish and maintain effective relationships with the various services, eg through a named person or key worker.

24. The procedures for non-statutory assessments prior to statutory assessments carried out under section 5 of the 1981 Act are largely a matter for schools and LEAs. Under section 2(5) of the 1981 Act, it is the responsibility of the governors of county and voluntary schools to try to ensure that any pupils with SEN are identified and that appropriate educational provision is made for them. The 1988 Act extends this duty to the governors of grant-maintained schools. In order to fulfil this responsibility schools will need fully to involve their teaching staff. Since every school is likely to have some pupils with SEN, LEAs will need to help governors to fulfil their duties by providing guidance to all county and voluntary schools in their area on the arrangements and procedures for identifying, assessing and meeting special educational needs. This guidance should include contact points for the specialist services to publicise referral routes. Grant-maintained schools will also need such guidance, and LEAs will need to formulate working arrangements with these schools, recognising their respective responsibilities. Policies are being developed in some areas to raise the awareness of all teachers in a school and this to improve the provision made for children with special educational needs. Under such policies, every school should have a teacher designated to help and advise colleagues on the provision for children with SEN. The classroom teacher is in the key position to observe responses in the classroom, to recognise the child who is experiencing difficulties in learning, and to try out different approaches to help meet the child's needs. Where the interventions made at school do not seem to meet the child's needs, further investigation will be required. Teachers should be encouraged to keep full records of their pupils' progress and to include information about professional consultations and assessments under the 1981 Act. The LEA Training Grants Scheme has among its national priorities in-service training courses for designated teachers who will act as coordinators in schools. Many LEAs also use local priority funding for courses to extend the knowledge and competence of such teachers; grant-maintained schools will be able to seek Special Purpose Grant funding from the Department to replicate grant provided under the LEA Training Grants Scheme, and will receive their share of any additional LEA funding as part of their Annual Maintenance Grant.

25. Arrangements for assessment made by LEAs must take account of local circumstances. They should allow for the progressive extension of professional involvement from the class teacher to the headteacher, and then, as appropriate, to a specialist teacher, the educational psychologist, the school doctor and nurse, and other professionals in the education, health and social services, including therapists. Parental involvement in assessment is vital since information in the possession of the parent may be crucial to the assessment. The parent should also be kept fully informed at every stage.

26. Clearly identified channels of communication are essential to enable schools to gain access to specialised support and advice when required. This means close

involvement between teachers, the school health service and social services departments. The aim should be to provide assistance before the situation becomes critical. Assessment should always be closely related to education, and teachers and other professionals should work closely together, bearing in mind that a child's special educational needs are likely to change and that assessment is not a single event but a continuous process.

27. The 1988 Act provides assessment arrangements for all pupils which differ in kind from assessment under the 1981 Act. Mechanisms for assessment under the 1988 Act will provide regular monitoring of each pupil's progress. Where pupils may have special educational needs, these new arrangements may help to identify such children. Headteachers should, nevertheless, continue to identify any child who, in their opinion, may need to be assessed under the 1981 Act, or whose current statement may need revision. Headteachers will have powers conferred by the regulations made under Section 19 of the 1988 Act to give directions to modify or disapply the National Curriculum for a temporary period of up to 6 months in specified circumstances.

STATUTORY PROCEDURES UNDER THE 1981 ACT

28. The 1981 Act lays down procedures for the assessment of children whose needs are, or probably are, such as to require LEAs to determine their special educational provision. The advice which LEAs should seek in making assessments, the matters they should take into account, and the contents and form of the statement are prescribed in the Education (Special Educational Needs) Regulations 1983. Annexes 2 and 3 to this Circular give guidance on the form and content of statements. Provision for children under five is dealt with paragraph 78.

29. Lack of progress by a child points to a need to initiate assessment procedures. The Act lays down formal procedures for this purpose. These procedures focus upon a group of children within the larger group of children with special educational needs. It is not possible to prescribe precise limits for this smaller group. The factors which will influence the LEA's decision whether or not they should determine the special educational provision for an individual child will vary from area to area depending on how the LEA aims to meet SEN, either through central provision (by means of special schools or the use of support teams, for example) or through support already available in mainstream schools. Formal procedures under Section 5 should always be initiated where there are prima facie grounds to suggest that a child's needs are such as to require educational provision additional to, or otherwise different from, that made generally in LEA maintained schools in the area.

30. LEAs have a duty under section 7(1) of the 1981 Act to afford the protection of a statement of special educational needs to any child they have assessed under section 5 of the Act, if that assessment leads them to conclude that they should 'determine the special educational provision that should be made' for that child, for example by placing the child in a special school and prescribing the special educational provision that should be made for the child in that school.

30(a). It has been held (by the Court of Appeal in the case of R v Secretary of State for Education and Science Ex Parte L. (1987)) that an LEA's decision under section 7(1) of the Act as to whether they should determine the special educational provision that should be made for a child is a decision as to whether the authority will, in exercise of their discretion, determine the special educational provision required, or will leave that provision to others – for example the Head Teacher and Governing Body of the school which the child attends.

30(b). In a more recent ruling of the Court of Appeal (in the case of R v Secretary of State for Education and Science Ex Parte E (1991)) it has been established that once an LEA have decided, following a section 5 assessment, that they are required to determine **some** special educational provision for a child they must maintain a statement of special educational needs for that child. The statement must include **all** of the child's special educational needs as assessed by the LEA under section 5 of the 1981 Act and must specify the special educational provision that should be made for each and every one of those needs. This applies even where some of the provision is to be made by direct intervention on the part of the authority and some is to be made by the child's school.

30(c). For the child with a statement, extra resources allocated in order to make the specified special educational provision for the child, which might commonly include additional support or equipment, may be provided from resources held centrally by the LEA or, where the LEA has delegated to schools the resources for pupils with statements, through the operations of the LMS formula. In the latter case, grant maintained schools will normally receive the equivalent funding as part of their Annual Maintenance Grant.

31. The Secretary of State would expect that children in special schools would normally be afforded the protection of a statement. Statements may not be needed where ordinary schools themselves determine and make special educational provision from their own resources. Nor would statements be required where children from ordinary schools attend for short but regular periods at tuition centres away from the school; or where the need for extra help is part-time and of short duration; or where as part of the assessment process and by agreement with the parent the child is placed temporarily and for a short period in a special school or unit.

32. Statutory assessment procedures under Section 5 of the 1981 Act may be required for some children with learning difficulties in hospital, other health care provision or being educated in a social service setting such as a residential care home, for example:

- (i.) if the child has a medical condition likely to affect future learning ability;
- (ii.) if the child has been admitted in connection with a social condition which is likely to affect future learning ability (such as social deprivation, whether negligence, neglect or child abuse);
- (iii.) if a child is receiving treatment likely to affect future learning ability;
- (iv.) if the child has been admitted to a children's or adolescent psychiatric ward.

In all these circumstances, the hospital authorities should liaise with the DHA-designated Medical Officer, so that he or she can inform the LEA, and LEA can form a judgement as to whether the child should be assessed or reassessed.

INITIAL STAGES

33. Parents may request an LEA to undertake an assessment of their child's educational needs and the LEA are bound to comply unless they regard the request as unreasonable. Where the LEA initiate the action, the serving of a formal notice under section 5 of the 1981 Education Act should never be the first indication to a parent that the child has learning difficulties. Before the notice is issued there should usually be a period of initial assessment and every possible

effort should be made to effect initial contracts between the teacher, or any other professional making the referral, and the child's parent.

34. Wherever possible, assessments should take place in surroundings familiar to the child, either at home or at school. A supported mainstream placement for assessment purposes may, if parents agree, be appropriate. Children should not remain for long periods in assessment placements and their progress should be monitored. Such placements should not be used as a long-term solution for disruptive or disturbed children with or without statements.

35. Section 5(3) of the 1981 Act provides that the parent should be informed of the LEA's proposal to assess the child and the full procedures to be followed in assessment. The parent should be given the name of an LEA officer from whom further information is available, and be notified in straightforward language of the right to make representations within a minimum period of 29 days after the date of notification. When notifying parents of this right, LEAs should encourage representations from parents, pointing out the importance of their contributions. LEAs may invite parents to indicate formally if they do not wish to make or add to representations, in which case parents should be told that the LEA understands that the right is not to be exercised and assessment can proceed without delay. Where parents do wish to make representations, they may need help in doing so. Where representations are made orally to the named officer, a written summary by the LEA should be agreed with the parent concerned. Alternatively, the LEA may suggest to the parent the name of a voluntary organisation, an Education Welfare Officer, or an employee of a statutory body who could help in this way. Voluntary organisations may be contracted on the parents' behalf if the parent consents. Outcomes tend to be more satisfactory for all parties when such bodies are involved at an early stage, so as to avoid misunderstandings.

36. 'Parent' is defined in Section 114(1) of the Education Act 1944 (the 1944 Act) to include a guardian and every person who has the actual custody of the child or young person. It is important to recognise the width of this definition. In this Circular the word 'parent' should be taken to include:–

(a.) both of the child's legal parents;

(b.) any guardian appointed by deed, will or order of a court;

(c.) any person. eg a foster parent, with whom the child is living, whether or not a custody order is in force in that person's favour;

(d.) when the child is in the compulsory care of a local authority under a care order, a committal to care made in divorce or other family proceedings or following a parental rights resolution, that local authority or in the case of a child in a children's home, the key worker; and

(e.) when the child is in care of a voluntary organisation, in whom the parental rights and duties have been vested by resolution, that voluntary organisation.

It should be noted that where a child is in the voluntary care of a local authority, that authority is not the 'parent'. Moreover, where a child is a ward of court it should always be remembered that no major step in the child's life should be taken without the prior permission of the court. It is for the local education authority to decide at what stage a local authority's social services department or the wardship court should be consulted on the matters covered in this Circular. The Government are proposing in the Children Bill to amend the definition of parent in the 1944 Act and reference should be made to the Bill if it is enacted. This will be the subject of guidance in due course.

SEEKING ADVICE

37. Under Regulation 4 of the 1983 Regulations, LEAs must seek educational, medical and psychological advice, together with advice from any other source they consider desirable in making an assessment under section 5 of the 1981 Act. 'Advice' must be written advice on the features of the case which are relevant to and which affect the child's special educational needs and on the ways of meeting those needs. The LEA must provide professionals with copies of any representations or evidence submitted by or on behalf of the child's parent, including any written summary of oral representations. It falls to the professional advisers to consult others, including any persons specified by the LEA, and to collect and collate any relevant information obtained from their area of responsibility and to submit it to the LEA. There is no prescribed form in which advice should be presented but, as required by the 1983 Regulations, it should be written. If LEAs devise structured forms for the collection of professional advice, they should draw them up in consultation with the professional concerned, and provide adequate space for individual comment. Some LEAs have already provided checklists or profiles for parents to use to help them contribute to assessments. These can be helpful to parents although they should not restrict parents from giving evidence in some other format if they so wish.

38. A satisfactory and speedy conclusion to the assessment and statement process is in the child's interest. Any delay puts the child at a disadvantage. The Secretary of State for Education and Science therefore expects that the period of time from the initial notification by the school or the parents to the LEA that an assessment might be necessary to the production of the draft statement for the parent's consideration should not exceed 6 months. Where LEAs propose target dates for the providers of advice, those professionals should recognise the need for prompt action in order to comply. In the latter situation, where the parent is a Serviceman he should consent to the Service Children's Education Authority being informed so that the family does not become subject to a posting order during this very sensitive assessment period.

39. To encourage the continued use of a common approach to advice on special educational needs, it is recommended that within the area of his/her specialism each professional adviser should provide details as specified in paragraph 18. Annex 1 to this Circular offers a checklist of the points to be considered as part of this approach. The checklist is intended as an aide-memoire. Not all points will apply to each child and the checklist dies not claim to cover all possibilities. It is open to individual professionals to select the points which are relevant to their own specialisms and to the circumstances of particular cases, and to advise whether some of the needs they have identified are more important than others or require more urgent attention.

EDUCATIONAL, MEDICAL AND PSYCHOLOGICAL ADVICE AND PARENTAL EVIDENCE

40. Where possible, *educational advice* must be sought from the head teachers of all the schools the child has attended at some time in the preceding 18 months. Evidence from assessments made under the National Curriculum arrangements may be relevant. The headteacher may consult other teachers who have taught the child during that period, and must do so where he or she has not personally taught the child. Where it is thought that the child may have a sensory impairment, the headteacher's advice must be given after consultation with a

person who is qualified to teach deaf or blind children, if the headteacher is not so qualified. If the child is not attending school, educational advice must be sought from someone with experience of teaching children with special educational needs, and knowledge of the different forms of special educational provision which might meet the needs of that child.

41. All *medical* and other *health* advice should be sought from the medical officer designated for this purpose by the DHA. Advice should be concise and relevant to the child's educational needs. Before submitting advice the medical officer should co-ordinate information from all the doctors concerned in the assessment of the child's special educational needs which will be attached at Appendix D to the Statement. Any psychiatric advice will also be included in the medical advice, either verbatim or in summary form, if its provider is content. It is helpful to the LEA if the designated medical officer indicates by name and profession those medical specialists from whom advice has been sought.

42. Advice about non-medical support services provided by the DHA eg. all therapy and nursing services, should also be sought through the medical officer and collected and passed in full to the LEA to be attached at Appendix G to the statement. The complexity of needs of some individual children may call for involvement of additional professional help including the family doctor.

43. DHAs should continue to strengthen the multi-disciplinary approach to the needs of severely disabled children, including under fives. Where they exist, District Child Development Teams, District Handicap Teams or Community Mental Handicap Teams may offer a suitable vehicle for the assessment of these children's special educational needs. The local child, adolescent and family psychiatric services, whether hospital or community based, may be an appropriate source of advice about children with emotional and behavioural problems. The specialist assessment facilities available in some schools, units and nurseries will also continue to serve these needs.

44. *Psychological advice* must be sought from an educational psychologist employed by the LEA or engaged by the LEA for the purpose of any particular case. Where other psychologists (eg a clinical or occupational psychologist) have relevant knowledge or information about the child, they must in accordance with Regulation 7(2) of the 1983 Regulations be consulted by the educational psychologist, and their advice recorded. LEAs will provide the services of educational psychologists to pupils in grant-maintained schools as to those in other schools in their areas.

45. *Parental representations* may be submitted direct by the parent or may take the form of evidence submitted by another person or organisation acting on the parent's behalf. The parental contribution, based on informal, intimate and detailed knowledge of the child's personal characteristics and needs, may include the opinion of others known to the child; it provides an important complement to the professional advice.

OTHER ADVICE

46. When the LEA notify the parent of their decision to assess a child's special educational needs, a copy of the notification should be sent to an officer nominated for this purpose by the Social Services Department. This is intended to enable them to consider whether they know of any problems affecting the child in their respective spheres and to indicate to the LEA whether they have information relevant to the assessment of the child's special educational needs.

Any advice furnished to the LEA will be attached at Appendix G to the statement. It will also be open to the LEA to seek advice from these services where it has not been volunteered.

47. The complexity of needs of some individual children may call for the involvement of additional professional help including the family doctor. Authorities are reminded of the advice given in DHSS Circular HC(78)5 that District Handicap Teams (DHTs) (or District Child Development Teams where they exist) should strengthen the multi-disciplinary approach to the needs of severely disabled children including under-fives. Where they exist, DHTs may offer a suitable vehicle for the assessment of these children's special educational needs. Community Mental Handicap teams may have a role to play. The local child, adolescent and family psychiatric services, whether hospital or community-based, may be an appropriate source of advice about children with emotional or behavioural problems. The specialist assessment facilities established by some authorities in schools, units and nurseries will also continue to serve these needs. Where sensory impairment is part of a complex of needs, the advice of a specifically qualified teacher may be needed. Education Welfare Officers may often have relevant knowledge.

COOPERATION

48. Professional assessment under the 1981 Act requires a systematic yet flexible approach. It may be organised in a variety of ways according to local circumstances and the requirements of individual cases. All contributors will need to bear in mind the need for prompt action and the expectation that assessment be completed within 6 months. Professional advisers may submit their evidence separately to the LEA, copying their advice to other colleagues involved in the assessment. It may be desirable for professional assessment to proceed in sequence, educational advice being followed by medical advice and then by psychological advice, but this is not obligatory. Adherence to this sequence should not be allowed to delay the process of assessment.

49. The relations between professional advisers and parents during the process of assessment are of crucial importance. Parents should be encouraged to feel that they are partners in the process. Paragraph 2(4) of Schedule 1 to the 1981 Act gives the parents the right to be present at examinations for assessment purposes and prescribes a penalty which may be payable by parents who refuse to allow their child to be examined. It is better for the LEA to seek the parent's cooperation, rather than to advise him or her at the outset of statutory penalties for falling to allow the child to be examined. Parents should be made aware that some forms of psychological testing might be carried out without the presence of any observers, although they may insist on exercising their right to attend.

50. In some cases professional advisers may find that, after their individual consideration, a case conference may best help them achieve the precise identification of a child's needs. LEAs may involve various groupings of professionals. Although parents have no legal right to attend such case conferences, there are obvious advantages, in terms of maintaining trust and cooperation, in parents being invited to attend, with a friend or adviser if they wish, and to take part in the conference. Where consolidated advice is provided in consequence of such conferences, the Regulations require identifiable contributions from the relevant services and the parent, if he or she is attending. All contributors should be asked to record at the time any reservations they may have about the advice or conclusion. Parents may need help with this.

51. By bringing together the skills, perceptions and insights of professionals in different disciplines, as well as those of the parent, it should be possible to arrive at a more complete understanding of a child's special educational needs. Effective multi-professional work requires cooperation, collaboration and mutual support on the part of all contributors. Each professional adviser needs to be aware of the roles of other contributors and should seek to reach agreement with them on their several roles and functions. It follows that the advice given by each one should reflect his or her concerns, leaving others to concentrate upon their particular area of expertise. For example, doctors should draw attention to the implications that the child's medical condition has on the child's ability to learn, to take part in school life and to benefit from the school curriculum, and also to the support and facilities the child may need. Advice should be relevant and usable in and educational context, and available to teachers to enable them to plan a detailed programme of education for the pupil. Advice should not be influenced by consideration of the eventual school placement to be made for the child, since that is a matter to be determined by the LEA at a later stage. Discussions between individual advisers and parents about the child's needs should include decisions about the provision and placement to be made.

52. The ultimate responsibility for formulating an assessment of the child's special educational needs rests with the LEA. It therefore falls to the LEA to coordinate and summarise the advice, evidence, representations and information received about the child. Where there is conflict in the professional advice submitted to the LEA, or where it is clear that further consideration is required to lead to a full understanding of the child's special educational needs, the LEA should arrange further discussions among the professional advisers to resolve any conflict or uncertainty about them. Where it proves impossible to reconcile differences it falls to the LEA to determine the special education provision they will make for the child. They should then clearly set out the reasons for their decision in the draft statement or other written communication with the parent.

53. The professional advice and parental evidence on the basis of which the LEA make their decision must be copied verbatim in the appendices to the statement. All those contributing should be aware that their full advice will be made available to the parent, and in the event of an appeal, to the appeal committee. LEAs are reminded that the contributing professional value feedback on the outcome of assessment procedures as it enables them to plan for and provide the necessary services. All designated officers receiving such information should ensure that it is passes on to the professionals who contributed to the assessment process.

PREPARATION OF A STATEMENT

54. The two stages in the preparation of a statement are:

(i.) the draft statement, on which the parent's comments must be invited, and

(ii.) the final statement.

55. Research and experience have shown that LEAs need to give careful attention to the wording of the draft and the final statement, so as to ensure that its meaning is precise and clear to parents and those who have to carry out its provisions. Help should be given to those parents who require it, so that they understand the assessment made, the provision proposed and the immediate and longer term significance for their child's progress. LEA officers, teachers or headteachers, educational psychologists, social workers, members of the Education Welfare

Service or representatives of special needs bodies – parents' self-help groups or voluntary organisations – may be able to provide this help.

56. Section 7(3) of the 1981 Act requires the LEA to submit the draft statement to the parent informing him or her of the right to make representations within 15 days and to ask for an interview to discuss the draft statement with an LEA officer. Such a meeting is the parent's opportunity to question the LEA's advisers and gain further information on their reasoning, to put his or her point of view and to challenge the proposals if so desired. If the parent, having attended the meeting or meetings, disagrees with any part of the draft statement he or she may require the LEA to arrange further joint consideration with the person or persons who provided the LEA with the relevant advice or with some other appropriate person.

57. An authorised officer of the LEA (or where the responsibility is not delegated, the relevant Committee of the LEA) should complete, sign and date the statement after completing any necessary consultations with the other agencies involved in providing for the child. The language of the statement needs to be clear, concise and jargon-free. Precise reference to the child's current educational attainments and general development is needed to enable progress to be monitored, reviewed and reassessed against specific aims and objectives.

FORM AND CONTENT OF THE STATEMENT

58. Regulation 10 of the 1983 Regulations prescribes the contents of a statement and, in the Schedule, sets out the form of the statement that should be used. Annex 2 to this Circular shows the format of the statement. A common and consistent format for writing statements, using the same 5 headings and numberings shown below is desirable, otherwise two problems may result:

(i.) the statement may be misinterpreted when the child transfers between LEAs; and

(ii.) the courts may find difficulty in applying accepted case-law interpretations.

Regulations 10(2) allows for variation to the form of the statement shown in the Schedule; what is important is that it should be accurate and communicate its meaning unequivocally to parents and teachers.

I Introduction

59. This will identify the child and the parents and the Social Services Department if the child is in their care. Mention should also be made of the statutory provision under which the statement is made.

II Special Educational Needs

60. In reaching their conclusions, the LEA will have considered the following information: –

(i.) educational, medical and psychological advice,

(ii.) any evidence or representations from the child's parents,

(iii.) any material provided by a District Health Authority (DHA) or Social Services Department (SSD),

(iv.) any other relevant advice.

Where a statement results, copies of all these documents must be appended to it, since all this information forms part of the statement. Where the advice of the professional advisers is in accord and the LEA adopt this as their assessment, they should state this in Section II of the statement together with a full summary of the child's needs and functioning. They should indicate that their decision is in accordance with the advice, and may use references such as 'see appendices'. They must ensure that what they are adopting makes sense, is clear and unambiguous, and is not internally contradictory. Where there is any doubt or conflicting professional advice, the LEA should state in section II their decision about the child's special educational needs, and the reason for it.

Section II must detail all of the child's special educational needs. It should include reference to all special educational needs identified during the formal assessment. There may be cases where in the interests of meeting the child's needs effectively, it is helpful to use diagnostic terms in the statement or supporting advice. The 1981 Act, while it abolished 'categories of handicap', does not rule out the use of such terms. It may be helpful to refer to specific disabilities but the statement should nevertheless go on to amplify clearly the nature of the child's educational needs.

Section II should provide a summary of the material outlined in paragraph 18 and include:

(i.) a description of the child's functioning – what the child can do as well as what he or she cannot do, and

(ii.) a description of the main educational and developmental short term, and longer term, objectives the child is expected to achieve.

Section II must detail the child's SEN. It should include reference to all SEN identified, whether or not the LEA feel able to make provision for those needs in Section III. There may be cases where in the interests of meeting the child's needs effectively it is helpful to use diagnostic terms in the statement or supporting advice. The 1981 Act, while it abolished 'categories of handicap', does not rule out the use of such terms. It may be helpful to refer to specific disabilities but the statement should nevertheless go on to amplify the nature of the child's educational needs.

Section II should provide a summary of the material outlined in paragraph 18 and include:

(i.) a description of the child's functioning – what the child can do as well as what he or she cannot do, and

(ii.) details of the educational and developmental objectives the child is expected to achieve, stating which are short and which longer-term.

III Special Educational Provision

61. The LEA are legally bound to provide whatever is specified in Section III, which should specify in detail the special educational provision that they consider appropriate for the special educational needs identified in Section II. It is important that this information should easily be understood by all those involved in the child's education, including the parents, so that they know exactly what is required. Statements that fail to specify in detail what provision the particular child requires are of little use to parents and to the professional who are to act upon them. Provision should be specified in terms of facilities and equipment, staffing arrangements, teaching methods and approaches. Where relevant, educational environment and access and, if necessary, transport should be specified.

Section III of the statement should specify, in accordance with Section 18 of the 1988 Act:

(a) any exceptional arrangements modifying the application of the National Curriculum to the individual pupil. Modification may apply to the attainment targets, programmes of study, or to the assessment and testing arrangements, and

(b) any exceptional arrangements disapplying any aspect of the National Curriculum from the individual pupil.

IV Appropriate School Or Other Arrangements

61(a). Section III of the statement should specify, in accordance with section 18 of the Education Reform Act 1988 (the 1988 Act) and Regulation 10(1)(a) of the Education (Special Educational Needs) Regulations 1983 as amended by the Education (Special Educational Needs) (Amendment) Regulations 1990:

(i.) any modifications to the provisions of the National Curriculum (in terms of attainment targets, programmes of study and assessment arrangements) in their application to the child which the LEA consider necessary to meet the child's special educational needs and,

(ii.) any exclusions from the application of the provisions of the National Curriculum (in terms of attainment targets, programmes of study, assessment arrangements and foundation subjects) which the LEA consider necessary in view of the child's special educational needs and,

(iii.) the provision which the LEA propose to substitute for any such exclusions in order to maintain a balanced and broadly based curriculum for the child which promotes the child's spiritual, moral, cultural, mental and physical development and that of society as a whole, and which prepares the child for the opportunities, responsibilities and experiences of adult life.

61(b). It is important that all of the information in section III should be easily understood by all those involved in the child's education, including the parents, so that they may know exactly what is required. Statements that fail to specify in detail what provision the particular child requires are of little use to parents and to the professionals who are to act upon them. Modifications to and exemptions from the application of the provisions of the National Curriculum are likely to be more clearly understood if they are made in the context of clear, published guidelines from the LEA.

62. The LEA must describe in section IV, the type of school they consider appropriate for the child, and name the particular school if known, or the provision to be made for the child's education, if the child is to be educated otherwise than at school. Very often the named school will be the child's present school. The type of school or named school specified by an LEA in section IV as being appropriate for meeting the child's special educational needs as set out in section II of the statement, and the special educational provision in terms of facilities and equipment, staffing arrangements, curriculum or otherwise as specified in section III, are both part of the special education provision.

62(a). Where a child has a statement, the provision made in section 6 of the Education Act 1980 (the 19080 Act) requiring LEAs, subject to certain conditions, to comply with parental preferences in school admissions is overridden by the duties laid on them in the 1981 Act to arrange for the special educational provision which the child needs. The parents of children with statements will not therefore have the right to appeal to a local appeal committee constituted under section 7 of the 1980 Act against the decision of an LEA not to place their child at their preferred choice of school. Notwithstanding this, parents do have the right of appeal to a local committee constituted under section 8(2) of the Education Act 1981 against the special education provision specified in their child's statement which includes the type of school or, where specified by the LEA, the school named in section IV (see paragraph 65).

Where a child has special educational needs but no statement, the LEA must act in accordance with the provisions of sections 6–9 of the Education Act 1980 in relation to parental preferences in school admissions. Even where a child has a statement, the LEA will wish to observe the parents' preference in choice of school wherever they can. But they are not bound by the 1980 Act to do so. In all cases LEAs are to have regard to the general principle set out in section 76 of the Education Act 1944, that pupils are to be educated in accordance with their parents' wishes, so far as is compatible with the provision of efficient instruction and training and the avoidance of unreasonable public expenditure.

62(b). The Secretary of State expects parents to take part in the consultations leading to school placements for children with special educational needs and they should be encouraged to visit the proposed school. Where the LEA have selected a school which is suitable for making the special educational provision which the child needs, they are not then obliged to meet the parents' wishes for a placement in another school in their area, a school in the area of another LEA, a grant maintained school, city technology college, a fee paying school, or a school with particular religious or cultural affiliations, although they may do so if they wish. The LEA will need to consider, however, whether the religious or cultural affiliations of the child and his family may be relevant in considering how he or she will benefit in a school which does not share those affiliations.

62(c). LEAs have powers under section 3 of the 1981 Act to make arrangements for provision otherwise than in a school. Parents may choose to have their child educated at their own expense. Where parents do so choose, the LEA must satisfy themselves that the parents' choice of school or other provision is suitable to meet the special educational provision specified in the child's statement. If that is so, the statement need not specify a particular school. The school should be named in section IV in all cases where the LEA are prepared to meet the cost and in cases where they consider that a particular school is the appropriate one for the child, and especially where section III of the statement indicates directly or indirectly that a particular school is the appropriate one, or where there is no other appropriate LEA maintained school.

62(d). Close consultation with the Social Services Department (SSD) is essential in reaching decisions on the special educational provision and placements to be made for children in care or children under statutory or voluntary supervision. The importance of such cooperation is emphasised in the guidance published by the Department of Health on the Children Act 1989 ('Volume 6 – Children With Disabilities'). Where the child with a statement is placed by an LEA, a SSD, or by his parents in a school which is not maintained by the LEA responsible for the statement, that LEA must still keep the child's statement under review at least annually. The LEA must also carry out a full reassessment of the child's needs as required under Regulation 9 of the Education (Special Educational Needs) Regulations 1983 as amended. The Regulation specifies that where a child's needs have not been assessed since before the child attained the age of 12 years and six months then, during the period of twelve months beginning with the day on which the child attains the age of 13 years and six months, the LEA shall reassess the child's needs.

V Additional Non-educational Provision

63. Regulation 10(1)(c) of the 1983 Regulations require section V to provide details of any non-educational provision which the LEA consider advantageous to the child and which the LEA either propose to make available, or which the LEA are satisfied, by arrangement or otherwise, will be provided by the District Health Authority (DHA), Social Services Department (SSD) or some other body. Paragraph 83 of Schedule 12 to the 1988 Act amends section 7(2) of the 1981 Act to make it clear that LEAs may arrange for such provision to be made.

63(a). In the case of speech therapy, LEAs should be aware that in the case of R v Lancashire County Council Ex Parte CM (1989) the Court of Appeal ruled that speech therapy could be considered as either educational or non-educational provision, depending upon the circumstances of each individual case. The Court said 'to teach an adult who has lost his larynx because of cancer might well be considered as treatment rather than education. But to teach a child who has never been able to communicate by language, whether because of some chromosomal disorder...or because of social cause...seems to us just as much educational provision as to teach a child to communicate in writing'.

63(b). Where the LEA determine that speech therapy forms part of the special educational provision in a child's statement, they will have a statutory duty under section 7(2) of the 1981 Act to arrange that such provision is made unless the child's parents have made suitable arrangements. In those circumstances, the LEA should normally call upon the DHA to secure the provision of speech therapy services for the child in view of the National Health Service's general duty to provide services to LEAs to enable them to carry out their duties under the Education Acts. However, where the DHA, for whatever reason, cannot provide speech therapy for a child whose statement specifies it as educational provision, the LEA must arrange it in order to fulfill their statutory duty under section 7(2) of the 1981 Act. The Lancashire judgement made this clear, when the Court said:'...there is nothing in the National Health Reorganisation Act 1973 which prevents a local education authority from employing speech therapists if that should prove necessary to enable it to comply with its statutory duties; alternatively it can go to other district health authorities or to private speech therapists'.

63(c). LEAs and DHAs are encouraged to cooperate closely in relation to the arrangements for the provision of speech therapy and other allied services for children with special educational needs. It is important that the nature and extent of provision required for individual children should be examined very carefully and that full consideration is given as to how such provision can best be delivered. In some cases, for example, children may need regular and continuing help from a speech therapist, either individually or in a group. In other cases it may be appropriate for the staff at the child's school to deliver a programme of support under the guidance and supervision of a speech therapist.

PLACEMENT AND FURTHER ADVICE

64. Every effort should be made to ensure that a permanent placement is arranged as soon as possible. In some cases, however, it will be necessary or desirable to arrange a provisional placement for the child pending the making of the final assessment. Such placements may be made as part of the process of assessment where, for example, the child experiences severe emotional or behavioural problems, or where the assessment is likely to be protracted. Provisional

placements should be made for a stated period only, at the discretion of the LEA. If, after the parent of the child has been given the opportunity to exercise his or her rights, the LEA decide to make a statement, section 7(9) of the 1981 Act requires them to send a copy to the parent, to inform the parent of the right to appeal under section 8, and to provide the name of a person to whom he or she can apply for information and advice about the child's special educational needs. The Act does not prescribe the identity of this person but LEAs should ensure that the named person has sufficient knowledge and experience of the education service to be familiar with the kinds of difficulties encountered by children with special educational needs, and is likely to be able to establish good relationships with parents.

APPEALS

Procedures under the 1981 Act include many opportunities for the discussion of problems and it is desirable that disputes should be resolved informally and at local level where possible. Appeals to the Secretary of State for Education and Science should be seen as a last resort. LEAs are encouraged to refer parents to organisations which can help them with appeals, and to indicate where these services area available free of charge. Parents have the right to appeal in the following circumstances:

(i.) If, after an assessment under section 5, the LEA decide that they are not requires to determine the special educational provision that should be made for a child, the parents may appeal to the Secretary of State against their decision. Under this section, the Secretary of State may direct the LEA to reconsider their decision. [1]

(ii.) Under section 8, if the parent disagrees with the special educational provision specified in a child's statement, which includes the type of school or named school in section IV, he or she may appeal to a local appeal committee constituted in a similar way as an appeal committee under the 1980 Act. The judgment in the case of R v Secretary of State for Education and Science Ex Parte O (1988) makes clear that an appeal against the special educational provision in the statement can also cover the special educational needs in section II in so far as an incorrect specification of needs leads to inappropriate provision being specified to meet them.

(iii.) Paragraph 84 of Schedule 12 to the 1988 Act amends section 8 of the 1981 Act to provide the parent with a right of appeal when the LEA amends the special educational provision in an existing statement, including when they modify or disapply all or part of the National Curriculum. The LEA must inform the parent of his or her right to appeal as described above. The requirement for an appeal against an amended statement to be heard by a local appeal committee does not apply in a case where the LEA notifies a parent of their decision to amend a statement having reconsidered a case which has already been remitted to them by a local appeal committee under section 8(5) of the 1981 Act for reconsideration in the light of the appeal committee's observations (see iv below). In such cases, the parent,

---

[1] Parents may also complain to the Secretary of State under Sections 68 and 99 of the 1944 Education Act if they believe that the LEA have acted unreasonably or are in breach of their statutory duty in deciding not to assess their child under Section 5 of the 1981 Act.

having been informed of the LEA's decision, may appeal direct to the Secretary of State.

iv. Local appeal committees can either confirm the special educational provision in the statement or ask the LEA to reconsider the case in the light of the committee's observations. After reconsideration the LEA must inform the parent of their decision. If the parent remains dissatisfied, he or she may appeal to the Secretary of State who can confirm the specified provision (see paragraph 62); make other such consequential amendments to the statement as are considered to be appropriate; or direct the LEA to cease to maintain it.

66. Local appeal committees which are considering appeals under section 8 should include members who have relevant knowledge of the range of provision for special educational needs. Committees should be convened and conducted in accordance with the recommendations on procedural and constitutional practice included in the Code of Practice on Appeals prepared by the Council on Tribunals and the Local Authority Associations. Any reports presented to the Appeal committee must also be made available to the child's parent who may seek disclosure of documents. Similarly any further evidence provided by the parent must also be made available to the LEA who should ensure that it is passed to the appeal Committee.

67. When the Secretary of State is considering appeals under section 5 and 8, the LEA and the parent will each have the opportunity to present their version of the facts and be enabled to comment on all relevant material presented to the Secretary of State by the other party.

68. Paragraph 5 of Part II of Schedule 1 to the 1981 Act requires LEAs to review statements at least annually. Reviews should normally be based on reports prepared by the school the child attends and should include where appropriate the views of teachers and other professionals who work with the child and the assessments made under the 1988 Act with reference to the National Curriculum. The views of the child's parents, and wherever practicable those of the child, should be included in formulating the outcome of the review and their attendance at reviews encouraged. The review should check whether the provision prescribed in the statement is meeting the stated aims and objectives for the child and whether the school placement remains appropriate. For those in special schools, the option of a supported mainstream placement should be considered. Any amendments should be notified to parents. As the attainment targets and programmes of study for each subject of the National Curriculum are published, annual reviews will need to take these requirements into account and the need for any amendment to the statement will also have to be considered. Teachers will need to be made aware of any educational implications identified in the review.

REASSESSMENTS

69. A reassessment will normally be appropriate where there has been a significant change in the circumstances of the child. A reassessment may be made as a result of an annual review or in compliance with a request from the parent, who may be of the opinion that the child's needs have changed significantly since the previous assessment. A headteacher may institute a re-assessment of a child's special educational needs. It is open to the head to exercise his or her powers under Section 19[1] of the 1988 Act (as detailed in paragraph 10(iii) above) if he or she

---

[1] Details can be found in DES Circular 15/89, entitled "Education Reform Act 1988: Temporary Exceptions from the National Curriculum."

considers it essential to modify or disapply the National Curriculum while a reassessment is carried out.

70. In addition, Regulation 9 of the 1983 Regulations prescribes that where the LEA maintain a statement in respect of a child whose educational needs have not been assessed since before the child reached the age 12 years and 6 months, they should reassess those needs during the period of one year beginning with the day on which the child reaches the age of 13 years and 6 months. This provides the opportunity for the child, and all concerned with his or her future, to consider the arrangements to be made for the remainder of the child's time at school and for preparation for transition to adult life; and to determine the nature of the further education, vocational training, employment or other arrangements to be made.

71. Under Section 5 of the Disabled Persons (Services, Consultation and Representation) Act 1986, LEAs must obtain an opinion from the SSD as to whether a child is or is not a disabled person as part of the first annual review or assessment or reassessment after the child's 14th birthday. LEAs are required to notify SSDs 8 months before the date when a young person with disabilities is likely to leave full-time education, and to keep the date under review. SSDs are required to carry out a multi-disciplinary assessment within 5 months of the LEA notification unless the young person or parent does not want it.

72. Irrespective of the arrangements for statutory review or reassessment, schools should be sensitive to the changing needs or circumstances of their pupils, and LEAs and schools should be ready to allow for the possibility of transfers between schools to meet such changes. Paragraph 6 of Part II of Schedule 1 to the 1981 Act as amended by paragraph 85 of Schedule 12 to the 1988 Act requires LEAs to serve notice on parents of their proposal to amend or cease to maintain a statement, so as to give them the opportunity to make representations. In arriving at any decision, the LEA should take account of all the professional advice normally available to the child's school. The child's subsequent progress should be monitored carefully. If a child placed in a mainstream school is unable to make satisfactory progress, additional support or a return to a special school should be considered. Details of the parents' right of appeal if any changes are made to their child's special educational provision are given earlier.

TRANSFERS

73. Regulation 12 of the 1983 Regulations (as amended by SI 1988/1067, The Education (Special Educational Needs) (Amendment) Regulations 1988) prescribes that when a child with a statement moves from the area of the LEA which made the statement (the old authority) to the area of another LEA in England or Wales (the new authority), the old authority shall transfer the statement to the new authority. They must also transfer any opinion they may have received under the Disabled Persons (Services, Consultations and Representation) Act 1986 that the child is disabled. Under the 1981 Act, the new authority have a duty to identify the child under section 4 and to assess his or her needs under Section 5. Where they propose to amend the special education provision to be made for the child, the new authority must serve notice on the child's parent under section 5(3) of the 1981 Act and seek the parent's views. Where the old authority consider that the child's special educational needs have not changed, it will be open to them to advise the new authority that the advice appended to the statement should apply, and to include any additional relevant information derived from annual reviews. Schools are well-placed to make

parents aware of the implications of their proposed move for the educational provision to be made for children with SEN in the new LEA.

74. Where a child covered by a statement becomes the responsibility of an education authority in Scotland, or of an education and library board in Northern Ireland, it is recommended that the LEA which made the statement should, if the parent agrees, send a copy of it to that authority or board for information. Reciprocal arrangements exist for the Scottish record of needs to be copied to LEAs in England and Wales.

KEEPING AND DISCLOSURE OF STATEMENTS

75. Regulation 11 of the 1983 Regulations provides that a statement should not be disclosed without the consent of the child's parent except for certain statutory purposes, or in the child's educational interest. Statutory purposes would included appeals under section 8 of the 1981 Act and, as a result of the Education (Special Educational Needs) (Amendment) Regulations 1990, a child's statement may also be disclosed for the purposes of a local authority in the performance of their duties relating to safeguarding and promoting the welfare of children imposed upon them by the Children Act 1989. The child's educational interest include the provision of information to the child's school and teachers. Feedback to contributing professionals is valuable both to future work with the individual child and for similar casework. Subject to the safeguards set out in Regulation 11(1)(c), LEAs may also give access to the statement to persons engaged in research on special education needs. The arrangements for keeping statements must ensure, so far as is reasonably practicable, that unauthorised persons do not have access to them.

76. DHSS Circular LAC(88)1, DES Circular 2/88 and Welsh Office Circular 3(88) detail the impact of parts of the Disabled Persons (Services, Consultation and Representation) Act 1986 on disabled young people leaving full-time education. As a result of the passing of that Act, the 1983 Regulations were amended by SI 1988/1067 so as to permit the disclosure by an LEA to a Social Services Department who need to know for the purpose of assessing the needs of that child with respect to the provision of statutory services under the welfare enactments as defined in Section 16 of the 1986 Act. Where information likely to prove distressing to the child is included, such as limited life expectancy or a prognosis of deteriorating powers, SSD officers are asked to treat that information in strict confidence. Whilst the Data Protection (Miscellaneous Subject Access Exemptions) Order (1987) provides that the contents of the statement when held on a computer do not need to be revealed in accordance with the Data Protection Act 1984 Subject Access Provisions, this Order applies only to the LEA and cannot be relied upon by the SSD. However, the provisions of the Data Protection (Subject Access Modification) (Social Work) Order 1987 may be relevant, where the statement is held on computer for social work purposes. In these circumstances the withholding of information, on the grounds of potential harm to the physical or mental health or emotional condition of the child, is allowed.

AGES OF CHILDREN TO WHOM THESE PROCEDURES APPLY

77. The 1981 Act covers all children from birth to the upper limit of compulsory school age at 16, and any pupils over 16 up to their nineteenth birthday who continue to be registered pupils at a school. The National Curriculum, however, applies to children aged 5 to 16.

CHILDREN UNDER 5

78. Section 10 of the 1981 Act places on health authorities a duty to inform the child''s parent when they form the opinion that a child under 5 has, or is likely to have, special educational needs, and of the authority's duty, after discussion with the child's parent to bring that opinion to the attention of the LEA. Normally this duty will be discharged by the designated medical officer of the health authority. Where the health authority considers that a child with special educational needs could be assisted by a particular voluntary body, they are under a duty under Section 10(2) of the 1981 Act to inform the parent accordingly. Voluntary bodies have a special role to play in counselling the parents of children with special educational needs and they are encouraged to provide full information about their services to DHAs, SSDs and LEAs.

79. For children under 5, a distinction is made between those under 2 and those between 2 and 5. Under section 6 of the 1981 Act, a child under 2 may be assessed by the LEA if the parent agrees, and must be assessed if the parent requests it. Assessments for the under-2s may take whatever form the LEA consider appropriate. It will be open to the LEA to decide whether and in what way to make and maintain a statement for a child under 2, and the statement will not be subject to the provisions of section 8 of the Act. 'Special educational provision' for a child under 2 means any kind of educational provision including support and advice to help parents to help their children. Mother and toddler groups, opportunity groups, and other forms of provision by social services and voluntary bodies are important in the educational context. Maximum flexibility will be required in order to meet the needs of the child in a way which also provides support for the family.

80. Section 4(2) of the 1981 Act gives LEAs responsibilities towards children with SEN from age 2 to the end of compulsory school age. The arrangements to be made for a child between the ages of 2 and 5 must comply with the requirements of sections 5 and 7 of the 1981 Act. The early identification of special educational needs is crucial for the young child with disabilities and/or delayed development since prompt and appropriate provision from the time of discovery can enhance the child's future progress. LEAs should give priority to children with special educational needs in admitting children to nursery provision. Where a child with significant learning difficulties is placed in such a school or class, the provision of any support services or additional help should be clearly specified in the statement. Early speech and language difficulties are often associated with later learning problems. Careful observation and recording at the nursery stage can assist in later provision. This, liaison between the school health services, social services, family doctor, health visitor, therapist, or any other specialists, the parent, any voluntary organisation involved, and the teacher is important. Such specialists should work together with the teacher and parent in meeting special educational needs.

81. As part of the continuing assessment of provision for children under 5 with disabilities, many Local Authorities now operate Portage or other pre-school parent support and home-based learning programmes. Their clearly defined organisational structures and goal-orientated programmes have advantages, not only to the child in the most important developmental period of his or her life, but also to the parent in encouraging positive contributions to the child's development. Close cooperation and understanding between the parent and the providing agencies, education, health and social services, is integral to the success

of such projects. Adaptations to Portage methods may be necessary to meet the needs of particular children, and especially those with visual impairment.

YOUNG PEOPLE OVER AGE 16

82. LEAs are required to maintain statements for young people over 16 if they remain at school, but not if they are in further education. Where an LEA considers it appropriate to forward an existing statement to a college which the young person is to attend, the prior permission of the intending student and the parent should be obtained. Sections 8 and 114 of the 1944 Act make clear that schools are institutions for providing education only up to age 19. The 1988 Act makes explicit, but does not extend, the duties of LEAs to provide full-time education for all who seek it, up to the age of 19, either in schools or in the further education. This applies to all pupils, including those with SEN. The 1988 Act requires LEAs in securing the provision of adequate facilities for further education, to have regard to the requirements of persons over compulsory school age who have learning difficulties. Section 41(10) of the 1944 Act (as inserted by section 120(2) of the 1988 Act) refers. For all young people in education after age 16, LEAs and SSDs are reminded of their duties under Section 5 and 6 of the Disabled Persons (Services, Consultation and Representation) Act 1986.

CHILDREN WITH STATEMENTS OF SPECIAL EDUCATION NEEDS AT GRANT-MAINTAINED SCHOOLS, INDEPENDENT SCHOOLS, NON-MAINTAINED SPECIAL SCHOOLS, AND CITY TECHNOLOGY COLLEGES

83. Where a statement under the 1981 Act has been issued, LEAs have a duty under section 7 of that Act to secure that the special educational provision specified in the statement is made for the child. The school named in a statement may be an LEA maintained primary, secondary or special school within or outside the area of the home LEA, or it may be one of the types of school listed above. In the case of any of the schools listed, admission arrangements are the responsibility of the Governors and the Headteacher.

84. Grant-maintained schools will be expected to follow the policy towards the admission of pupils with special educational needs which operated prior to their change of status. The governors and headteacher of a grant-maintained school must observe the requirements of the 1981 Act in respect of all their pupils. In fulfilling these duties they may be assisted by the educational psychologist service of the pupil's LEA; LEAs are responsible for providing this service to pupils at grant-maintained schools on the same basis as to pupils at other maintained schools. Where a child with a statement is admitted to a grant-maintained school, the child's LEA is responsible for providing direct to the school and pupil any additional support specified in the statement. This support may be in the form of grant to the school to enable it to make the necessary provision, or in the form of direct provision by the LEA of staff, equipment etc.

85. The LEA maintaining a child's statement have a duty to undertake annual reviews and the statutory 13+ reassessment of each child with a statement registered at one of the above schools. If the parent elects to make private arrangements for the child's placement, the LEA must ensure that the parent's arrangements are and continue to be suitable, and that reviews and 13+ reassessments are carried out.

86. Where LEAs are satisfied that a child has special educational needs and that it is expedient in his interests that special educational provision should be made

for the child at a school not maintained by them or another LEA, they have a duty under section 6 of the Education (Miscellaneous Provisions) Act 1953, to pay the whole of the fees payable in respect of arrangements they have made for the education of the child at that school. They may make placements at independent schools only where the school currently has the approval of the Secretary of State for Education and Science under section 11(3)(a) of the 1981 Act and for the purposes of Schedule 1 to the Education (Special Education Needs) (Approval of Independent Schools) Regulations 1991 for the admission of pupils with statements or where the Secretary of State's prior consent under section 11(3)(b) of the 1981 Act to the placement of each individual child has been obtained by the LEA.

86(a). LEAs also have discretionary powers, under section 81 of the Education Act 1944, and for the purposes of Regulation 4 of the Scholarship and Other Benefits Regulations 1977 (SI 1977/1443 as amended), to pay the whole of any tuition fees and the whole or part of any approved board and lodging fees and expenses which are related to a child's attendance at a fee paying school where this is for the purpose of enabling such pupils to take advantage without hardship to themselves or their parents of the education facilities there. Such payments must be made in order to prevent or relieve financial hardship and relate to the means of the child's parents. The LEA must also be satisfied that the course of education to which the payments relate is suitable for the child.

86(b). Section 3A of the 1981 Act, as inserted by the Children Act 1989, empowers LEAs to make arrangements for children with statements to attend establishments outside England and Wales specialising in providing for children with special needs and to provide material assistance to parents in respect of such attendance, including contributing towards or paying fees, travelling and other expenses.

86(c). The National Curriculum does not apply in non-maintained special schools, independent schools, maintained special schools established in hospitals or Children's Homes with education. However, the Secretary of State encourages such schools and other hospital and home education services, wherever practicable, to seek to provide the National Curriculum. Any statement of special educational needs should make clear what curriculum is expected to be provided for the pupil and what modifications or disapplications apply. Where it is intended that the pupil will subsequently transfer to another school, it is essential to ensure continuity of curricular coverage and to minimise the disruption of transferring between schools.

CHILDREN IN CARE

87. Where a child is the subject of a care order, or is in the voluntary care of the SSD, the LEA must continue to carry out their duties under the 1981 Act. The two departments of the local authority must recognise the need to co-operate in the best educational, emotional and social interests of the child. To help to ensure the child's educational development, SSDs should consult the LEA in advance if practical and in any case should inform LEAs about every placement they make and should keep that information up to date. Every placement by an SSD in the independent school sector of a child with a statement. In their turn, LEAs should inform SSDs of the outcome of the assessment process for all children known to be the subject of a care order, in voluntary care, or supervised by the SSD, wherever the child is placed, whether at home or in residential accommodation, and should give full weight to the social and emotional needs of the child. The

Children Bill proposes to strengthen these requirements by a system of statutory notifications. Guidance on this will be issued in due course.

LANGUAGE OF INSTRUCTION

88. The 1981 Act makes clear that a child should not be taken to have a learning difficulty because the language or form of language of the home is different from the language of instruction in the school. The problems experienced by such children are essentially linguistic: they should not be equated with learning difficulties in the terms of the Act. LEAs may find it difficult to determine whether a child who is not yet fluent in the language of instruction may have special educational needs, and every attempt should be made in such a case to communicate with the child in a language with which he or she is conversant. In assessing the child's special educational needs, it is important to take account of the possibility that cultural differences may mask the child's true learning potential or indeed the nature and extent of his or her special needs. Authorities should ensure that the language in which notices are served on the child's parent is one with which the parent will be familiar or, failing that, a language for which he or she can readily obtain a interpreter. LEAs may find it helpful to make special arrangements to bring in a person with knowledge of the language and cultural background of the child and the parent in the various stages of assessment.

SERVICE CHILDREN

89. Where section 5 assessment procedures have been initiated for a child whose parent is serving in the Armed Forces, the LEA concerned is requested to obtain the parent's consent prior to notifying the Service Children's Education Authority (SCEA) using form SEN 1. This form gives SCEA advanced warning of children with SEN whom they might find difficulty in placing in Service schools should be sent to SCEA, together with a copy of the statement if one is made. SCEA may wish to obtain further information about the child's precise needs and it is expected that LEAs will assist with such enquiries. Copies of the special Form SEN 1 can be obtained from the Department of Education and Science.

CO-OPERATION BETWEEN EDUCATION, SOCIAL SERVICES AND HEALTH AUTHORITIES

90. Section 22 of the National Health Service Act 1977 requires health and local authorities including both education and social services to co-operate in exercising their respective functions, and it provides for the establishment of joint consultative committees to advise them.

91. Any new arrangements on the structure and organisation of the NHS will not affect the policies that have been established for the provision of services for children. Health authorities will remain responsible for discharging their responsibilities set out in this circular.

92. The best means of collaboration for each locality needs to be settled locally, but in relation to child health services, Health Authorities should ensure that there continue to be appropriately qualified and experienced medical and nursing staff who would have among their functions specific responsibility for advising LEAs. They will have a crucial function in the process of assessment, in co-ordinating the advice of their respective clinical colleagues, and in acting as a point of contract for LEAs. To assist liaison, the Secretaries of State urge LEAs and SSDs to make similar appointments and to nominate officers to act as the points of contact for the purpose of assessments of special educational needs. All services should

therefore review their patterns of work and agreed procedures in order to avoid unnecessary duplication and delay and to help ensure that the appropriate professionals can be involved quickly at any stage.

ADVICE ON SPECIAL EDUCATIONAL NEEDS: SUGGESTED CHECKLIST

(a) DESCRIPTION OF THE CHILD'S FUNCTIONING

1. Description of the child's strengths and weaknesses

    Physical State and Functioning
    (physical health, developmental function, mobility, hearing, vision and continence)

    Emotional State
    (link between stress, emotions and physical state)

    Cognitive Functioning

    Communication Skills
    (verbal comprehension, expressive language speech)

    Perceptual and Motor Skills

    Adaptive Skills

    Personal and Social Skills

    Approaches and Attitudes to Learning

    Educational Attainments

    Self-image and Interest

    Behaviour

2. Factors in the child's environment which lessen or contribute to his or her needs

    In the Home and Family, and including the language of the home

    At School

    Elsewhere

3. Relevant aspects of the child's history

    Personal

    Medical

    Educational

(b) AIMS OF PROVISION

1. General area of development
   (Reference should be made to the relevant attainment targets of the National Curriculum wherever possible.)

    Physical Development
    (eg, to develop self-care skills)

    Motor Development
    (eg, to improve co-ordination of hand and fingers, to achieve hand – eye co-ordination)

    Cognitive Development
    (eg, to develop the ability to classify)

Language Development
(eg, to improve expressive language skills)

Social Development
(eg, to stimulate social contact with peers)

2. Any specific area of weaknesses or gaps in skills acquisition which impede the child's progress

Eg, short-term memory deficits

3. Suggested methods and approaches

Implications of the Child's Medical Condition
(eg, advice on the side-effects of medication for epilepsy)

Teaching and Learning Approaches
(eg, teaching methods for the blind or deaf, or teaching through other specialised methods)

Emotional Climate and Social Regime
(eg, type of regime, size of class or school, need for individual attention)

(c) FACILITIES AND RESOURCES

1. Special Equipment

(eg. physical aids, auditory aids, visual aids)

2. Specialist Facilities

(eg, for incontinence, for medical examination, treatment and drug administration)

3. Special Education Resources

(eg, specialist equipment for teaching children with physical or sensory disabilities, non-teaching aids)

4. Other Specialist Resources

(eg, Nursing, Social Work and Welfare Support, Speech, Therapy, Occupational Therapy, Physiotherapy, Psychotherapy, Audiology, Orthoptics)

5. Physical Environment

(eg, access and facilities for non-ambulant pupils, attention to lighting environment, attention to acoustic environment, attention to thermal environment, health care accommodation, privacy of continence care)

6. School Organisation and Attendance

(eg, day attendance, weekly boarding, termly boarding, relief hostel accommodation)

7. Transport

STATEMENT OF SPECIAL EDUCATIONAL NEEDS

I – Introduction

1. In accordance with section 7 of the Education Act 1981 and the Education (Special Educational Needs) Regulation 1983, the following statement is made by the ________________ council ('the education authority') in respect of the child whose name and other particulars are mentioned below.

Child

Surname .... Other names ....
Home address ....

....

.... Sex ....
Date of birth .... Religion ....
.........................Home language ....
Child's parent or guardian
Surname .... Other names ....
Home address .... Relationship to child ....

....

....

Telephone No. ....

2. When assessing the child's special educational needs the education authority took into consideration, in accordance with Regulation 8 of the Regulations, the representations, evidence and advice set out in the Appendices to the statement.

II – Special educational needs

(Here set out in accordance with section 7 of the 1981 Act, the child's special educational needs as assessed by the education authority.)

III – Special educational provision

(Here specify, in accordance with Regulation 10(1)(a),
(a) the special educational provision which the education authority consider appropriate to meet the needs specified in Part II.

(Here specify, in accordance with Section 18 of the Education Reform Act, 1988)
(b) any modifications to the National Curriculum necessary to meet the child's special educational needs, in terms of programmes of study, attainment targets and assessment and testing
(c) any exemptions from foundation subject (specify which)
(d) details to indicate how it is proposed to replace the exempted programme in order to maintain a broad, balanced curriculum.)

IV – Appropriate school or other arrangements

(Here specify, in accordance with Regulation 10(1)(b), the type of school and any particular school which the education authority consider appropriate for the child or the provision for his or her education, otherwise than at a school, which they consider appropriate.)

V – Additional non-educational provision

(Here specify, in accordance with Regulation 10(1)(c), any such additional provision as is there mentioned or record that there is no such additional provision. Where provision is mentioned, state the providing Authority.)

(Signature of authenticating Officer)

....

A duly authorised officer of the education authority

(Date)

....

APPENDICES TO THE STATEMENT OF SPECIAL EDUCATION NEEDS

Appendix A: Parental representations

(Here set out any written representations made by the parent of the child in pursuance of section 5(3)(d) of the 1981 Act and summary which the parent has accepted as accurate of any oral representation so made or record that no such representations were made. Any representations from the child may also be included.)

Appendix B: Parental evidence

(Here set out any written evidence either submitted by the parent of the child in pursuance of section 5(3)(d) of the 1981 Act or submitted at his or her request or record that no such evidence was submitted.)

Appendix C: Educational advice

(Here set out all the advice obtained in pursuance of Regulation 4(1)(a).)

Appendix D: Medical advice – furnished by DHA designated medical officer

(Here set out all the advice obtained in pursuance of Regulation 4(1)(b).)

Appendix E: Psychological advice

(Here set out all the advice obtained in pursuance of Regulation 4(1)(c).)

Appendix F: Other advice obtained by Education Authority.

(Here set out any advice obtained in pursuance of Regulation 4(1)(d) or record that no such advice was sought.)

Appendix G: Non-medical information furnished by District Health Authority or information from the Social Services Department.

(Here set out any such information as is mentioned in Regulation 8(d) or record that no such information was furnished.)

Note

The above list follows the wording of the Education (Special Education Needs) Regulations 1983. The educational, medical and psychological advice will be reproduced in Appendices C, D and E respectively. Appendices A, B, F and G will consist of copies of the relevant documents, or where none have been submitted, of a note to that effect.

WHAT LEAS NEED TO TELL PARENTS OF CHILDREN WITH SPECIAL EDUCATIONAL NEEDS

1 About the 1981 Act Procedures, and

2 About the 1988 Education Reform Act and its Implications for their Children

3 About complaints under the 1944 Act.

1. 1981 ACT

a. *Definitions and Duties*

Definitions of special educational needs, learning difficulties, special educational provision.

Procedures for children with SEN.

Duties of LEA to make and review provision for pupils with SEN.

Duties of LEA provide for children under age 2 and under 5.

Duties of LEA to make integrated placements, subject to the caveats in Section 2(3).

Duties of LEA under the 1981 Act for young people at school to age 19.

Rights of parents to contribute to assessments and inform discussions.

Rights of parents to have confidentiality.

b. *Assessment*

Rights of parent to request assessment. Need to prepare parents and to explain proposals to assess. The named officer contact.

Parent's right to a minimum period of 29 days within which to comment on the LEA's proposal to assess the child. Translations of procedures and meeting into other languages.

Duty of parent to submit child for assessment, and parent's right to attend such examinations.

c. *Statements*

Parent's right to see all the advice on the assessment of the child following a draft statement.

Significance of proposed (or draft) statement and final statements.

Parent's right to a maximum of 15 days within which to make representations to the LEA on the draft statement.

Content of the statement.

Parent's right to receive a copy of the statement.

Consultation procedures.

Identification of any named persons or key workers.

Annual reviews.

13+ reassessments and their significance for the Disabled Persons (Services, Consultation and Representation) Act 1986.

Parent's right to make representations where the LEA propose to amend or cease to maintain a statement.

d. *Appeals Procedure*

Explain appeals procedure.

Right of parent to appeal where no statement is made.

Right of parent to appeal against the special educational provision in the statement.

Details of appeals committees.

Details of appeals committees' responsibilities.

Right of parent to appeal to the Secretary of State.

2. 1988 ACT

National Curriculum

Explanation of : Subjects comprising the national curriculum

Attainment Targets

Programmes of Study

Testing and Assessment

Modification and/or disapplications to the National Curriculum recorded in the statement and alternative provision being made.

Appendix 7

Children Act 1989

PART I INTRODUCTORY

Welfare of the child

1. – (1) When a court determines any question with respect to –

(a) the upbringing of a child; or

(b) the administration of a child's property or the application of any income arising from it,

the child's welfare shall be the court's paramount consideration.

(2) In any proceedings in which any question with respect to the upbringing of a child arises, the court shall have regard to the general principle that any delay in determining the question is likely to prejudice the welfare of the child.

(3) In the circumstances mentioned in subsection (4), a court shall have regard in particular to –

(a) the ascertainable wishes and feelings of the child concerned (considered in the light of his age and understanding);

(b) his physical, emotional and educational needs;

(c) the likely effect on him of any change in his circumstances;

(d) his age, sex, background and any characteristics of his which the court considers relevant;

(e) any harm which he has suffered or is at risk of suffering;

(f) how capable each of his parents, and any other person in relation to whom the court considers the question to be relevant, is of meeting his needs;

(g) the range of powers available to the court under this Act in the proceedings in question.

(4) The circumstances are that –

(a) the court is considering whether to make, vary or discharge a section 8 order, and the making, variation or discharge of the order is opposed by any party to the proceedings; or

(b) the court is considering whether to make, vary or discharge an order under Part IV.

(5) Where a court is considering whether or not to make one or more orders under this Act with respect to a child, it shall not make the order or any of the orders unless it considers that doing so would be better for the child than making no order at all.

PART III LOCAL AUTHORITY SUPPORT FOR CHILDREN AND FAMILIES

Provision of services for children and their families

Provision of services for children in need, their families and others.

17. – (1) It shall be the general duty of every local authority (in addition to the other duties imposed on them by this Part) –

(a) to safeguard and promote the welfare of children within their area who are in need; and

(b) so far as is consistent with that duty, to promote the upbringing of such children by their families,

by providing a range and level of services appropriate to those children's needs.

(2) For the purpose principally of facilitating the discharge of their general duty under this section, every local authority shall have the specific duties and powers set out in Part 1 of Schedule 2.

(3) Any service provided by an authority in the exercise of functions conferred on them by this section may be provided for the family of a particular child in need or for any member of his family, if it is provided with a view to safeguard or promoting the child's welfare.

(4) The Secretary of State may by order amend any provision of Part I of Schedule 2 or add any further duty or power to those for the time being mentioned there.

(5) Every local authority –

(a) shall facilitate the provision by others (including in particular voluntary organisations) of services which the authority have power to provide by virtue of this section, or section 18, 20, 23 or 24; and

(b) may make such arrangements as they see fit for any person to act on their behalf in the provision of any such service.

(6) The services provided by a local authority in the exercise of functions conferred on them by this section may include giving assistance in kind or, in exceptional circumstances, in cash.

(7) Assistance may be unconditional or subject to conditions as to the repayment of the assistance or of its value (in whole or in part).

(8) Before giving any assistance or imposing any conditions, a local authority shall have regard to the means of the child concerned and of each of his parents.

(9) no person shall be liable to make any repayment of assistance or of its value at any time when he is in receipt of income support or family credit under the Social Security Act 1986.

(10) For the purposes of this Part a child shall be taken to be in need if –

(a) he is unlikely to achieve or maintain, or to have the opportunity of achieving or maintaining, a reasonable standard of health or development without the provision for him of services by a local authority under this Part;

(b) his health or development is likely to be significantly impaired, or further impaired, without the provision for him of such services; or

(c) he is disabled,

and 'family', in relation to such a child, includes any person who has parental responsibility for the child and any other person with whom he has been living.

(11) For the purposes of this Part, a child is disabled if he is blind, deaf or dumb or suffers from mental disorder of any kind or is substantially and permanently handicapped by illness, injury or congenital deformity or such other disability as may be prescribed; and in this Part –

'development' means physical, intellectual, emotional, social or behavioural development; and

'health' means physical or mental health.

PART V PROTECTION OF CHILDREN

Child assessment orders

43. – (1) On the application of a local authority or authorised person for an order to be made under this section with respect to a child, the court may make the order if, but only if, it is satisfied that –

(a) the applicant has reasonable cause to suspect that the child is suffering, or is likely to suffer, significant harm;

(b) an assessment of the state of the child's health or development, or of the way in which he has been treated, is required to enable the applicant to determine whether or not the child is suffering, or is likely to suffer, significant harm; and

(c) it is unlikely that such an assessment will be made, or be satisfactory, in the absence of an order under this section.

(2) In this Act 'a child assessment order' means an order under this section.

(3) A court may treat an application under this section as an application for an emergency protection order.

(4) No court shall make a child assessment order if it is satisfied –

(a) that there are grounds for making an emergency protection order with respect to the child; and

(b) that it ought to make such an order rather than a child assessment order.

(5) a child assessment order shall –

(a) specify the date by which the assessment is to begin; and

(b) have effect for such period, not exceeding 7 days beginning with that date, as may be specified in the order.

(6) Where a child assessment order is in force with respect to a child it shall be the duty of any person who is in a position to produce the child –

(a) to produce him to such person as may be named in the order; and

(b) to comply with such directions relating to the assessment of the child as the court thinks fit to specify in the order.

(7) A child assessment order authorises any person carrying out the assessment, or any part of the assessment, to do so in accordance with the terms of the order.

(8) Regardless of subsection (7), of the child is of sufficient understanding to make an informed decision he may refuse to submit to a medical or psychiatric examination or other assessment.

(9) The child may only be kept away from home –

(a) in accordance with directions specified in the order;

(b) if it is necessary for the purposes of the assessment; and

(c) for such period or periods as may be specified in the order.

(10) Where the child is to be kept away from home, the order shall contain such directions as the court thinks fit with regard to the contact that he must be allowed to have with other persons while away from home.

(11) Any person making an application for a child assessment order shall take such steps as are reasonably practicable to ensure that notice of the application is given to –

(a) the child's parents;

(b) any person in whose favour a contact order is in force with respect to the child;

(c) any other person caring for the child;

(d) any person in whose favour a contact order is in force with respect to the child;

(e) any person who is allowed to have contact with the child by virtue of an order section 34; and

(f) the child,

before the hearing of the application.

(12) Rules of court may make provision as to the circumstances in which –

(a) any of the persons mentioned in subsection (11); or

(b) such other person as may be specified in the rules,

may apply to the court for a child assessment order to be varied or discharged.

(13) In this section 'authorised person' means a person who is an authorised person for purposes of section 31.

SCHEDULE 2
LOCAL AUTHORITY SUPPORT FOR CHILDREN AND FAMILIES

PART I PROVISION OF SERVICES FOR FAMILIES

Identification of children in need and provision of information

1. – (1) Every local authority shall take reasonable steps to identify the extent to which there are children in need within their area.

(2) Every local authority shall –

(a) publish information –

(i) about services provided by them under sections 17, 18, 20 and 24; and

(ii) where they consider it appropriate, about the provision by others (including, in particular, voluntary organisations) of service which the authority have power to provide under those sections; and

(b) take such steps as are reasonably practicable to ensure that those who might benefit from the services receive the information relevant to them.

Maintenance of a register of disabled children

2. – (1) Every local authority shall open and maintain a register of disabled children within their area.

(2) The register may be kept by means of a computer.

Assessment of children's needs

3. Where it appears to a local authority that a child within their area is in need, the authority may assess his needs for the purposes of this Act at the same time as any assessment of his needs is made under –

(a) the Chronically Sick and Disabled Persons Act 1970;

(b) the Education Act 1981;

(c) the Disabled Persons (Services, Consultation and Representation) Act 1986; or

(d) any other enactment.

Prevention of neglect and abuse

4. – (1) Every local authority shall take reasonable steps, through the provision of services under Part III of this Act, to prevent children within their area suffering ill-treatment or neglect.

(2) Where a local authority believe that a child who is at any time within their area –

(a) is likely to suffer harm; but

(b) lives or proposes to live in the area of another local authority they shall inform that other local authority.

(3) When informing that other local authority they shall specify –

(a) the harm that they believe he is likely to suffer; and

(b) (if they can) where the child lives or proposes to live.

Provision of accommodation in order to protect child

5. – (1) Where

(a) it appears to a local authority that a child who is living on particular premises is suffering, or is likely to suffer, ill treatment at the hands of another person who is living on those premises; and

(b) that other person proposes to move from the premises, the authority may assist that other person to obtain alternative accommodation.

(2) Assistance given under this paragraph may be in cash.

(3) Subsection (7) to (9) if section 17 shall apply in relation to assistance given under this paragraph as they apply in relation to assistance given under that section.

Provision for disabled children

6. Every local authority shall provide services designed –

(a) to minimise the effect on disabled children within their area of their disabilities; and

(b) to give such children the opportunity to lead lives which are as normal as possible.

Provision to reduce need for care proceedings etc.

7. Every local authority shall take reasonable steps designed –

(a) to reduce the need to bring –

(i) proceedings for care or supervision orders with respect to children within their area;

(ii) criminal proceedings against such children;

(iii) any family or other proceedings with respect to such children which might lead to them being placed in the authority's care; or

(iv) proceedings under the inherent jurisdiction of the High court with respect to children;

(b) to encourage children within their area not to commit criminal offences; and

(c) to avoid the need for children within their area to be placed in secure accommodation.

Provision for children living with their families

8. Every local authority shall make such provision as they consider appropriate for the following services to be available with respect to children in need within their area while they are living with their families –

(a) advice, guidance and counselling;

(b) occupational, social, cultural or recreational activities;

(c) home help (which may include laundry facilities);

(d) facilities for, or assistance with, travelling to and from home for the purpose of taking advantage of any other service provided under this Act or of any similar service;

(e) assistance to enable the child concerned and his family to have a holiday.

Family centres

9. – (1) Every local authority shall provide such family centres as they consider appropriate in relation to children within their area.

(2) 'Family centre' means a centre at which any of the persons mentioned in sub-paragraph (3) may –

(a) attend for occupational, social, cultural or recreational activities;

(b) attend for advice, guidance and counselling; or

(c) be provided with accommodation while he is receiving advice, guidance or counselling.

(3) The persons are –

(a) a child;

(b) his parents;

(c) any person who is not a parent of his but who has parental responsibility for him;

(d) any other person who is looking after him.

Maintenance of the family home

10. Every local authority shall take such steps as are reasonably practicable, where any child within their area who is in need and whom they are not looking after is living apart from his family –

(a) to enable him to live with his family; or

(b) to promote contact between him and his family,

if, in their opinion, it is necessary to do so in order to safeguard or promote his welfare.

Duty to consider racial groups to which children in need belong

11. Every local authority shall, in making any arrangements –

(a) for the provision of day care within their area; or

(b) designed to encourage persons to act as local authority foster parents, have regard to the different racial groups to which children within their area who are in need belong.

Appendix 8

Further and Higher Education Act 1992

3. – (1) It shall be the duty of each council to secure the provision for the population of their area of adequate facilities for education to which this subsection applies, that is –

(a) part-time education suitable to the requirements of persons of any age over compulsory school age, and

(b) full-time education suitable to the requirements of persons who have attained the age of nineteen years,

Part-time education, and full-time education over 18.

where the education is provided by means of a course of a description mentioned in Schedule 2 to this Act.

(2) A council shall discharge that duty so as –

(a) to secure that facilities are provided at such places, are of such character and are so equipped as to meet the reasonable need for education to which subsection (1) above applies, and

(b) to take account of the different abilities and aptitudes of persons among that population.

(3) A council may secure the provision of facilities for education to which subsection (1) above applies where they are not under a duty to do so.

(4) A council shall discharge their functions under this section so as to make the most effective use of their resources and, in particular, to avoid provision which might give rise to disproportionate expenditure.

(5) In discharging those functions a council shall have regard to any education to which subsection (1) above applies provided by institutions outside the further education sector or higher education sector.

(6) The Secretary of State may by order amend Schedule 2 to this Act.

4. – (1) In exercising their functions under sections 2 and 3 of this Act, each council shall (subject to the provisions of those sections) do so in accordance with subsections (2) to (4) below.

Persons with learning difficulties.

(2) Each council shall have regard to the requirements of persons having learning difficulties.

(3) A council shall, if they are satisfied in the case of any person among the population of their area who has a learning difficulty

and is over compulsory school age but has not attained the age of twenty-five years, that –

(a) the facilities available in institutions within the further education sector or the higher education sector are not adequate for him, and

(b) it is in his best interests to do so,

secure provision for him at an institution outside those sectors.

(4) A council shall, if they are satisfied that they cannot secure such provision for a person as they are required to secure under subsection (3) above unless they also secure the provision of boarding accommodation for him, secure the provision of boarding accommodation for him.

(5) In exercising their functions under sections 2 and 3 of this Act in the case of any person who has a learning difficulty and is over compulsory school age, a council may –

(a) if they are satisfied that the facilities available in institutions within the further education sector or the higher education sector are not adequate for him, secure provision for him at an institution outside those sectors, and

(b) secure the provision of boarding accommodation for him.

(6) Subject to subsection (7) below, for the purposes of this section a person has a 'learning difficulty' if –

(a) he has a significantly greater difficulty in learning than the majority of persons of his age, or

(b) he has a disability which either prevents or hinders him from making use of facilities of a kind generally provided by institutions within the further education sector for persons of his age.

(7) A person is not to be taken as having a learning difficulty solely because the language (or form of the language) in which he is, or will be, taught is different from a language (or form of a language) which has at any time been spoken in his home.

Appendix 9

Legal aid and legal advice

LEGAL AID

1. There are some misconceptions about the availability of Legal Aid following the implementation of the Children Act 1989. The Regulations relating to Legal Aid were in fact changed in April 1990.
2. Legal Aid is available for Court proceedings only. This would consist of judicial review proceedings or an action in negligence against the Local Education Authority.
3. Assuming the child complies with the financial criteria (and most do having no income or capital) free Legal Aid will be available to the child.
4. It is important Parents are aware that although Legal Aid is available for judicial review proceedings such proceedings will in themselves not necessarily resolve issues with the Local Education Authority. The effect of judicial review is simply to quash the relevant decision whether it is of the LEA or the Minister who will then have to reconsider the matter afresh, perhaps in the light of some observations made by the Judge.
5. It is important to stress that Legal Aid *is not* available for any part of the statementing procedure, whether by way of appeal or appeals under it.
6. Legal expenses insurance arranged by the Parents has actually covered a 1981 Act appeal.

GREEN FORM LEGAL ADVICE

Advantages (not many!)

(i) Entitles Client to up to £80.00 worth of legal advice subject to any extension.

(ii) It can be possible to extend the limit so as to cover one expert's report (with difficulty).

Disadvantages

(i) Financial criteria is very strict both as to income and capital. For example rent and mortgage payments are not taken into account. For a Client with a wife and two children capital in excess of £1,570.00 puts one outside the scope of the scheme.

(ii) It is available to the Parents only not the child and is based on their income, not the child's.

(iii) The Client has to visit the Solicitor at his office in order to sign a Green Form. Difficult sometimes for people on income support. There is a procedure for allowing someone else to attend at the Solicitor's office to sign on the Client's behalf but there is a special form for this. I have not yet been able to obtain it from the Legal Aid Board.

(iv) £80.00 does not go very far when you consider that an expert's report can cost in the region of £200 to £300.

(v) It is necessary at each stage to negotiate with the Local Legal Aid Board to extend the limit under the Green Form to cover perhaps the cost of an expert's report and then to cover for example the cost of assisting Parent at an appeal hearing. As a Mckenzie Man the Solicitor cannot take a direct part in the appeal process.

(vi) With present constraints on public expenditure Legal Aid Boards are becoming more and more difficult to deal with in respect of extensions to the Green Form.

With thanks to
Robert Love,
A.E. Smith & Sons,
Solicitors.

Useful sources of help and advice other than LEAs

The **Voluntary Council for Handicapped Children** has a free information service, and a range of free publications, including a list of organisations concerned with specific disabilities and other leaflets. For a full list, send a large SAE to: Voluntary Council for Handicapped Children, 8 Wakley Street, London EC1V 7QE.

The **Advisory Centre for Education (ACE)**, 1b, Aberdeen Studios, 22 Highbury Grove, London N5 2EA (071–354 8321 – call between 2 and 5pm, Monday to Friday). Publishes guides for parents on the education system. For the *Education Law Advisers Service* contact C. Henson, ACE.

The **Centre for Studies on Integration Education (CSIE)**, 4th floor, 415 Edgware Road, London NW2 6NB (081-452-8642). Main task is the collection and dissemination of information about integration. Offers a free advice service.

LEGAL ADVICE

Network, 16, Princeton Street, WC1R 4BB (071–831 8031).

The **Children's Legal Centre** is an independent national body set up following international Year of the Child. Its work is concerned with laws and policies which affect children and young people in England and Wales. It provides a free advice and information service by telephone (2pm to 5pm, Mondays to Fridays) and letter. Children's Legal Centre, 20 Compton Terrace, London NW1 2UN (071–359 6251).

The **Law Society,** 113 Chancery Lane, London WC2, publishes a series of 28 booklets covering England and Wales, listing solicitors who do legal aid work and other sources of legal advice – citizens' advice bureaux, legal advice law centres – and giving basic details about legal aid. These booklets, which are updated annually (Legal Aid Solicitors' Lists), should be available in advice agencies and libraries. Education Law Advisers Service c/o C. Henson ACE. 1b, Aberdeen Studios, 22 Highbury Grove, London N5 2EA (071–354 8321).

EXPERT WITNESSES

Dyslexia Institute, 133 Gresham Road, Staines TW18 2AJ (0784–463 821).

If you do not agree with the advice prepared by professionals, *eg* doctors, education psychologists, teachers *etc*, for the authority, you may want to get a second, independent opinion from an expert. If you are seeking to challenge the suggested 'special educational provision' set out in a draft Statement, you may want to submit reports prepared by independent experts, and also ask them to appear as 'witnesses' for you at an appeal. Some voluntary organisations concerned with specific disabilities have informal lists of experts who may be able to help (see above). The **Association of Educational Psychologists** will supply details of psychologists in particular areas for parents who want second opinions. Contact: AEP, 3 Sunderland Road, Durham DH1 2LH (091–384 9512).

Independent Panel of Special Education Advice (IPSEA), c/o John Wright, 12 Marsh Road, Tillingham, Essex CM0 7SZ (0621–779 781), lists educational psychologists and other professionals with a knowledge of special needs who give direct support to parents and children (generally outside their employing LEA) on a voluntary basis. The help usually consists of giving an expert second opinion on a child's learning difficulties and/or commenting on the suitability or otherwise of the provision offered on a statement.

PARENTS' GROUPS

British Dyslexia Association, 98 London Road, Reading, Berks RG1 5AY (0734–662 677)

You may want to get together with other parents to discuss special education and other local issues – the strength of a group can influence local policy and ensure that the LEA 'keep under review' its arrangements for special educational provision **(S.2 (4) EA 1981). Network '81** is a national network of support groups run by and for parents. Write to: Liz Arrondale, 52 Magnaville Road, Bishops Stortford, Herts CM23 4DN (0279–503 244).

Parents in Partnership, Top Portcabin, Clare House, St George's Hospital, Blackshaw Road, London SW17 (081–682 1473) telephone between 9.30 and 3.00 weekdays. For parents of children with special needS who help each other by forming local groups mainly in the London area. Helps parents with the assessment and statementing procedure and runs training days.

You may be able to obtain information about other groups from, for example, your local **Community Relations Council** or coordinating body for voluntary organisations, or at your local reference library. There may also be a local group of the **Campaign for State Education (CASE)** in your area.

GOVERNMENT DEPARTMENTS AND OTHER OFFICIAL BODIES

Specific enquiries on special education should be addressed to: **Special Education Division,** Department of Education and Science, Sanctuary Buildings, Great Smith Street, London SW1P 3BT (071–925 5000).

WHERE TO FIND OUT MORE

Department of Education and Science (DES), Sanctuary Buildings, Great Smith Street, London SW1P 3BT (071–925 5000).

Welsh Office, Education Department, Phase 2, Government Buildings, Ty Glas Road, Llanishen, Cardiff CF4 5NE (0222–761 456).

Department of Health (DH), Alexander Fleming House, Elephant and Castle, London SE1 6BY (071–407 5522).

Council on Tribunals, 22 Kingsway, London WC2B 6LE (071–936 7045).

Commissioner for Local Administration (Ombudsman): England: 21 Queen Anne's Gate, London SW1 (071–222 5622); Wales: Derwen House, Court Road, Bridgend, Mid Glamorgan CF31 1BN (0656–613 25).

Parliamentary Commissioner for Administration and Health Service, Church House, Great Smith Street, London SW1P 3BW (071–212 6271).

Equal Opportunities Commission (EOC), Overseas House, Quay Street, Manchester M3 3HN (061–833 9244).

Commission for Racial Equality (CRE), Elliot House, 10/12 Allington Street, London SW1E 5EH (071–828 7022).

Children's Legal Centre, 20 Compton Terrace, London N1 2UN (071–359 6251).

Independent Panel of Special Educational Advisers (IPSEA), c/o John Wright, 12 Marsh Road, Tillingham, Essex CM0 7SZ (0621–779 781).

Law Centres Federation, 164 Gower Street, London NW1 (071–387 8570).

Centre for Studies on Integration in Education (CSIE), 4th floor, 415 Edgware Road, London NW2 6NB (081–452 8642).

Appendix 11

Index of cases